Safe at Home 2

MORE WINNING PLAYERS
TALK ABOUT
BASEBALL
AND THEIR
FAITH

DAVE BRANON
Foreword by Gary Carter

MOODY PRESS
CHICAGO

PHOTO CREDITS:

Photograph of Greg McMichael courtesy of Tom Pace.

All other photographs are courtesy of Anaheim Angels, Atlanta Braves, Baltimore Orioles, Cleveland Indians, Cincinatti Reds, Colorado Rockies, Detroit Tigers, Florida Marlins, Kansas City Royals, Los Angeles Dodgers, Milwaukee Brewers, New York Yankees, Philadelphia Phillies, San Diego Padres, San Francisco Giants, and Texas Rangers Major League Baseball clubs.

ISBN: 0-8024-7904-9

1 3 5 7 9 10 8 6 4 2

To a team that may not completely understand my love for baseball but who supports me 100 percent anyway: my wife, Sue, who always goes to bat for me when I'm sequestered in my basement office, banging out another book; Lisa, Julie, Melissa, and Steven, who share my excitement every time another interview is complete. If there was a World Series for families, you five would all be wearing championship rings.

To my prayer partners in any writing effort I undertake: Jim and Bert Jeffery; Harold and Patty Ploeg; Melissa and Dennis Hormell; Jim and Bonnie Gordon; Tim and Beth Nesseth; and Mike and Deb Williams.

Contents

Acknowledgments

Cooperation. That's the key word that describes what it takes to put together a book like this. If I did not have the cooperation of dozens of people, I would still be staring at a blank computer screen with nothing to write. That's why I am so grateful to the people who decided that this effort was worth helping.

Some friends were extremely helpful. People like Tim Cash, who, besides assisting me with Terry Pendleton, Brett Butler, and John Smoltz, was always right there when I needed to talk about baseball, players, and matters of faith. And Gari and Bobby Meacham, who are always so considerate. They were my liaisons for Walt Weiss and Joe Girardi. Rob Bentz, my right-hand man at *Sports Spectrum,* is always there when I need some advice. And Carol Curtis was so kind to contact her son, Chad, on my behalf.

Then a lot of people I don't know had to come on board to assist with this project, and I appreciate their cooperation—which gained for them nothing but the knowledge that they were being helpful.

Agents: Tommy Tanzer for Sterling Hitchcock; Alan Meersand for Travis Fryman; Tracy Codd for Todd Hollandsworth; and Joe Sambito for Andy Pettitte.

Media relations people for major league teams: John Blake of the Texas Rangers, who was extremely helpful in my talking with Dave Valle, Mark McLemore, and Kurt Stillwell. And Kurt himself was so generous to give me additional information when I needed it.

Carolyn LaPierre of the Anaheim Angels, who put up with a ton of phone calls from me and made sure I could talk with Rex Hudler, Shawn Boskie, and Tim Salmon.

Steve Gilbert of the Milwaukee Brewers, who made sure I talked with Dave Nilsson before he took off for Australia and who helped hook me up with Scott Karl.

Glen Serra of the Atlanta Braves, who contacted Greg McMichael for me. And Greg himself, who is so accommodating and classy, and who deserves much more than bad memories of his last outing with the Braves.

Brandy Lay of the Colorado Rockies stands out as a writer's dream PR person, calling to make sure I had everything I needed in regard to my interviews with Walt Weiss and Mike Muñoz.

Bart Swain of the Cleveland Indians set up an interview with Kevin Seitzer soon after the former Brewer arrived on the scene in Cleveland.

Steve Fink of the Kansas City Royals came through quickly in my request to interview Keith Lockhart. And Keith himself was accommodating to my needs as a nosy writer.

Stella Fiore of the New York Mets put to rest the idea that New York folks don't have heart, as she lined up my interview with Rico Brogna in record fashion.

Jim Moorehead of the San Francisco Giants made sure I heard from Mark Dewey.

Mentioning the agents and media relations people, though, does not go far enough. The players themselves are to be commended. There was nothing in it for them as they gave up their time to talk with me—except for the chance to allow people to learn more about their faith. It is gratifying to know that this is enough. My sincere thanks go to each player in this book for his cooperation.

As always, the resources of *Sports Spectrum* magazine and radio were invaluable assets to my writing. Information from both of those sources is spread throughout the book, and for those sources I am grateful.

Several other sources were cited as I researched the stories of these players, including media guides from each team represented, *The Sporting News Official Baseball Register, Sports Illustrated* magazine, and *Fastball* and *Sportsline USA* Internet services for verification of facts and historical incidents.

Foreword

When Safe at Home *was published in 1992, Gary Carter was one of the players profiled. Throughout his career, Carter made it a point to give a testimony about Jesus Christ whenever he had a chance. Now that he has retired from the game and is on the other side of the microphone, he is still using his platform in baseball to God's glory—as he does so clearly in this Foreword to* Safe at Home 2.

—DB

I still have a great love and passion for the game of baseball. I played for eighteen years in the major leagues, and to this day, I feel very fortunate and blessed that God gave me an opportunity to play the wonderful game of baseball for so long.

I was in the broadcast booth as a TV analyst for the Florida Marlins for the first four years after I retired. In 1996, I began working as a TV analyst for the Montreal Expos, the team I played for most of my career.

Let me go back to 1973, when Christ became my Lord and Savior. I knew all about God and went to church on a regular basis, but it wasn't until that year that I asked His Son, Jesus Christ, to come into my life.

It changed my outlook on life and how I approached the game of baseball—especially because of the talent God had given me. Knowing Him made me appreciate the game more and helped me represent the game in the best way possible. The fans, the media, and everyone around the game of baseball took on a different light.

I became involved with the Baseball Chapel, which held services every Sunday in team clubhouses. My faith continued to grow through the years with the help of Baseball Chapel and by reading the Bible. Currently, I am the president of Baseball Chapel and am grateful to give back some of what the organization provided for me. You can never stop learning and growing in God's Word.

Let me tell one story that illustrates how God was with me during my career. It was Game 6 of the 1986 World Series, and I was playing for the Mets. We were behind in the game 5–3 with two outs in the 10th inning. I could have been the last out of the World Series, with the victory going to the Boston Red Sox.

While in the on-deck circle, I really felt the presence of God right there. I normally prayed while in the on-deck circle, but this time I prayed maybe just a little bit more. With divine intervention, I was able to line a base hit into left field, which led to a rally and our winning the game 6–5. We then won Game 7 and the World Series.

Without God in my life, that moment may have never happened. With God, I felt I was the best ballplayer I could be. With His help, I became a better father and husband. I owe everything to God—especially having Jesus Christ in my life. Without Him, I would be nothing. I love Jesus Christ.

Included in this book are a couple dozen men who feel the same way I do. They have benefited from Baseball Chapel, as I have, and they want to serve Jesus Christ through baseball. They share my passion for the game, but they reserve their greatest love for the Lord Jesus Christ.

> Gary Carter
> President, Baseball Chapel

Gary Carter was an eleven-time All-Star who played for the New York Mets, the Montreal Expos, the Los Angeles Dodgers, and the San Francisco Giants in a stellar eighteen-year career. He hit more than 300 home runs and knocked in more than 1,200 runs during his time in the majors. He holds records for the most games played, putouts made, and chances accepted by a catcher in National League history.

Introduction

I had almost forgotten how much fun baseball can be.

A few Decembers ago, I packed my bags and headed out of the wintry Michigan gloom and into the bright sunshine of Kissimmee, Florida, the spring training site of the Houston Astros. Officials met me at the airport and whisked me off to the hotel where we players would be staying for the next few days.

I met my roommate, a player from Syracuse University.

The next morning, after we enjoyed a hearty training breakfast, the bus was ready to take us to the training facility. I walked into the locker room, and there above my locker was a card with my name and the number 23 on it. Inside my locker was my baseball uniform—just waiting to be worn onto the field of play.

For the next four days, it would be baseball from morning until evening for my teammates and me. Our days were filled with drills, exercises, hitting practice, fielding practice, intense instruction, and games.

No, I wasn't trying out for the Houston Astros. The childhood dream of suiting up for a major league baseball team had died decades earlier when I struck out three times against future Big Red Machine pitcher Don Gullett—while several big league scouts watched.

What I was doing during that December hiatus from the real world was attending a fantasy baseball camp sponsored by Athletes in Action.

In my "toughest" assignment as a writer, I was covering the camp for *Sports Spectrum* magazine.

It had been more than twenty years since I had played baseball for keeps. Yet it was amazing to find how easily the rust fell off the skills. If only the muscles could have returned to their eighteen-year-old form.

Growing up as I did, dreaming that one day I'd play shortstop for the Cincinnati Reds, my heart raced with excitement to realize how special this time was. Silly as it may sound, here I was a father of four who had passed his fortieth birthday, yet the thrill of playing baseball on the same diamond with major leaguers left me pinching myself.

It was just a temporary dream come true—a four-day tease. Yet nothing could change the fact that for those ninety-sixth hours I was on a big league field, playing with major league players. Full-time.

For four days, there was no real job to worry about. No mundane things, such as grocery shopping, to bother with. No distractions, such as getting the car fixed. Just baseball.

Imagine it.

Taking batting practice off Greg McMichael.

Sitting in the dugout and spinning stories with Jose Alvarez, formerly of the Braves.

Asking Randy Velarde and Andy Stankiewicz for help in turning the double play.

Having lunch with legendary college baseball coach and former major leaguer Jerry Kindall.

Playing golf with Gary Carter.

Relearning the mechanics of hitting from Brian and Blake Doyle, who took my swing apart as if they were rebuilding a carburetor. It didn't matter to them that I hit .538 in Little League; they thought I had some serious flaws in my approach to hitting.

As I sat in the dugout one day and reflected on what was happening, I couldn't help but appreciate anew the beauty of baseball. The symmetry of the baseball field with its focus at home plate spreading to its expansive outfield made me think of why it is indeed a field of dreams. The warmth of the Florida sun that even in December greens the perfectly cut grass reminded me that the summer game reflects the laid-back season in which it is played. The crisp report of ball on bat and the sharp sounds of players communicating reinforced my feeling that the sounds of baseball translate so perfectly to radio—and I thought back to the thousands of games I had listened to on my little transistor.

Baseball, I remembered, is a game played in the mind as well as on the field. I recalled the best advice I received in Little League: "Always know what you're going to do with the ball before it is hit to you." In the mind, the play was completed before it began. I recalled the exciting radio calls I had heard, allowing me to live those moments in my mind.

Harry Caray's call of Stan Musial's 3,000th hit.

Marty Brenneman's call of Pete Rose's last out against Gene Garber in his 44-game hitting streak—a radio moment that I could hear only when I took my radio out on the back deck of our Michigan home so I could receive the signal from WLW in Cincinnati.

Ernie Harwell's first broadcast of the season when he quoted from the Song of Solomon.

And the final call of the final broadcast of any baseball season—the sure harbinger of cold weather and more than 150 days of radio silence.

Yet even in the winter, when the only baseball games played are in the Caribbean, the game remains a game of the mind.

The Hot Stove League is a mind game. Trades. Free agent signings. Managerial moves. The game still exists in our imagination as fans everywhere dream of the possibility of success next season.

As I experienced baseball at that fantasy camp, I also noticed that baseball is increasingly becoming a game of the heart. In the case of the players at the camp, their hearts were not dedicated solely to the game. They also had hearts for Jesus Christ.

Working as I had with baseball players for *Sports Spectrum* and the first *Safe at Home* book, I knew that there were many players who had faith. But what I discovered was that these players haven't merely signed up for fire insurance. They want their faith in Jesus Christ to make a difference in their lives.

That's why so many of them are actively involved in Bible studies, team chapels, and outreach opportunities.

And that's why people like Chris Bando, Chuck Snyder, Tim Cash, Don Gordon, and John Weber are so important to them. These are men who spend a lot of time discipling major league baseball players. Bando, a coach for the Brewers, has spent much off-season time helping men like Tim Salmon and Shawn Boskie grow in their faith. Chuck Snyder and his wife, Barb, work closely with Seattle-area baseball players, helping them learn how to live out their faith. Cash and Gordon work with a ministry called Unlimited Potential, Inc. (UPI), which disciples players and then gives them ministry opportunities. Weber assists Dallas-area players who want to understand what living the Christian life is all about.

Baseball has an exciting array of big-name stars who love Jesus Christ and want to live for Him. And it has a number of young players who are just beginning to walk with the Lord.

That fantasy camp experience was just plain fun because I got to play baseball again. To roam shortstop and pretend to be Alan Trammell. To stand in the batter's box and assume my Frank Robinson stance that I had learned from watching big number 20 so many years before. To wear a baseball uniform again—perhaps for the last time.

But it was so much more. It gave me a new appreciation for the men of the game who stand up for Jesus Christ—who, despite the problems baseball has experienced, want people to know that the game is full of many good people, a large portion of whom play the game as a testimony.

It was good preparation for writing this book, for that is the same thing I discovered as I talked with the players you will read about. From John Smoltz, who has grown in his faith as he has grown as a pitcher; to Mark Dewey, who is not afraid to live out his strong convictions; to Chad Curtis, whose dream turned into a nightmare yet he became a stronger person for it; to Terry Pendleton, who understands the true spirit of servant leadership—the players in this book are eager to let Jesus show through them.

If you had forgotten how much fun baseball can be, I hope this book brings back some of the game's joy for you. It's a great game, and these players have the world's greatest message. Now get out there and have some fun!

Shawn Boskie
A Surprising Journey

VITAL STATISTICS

Born March 28, 1967, in Hawthorne, Nevada
6 feet 3, 200 pounds
Attended Modesto (Calif.) Junior College
Position: Pitcher
Throws right, bats right
Family: Wife, Pam, and two children, Brad and Anna
1997 Team: Baltimore Orioles

CAREER HIGHLIGHTS

- Established career highs in starts (28) and strikeouts (133) in 1996
- Won first five starts with California Angels (1995)
- Won back-to-back games against Chicago Cubs after being traded to Philadelphia (1994)
- Pitched a complete-game victory in first major league start

WARMING UP

One way Shawn Boskie stays strong spiritually is by surrounding himself with friends who share his faith. "The Lord is constantly putting people in my life at every stop. Not everyone has [encouraging Christians] in their lives." For instance, before he had even joined the Angels, Boskie had struck up a friendship with Tim Salmon. Together they had attended Bible studies near their Arizona homes with Chris Bando, a former major leaguer who coaches for Milwaukee. "For some reason, there have always been people in my life to help me," Boskie says.

FAVORITE BIBLE PASSAGE

"Do your best to present yourself to God as one approved, a workman who does not need to be ashamed and who correctly handles the word of truth" (2 Timothy 2:15).

Shawn Boskie

When Shawn Boskie was an eighteen-year-old infielder for Modesto Junior College in 1985, he could have taken everything he knew about Christianity and major league baseball and put it in the back pocket of his baseball uniform—with room left over for a batting glove.

This is not the story of a young man who grew up with baseball pennants lining his walls and Christian storybooks lining his shelves. It's about a kid from Reno, Nevada, who must be as surprised as anybody that he's a major league pitcher who uses his fame as a platform to talk about Jesus Christ. Neither concept ever entered his mind for the first twenty-one years of his life.

That's not to say, however, that Boskie did not know about either God or baseball as a kid. He attended Sunday school at the Reno church where his mom was the organist. Indeed, his mother taught her little boy the "now I lay me down to sleep" prayer and answered his questions about God. And Shawn knew enough to ask his dad why he was not a regular churchgoer. Yet as the boy grew into a teenager, his interest in spiritual things waned.

"As I got older, I didn't really seem to fit in with the people at church," he says. "I didn't really want to go to church. My parents started giving me a little more freedom in high school, and I chose not to go as often."

As so often happens with teenagers, new pursuits pushed out the old. "What was more important to me was fitting in with my schoolmates. I believed in God, but my lifestyle didn't reflect any standard other than what my parents had raised me with, which was a good, moral background." They weren't standards based on the Bible, though, leaving Shawn's world open to sinful habits that he would later find hard to break.

Although Shawn's dad was not inclined to push a spiritual agenda, he was still a strong influence on his only son's life. "The role my dad played in my life helped shape who I am today," Shawn says. "He was a great dad! He took time to be with me. Both of my parents were active in city league softball, so I was constantly around athletics. My dad never turned me down for a game of catch or wrestling on the floor after he came home from work. He showed me what a man should be like."

As a youngster, Shawn played both baseball and football, and his parents, he says, "were at all my games. At the time, I didn't realize that was so important."

While a student at Reno High School, Boskie seemed to have both sports open to him for the future. In football, he was recruited by some small schools and by UNLV as a cornerback and a quarterback. But baseball was his sport of choice. "I didn't necessarily like it better, but I played it better. It was clear that baseball was the way to go."

So off he went to Modesto, California, to play infield for Modesto Junior College. Boskie did not go with the idea that he would play a few games and waltz into a big-league contract. "Pro baseball wasn't even an option coming out of high school," he says. He was simply trying to get a college education and see where it would lead.

And he was also trying out his wings. "I remember the day I left for college; it was rather strange. I looked at it as my freedom. No more curfews. No more accountability. Leaving home wasn't any kind of tearjerker. Although I loved my parents, I felt like *I'm finally free*."

For Boskie, the results of his so-called freedom were evident right away. To assist the baseball players, Modesto Junior College lined up housing, and Shawn was hosted by a woman whose son was away at another college. As Boskie moved into the room, he discovered stacks of sexually explicit magazines in the closet. For someone seeking freedom from restraints, it was just what he wanted.

"I believed in God this whole time," Boskie says about that period of his life, which he now says is "ugly to talk about." And he recalls, "I probably would have said I was a Christian at that time. But I don't remember meeting up with anyone who was different—like a born-again Christian would have been different. I don't remember anybody challenging me on this issue."

This part of the "freedom" Boskie thought was so vital as an independent teenager would form a bondage that would later have to be dealt with.

On the baseball field and in the classroom at Modesto, things were going well. He felt that his life was in order. But then a surprising and gratifying opportunity came along in January 1986 that turned his plans upside down. The Chicago Cubs showed up and told Boskie that they were interested in drafting him as a pitcher. Earlier, Modesto had asked him to move from his infield position to the mound, but he had been reluctant to do so. "I didn't really want to pitch, but I said I would."

The Cubs sent a freelance scout to take a look at this young man who had pitched only sporadically throughout his youth baseball days. They asked him to pitch on the side—not even in a game—for fifteen or twenty minutes. "The next thing I knew," Boskie says, "they had picked me in the first round of the draft." He was the tenth player picked in the entire draft.

"That was the first time I ever watched baseball on TV and thought about playing in the major leagues," he says. "I didn't know anything about the Cubs. I hardly knew anything about any major league teams."

Jokes about the Cubs and their history of futility aside, the team saw in Boskie something that his fine major league career has proved to be true. "They knew I had a live arm and a body that was suitable," he says. They could teach him how to pitch.

As he began to wind his way through the back roads of minor league baseball, he became even more intent on exploiting his newfound freedom and lack of restraints. He thought he was doing what baseball players do naturally—traveling the nightclub circuit in search of the next available young woman. While playing at Winston-Salem in 1988, Boskie thought he was enjoying the double success that was expected of men in flannels. "I started having my best year as far as baseball and as far as women," he says, with clear regret in his voice. "I felt like everything was going great. I couldn't be doing any better in the nightclubs. I figured this was the typical baseball lifestyle. My main motive was sexual conquest."

Yet as much as Winston-Salem provided Boskie with opportunities to make poor choices, his time there also offered the hope of true happiness that he didn't even know he needed. It began with a chapel service. When Boskie heard about it, he thought, *I went to church as a kid, and I believe in God, so I'll go. It's a good thing to do.* That summer, he heard the message about having a personal relationship with Jesus and about being born again. "I remember thinking to myself, *I never heard any of this stuff before*. But then a player from another team gave his testimony. He had gone to USC or UCLA, and his life had been going in the wrong direction with drugs and with girls. I listened to this stuff, and I said to myself, 'I believe in God, but it sure doesn't sound like what he's talking about.' So I started getting curious about what I actually believed."

Later, he heard another talk, this time by former football player Jackie Brown. "He told us how he had gotten saved. I figured this guy could relate to me because he talked about the same things I did—women, drugs, and stuff. I hadn't gotten mixed up with drugs, but I drank a lot of alcohol. I figured, 'He'll know where I'm coming from.' Sure enough, he did. I talked to him and told him I didn't really know what I believed. I told him that I was either going to believe this or throw it out and go on. I remember him smiling and praying with me that God would clear things up in my mind. That was really strange, because I had never prayed out loud with anyone before."

Boskie was not yet ready to turn his life over to Jesus

Christ, but he was eager to learn more. His mother had given him a Bible when he was nine years old, and he had brought it with him to Winston-Salem.

"I decided I was going to read my Bible," he recalls. "I started reading Genesis, and by the time I got to the third or fourth chapter, I was out of gas. I began to wonder, *How does this relate to what Jackie and I talked about?* I started flipping around in my Bible, and I found a section in the back called, 'A Children's Introduction to the Bible' by Charles Ryrie. I didn't know who he was, but I thought, *This is perfect. I'm twenty-one years old, but I'm looking for something simple.* It explained that the Bible is a love letter from God. And it said we can know God. It also mentioned that although many people say we are all God's children, that isn't true. It said we are all created by God, but there is something called sin that has separated us from Him. It explained what sin is—going against God's law. And it had some key verses that led me through the salvation plan."

For Shawn, that straightforward explanation was exactly what he was looking for. He had known about God all his life, but now he discovered how he could *really* know Him. "A few nights later, while I was lying in bed, I prayed the sinner's prayer. I remember saying, 'Jesus, forgive me of my sins. Jesus, You take control. You lead me where You want me to be.' It was the first time since I was five or six years old that I thought God actually heard me pray. The next day, I felt like a huge burden had been lifted from my shoulders. I told my roommates about my salvation, and I told them about it rather passionately. There was evidence of my new faith just in my willingness to talk about it. I knew it was real."

Of course, his life did not turn around immediately. As a spiritual baby, Boskie still struggled with some lifestyle problems. "I didn't know the Bible, and I didn't know what God expected from me. I just knew that I had gotten saved and that Jesus was the answer." In fact, the freedom Boskie thought he had found during college in the pages of pornographic magazines was really bondage that thwarted his early spiritual growth.

After the season ended, Boskie lived in California. Because

he still held on to remnants of his old lifestyle, he sometimes found it difficult to feel close to God. "I remember praying for my salvation three or four times," he says. Although he still struggled, his roommate that winter, Lee Hancock, was a believer who helped keep Shawn moving in the right direction.

The next spring, Boskie was slated to go to his first major league camp with the Cubs. His 12–7 record with Winston-Salem in twenty-seven starts and his two shutouts had earned him a shot at making the big club. Before Boskie left for spring training, Hancock gave him a workbook for new Christians. Also, he experienced his first major league Christian fellowship with Scott Sanderson, Mitch Webster, and Rick Sutcliffe. With the help of more mature Christians, he was beginning to grow stronger in his faith.

"As a result of these things, my life started changing for the better." He had not completely conquered his old habits, but he was making progress.

Another significant event took place in Boskie's life at the end of spring training: He was sent to Charlotte. Although he would have preferred to stay in Chicago, he probably wouldn't have met Pam Russell if he had. Pam, a recent graduate of Appalachian State University, was working at a Charlotte restaurant when Shawn met her. After they dated for a while, Boskie asked her if she was a Christian. She said yes, but he wasn't convinced.

"She had grown up with a similar background to mine and had gotten off to where she was doing her own thing, like I had done. I loved her companionship, but at the same time, it was a struggle for me. We didn't have the same convictions."

Pam and Shawn continued to date, often talking about God and spiritual issues. It was a difficult time for both of them as they tried to sort out their relationship, knowing they did not share the same faith.

Things began to change for Shawn and Pam, though, after attending a service at Forest Hills Presbyterian Church in Charlotte. The pastor, David Chadwick, spoke that morning about some things Shawn knew he had not surrendered to God. "I was sitting in the church, and the message was aimed right at me. I thought, *Wow, it seems like I'm the only one in the church right now.* I think Pam was sensing the same thing."

During the service, communion was held. "I confessed my sins," Shawn recalls, "and I took the supper, but Pam didn't. Pastor Chadwick had made it very clear that if you're not a believer, you shouldn't. I thought that was good. After church, I told Pam my testimony." Then Boskie told his girlfriend that from then on their courtship would be based on biblical guidelines and that if the change resulted in the end of their relationship, then that's the way it would have to be.

"Then I went on a fourteen-day road trip and left her with that to chew on," Boskie says.

They continued to date under those conditions. After the season, Pam visited Shawn while he was playing in the Instructional League in Arizona. While there, they attended a church where Pam again heard the gospel. That night, she accepted Christ as her Savior.

That set the stage for the 1990 baseball season. On May 20, his long journey from a junior college infield to a major league mound was completed when the Cubs called him up from their Iowa farm team.

The Cubs were in Houston to take on the Astros, and Boskie was penciled in for his first major league appearance—a start in the Astrodome. Not surprisingly, a case of the jitters kept him from getting much rest the night before. "I was lying in bed, very nervous, thinking, *Okay, what do I have to do? I have a good fastball that I'll just throw low. I have a slider and a pretty good change-up. So I'll just use those and see what happens.* Then I would get more relaxed. Fifteen minutes later, I'd get really nervous again. Then I would go through my game plan and get more relaxed. This cycle kept going."

Although this is not a recommended pregame ritual, it seemed to work for Boskie. He pitched a complete game, recording a 5–1 victory over the home team. He gave up just five hits and even got two hits himself. As the season progressed, Shawn fashioned a 5–6 record with a 3.69 ERA before injuring his elbow in early August and missing the last two months. On August 20, he had surgery to remove chips from his elbow.

Besides that first-game win over the Astros, Boskie's other big day of 1990 came on November 3, when he and Pam were married. After all the successes Shawn has had over the years, he still considers 1990 his highlight year.

Boskie pitched for the Cubs the next three seasons, experiencing a mixture of success and frustration. In 1993, the Cubs turned him into a relief pitcher. Although he compiled a 4–2 record and kept his ERA under 3.00 as a reliever, this was not a career move for Boskie. It would take a trade to Philadelphia to put him back in the starting rotation. On April 12, 1994, the Cubs sent Boskie to the Phils for pitcher Kevin Foster.

"Getting traded was strange," Boskie says. "There were a lot of mixed emotions. It was hard to admit that I was leaving my home team. You can't beat playing for the Cubs, but I thought it was inevitable that I would be going someplace else."

The 1994 season presented a multitude of changes for the Boskies. About the same time they moved to Philadelphia, Pam discovered that she was pregnant. Then, in July, after Shawn had made eighteen appearances for Philadelphia, fourteen of them as a starter, the Phillies peddled him off to the Seattle Mariners. Three major league teams in three months.

A few weeks later, the baseball players went on strike, effectively ending his short career in the Emerald City. In November, the Mariners released Boskie. For the first time in his career, he was a man without a team.

"It was an unsettling feeling to be released. I thought, *How could they release me? I'm still young—just twenty-seven. I have a good arm.*"

During the strike, two good things happened to the Boskies. First, on January 30, their son, Brad, was born. And on March 5, Shawn signed with the California Angels. It was a minor league contract, but it would give him a chance to make the major league team when the strike ended. And that's what happened: Boskie had a great spring training and made the Angels' squad.

What began as a potentially great season, though, deteriorated into a period that Boskie calls "one of the toughest points of my career." After winning his first five decisions and posting a 6–2 record by the All-Star break, Boskie injured his elbow and did not come off the disabled list until September. By then, the Angels, who had been in first place most of the season, had seen their pennant hopes flicker. They were in a dogfight with Seattle for first place in their division. Hopeful of coming into the final stretch ready to help the Angels get into postseason play, Boskie was excited to be back in the rotation. However, the Angels suffered through an 11–17 September. "I figured I could come in and help," Boskie recalls. "But I contributed to the collapse." ·

Although the Angels won their last five games to force a one-game playoff with the Mariners, they lost that game and had to settle for second place. "I really didn't understand," Boskie says. "I was mad at God, but didn't know how to express it. I felt like I didn't have any right to be mad at Him because He had blessed me so much. I had this battle going on inside of me. I held it in and kept getting kind of depressed. It ended up being a great growing time, though. I was forced to think about and examine who God is and how to get to know Him better."

Through that time of trial, he learned how valuable Pam was to him. "It was a tough time, but my wife was my greatest support. She went through everything I went through and was a huge help."

The Angels' 1996 season was an extension of the collapse of '95. Seemingly loaded with talent, they nonetheless skidded into a below-.500 season that confused everyone. One of the bright spots for the Angels, though, was Boskie, who won twelve games that year.

So much has changed since Shawn Boskie threw his belongings into his pickup truck and headed to Modesto in the fall of 1985. The infielder has become a major league pitcher. The ladies' man has become a committed family man. The college student who thought he found freedom in sexually explicit material has discovered *true* freedom in Jesus Christ. The kid whose only prayer was "now I lay me down to sleep" is telling others about faith in God.

Potential is such an unpredictable thing. Shawn Boskie is a clear testament to the importance of letting God control one's destiny. His success in baseball and in matters of faith far out-distance what could have been predicted for him in his late teens. He's an example of what can be done in the life of anyone who will turn his heart over to Jesus Christ.

Q & A WITH SHAWN BOSKIE

Q: *What kind of ministry are you involved in?*
Shawn: I help with a ministry called Cry the Caribbean in the Dominican Republic. It's a center for street kids. It's not an orphanage, because some of the kids have parents who just can't take care of them. It's awesome to see these kids' lives transformed.

Q: *When you first got saved, you still struggled with some bad habits. What was something that changed right away for you for the better?*
Shawn: One of the first things that changed when I became a Christian was my language. The bad words just kind of got filtered out. I just didn't like those words that I used to sprinkle throughout my sentences. They didn't taste good coming out of my mouth anymore.

Q: *What is one of the toughest temptations Christian players face on the road?*
Shawn: The toughest thing is the sexual immorality. I face it like it's an addiction. Society would never have us believe that, but this is something that is constantly an issue. We have movie channels in the hotel rooms, so we can watch anything. That has been a battle my whole career. There are some key verses that gave me a wake-up call from God. There's a verse in Romans 13 that says to make no provision for the flesh. There's a verse in Psalm 66 where David says, "If I had cherished sin in my heart, the Lord would not have listened." If we hang on to sin in our heart and give lip service to it like we're trying to beat it, that's not the answer. There's another verse in the Psalms that says, "I will set no worthless thing before my eye." It seems like those are verses directly from God to me.

Q: *You gave up quite a few home runs in 1996. Why do you think that is, and why are there so many home runs being hit these days?*
Shawn: For me, a lot of it is because I'm a fastball pitcher. My ball doesn't sink. If my control is not there, then guys can get my fastball. The home run explosion is a combination of things. I think one thing is the strike zone. It's too small. And the hitters are stronger.

THE ROAD TO THE MAJORS

- Selected by the Chicago Cubs in the first round of the 1986 draft
- Traded to the Philadelphia Phillies on April 12, 1994
- Traded to the Seattle Mariners on July 21, 1994
- Signed as a free agent by the California Angels on March 5, 1995
- Signed as a free agent by the Baltimore Orioles on December 16, 1996

Minor league stops: Wytheville, Peoria, Winston-Salem, Charlotte, Iowa, Lake Elisnore, Vancouver

Minor league highlight: In 1988, he ranked second in the league in strikeouts with 164.

THE BOSKIE FILE

Year	Team	W	L	PCT	G	SV	IP	H	R	ER	HR	BB	SO	ERA
1990	ChiC	5	6	.455	15	0	97.2	99	42	40	8	31	49	3.69
1991	ChiC	4	9	.308	28	0	129.0	150	78	75	14	52	62	5.23
1992	ChiC	5	11	.313	23	0	91.2	96	55	51	14	36	39	5.01
1993	ChiC	5	3	.625	39	0	65.2	63	30	25	7	21	39	3.43
1994	ChiC	0	0	- - -	2	0	3.2	3	0	0	0	0	2	0.00
	Phi	4	6	.400	18	0	84.1	85	56	49	14	29	59	5.23
	Sea	0	1	.000	2	0	2.2	4	2	2	1	1	0	6.75
1995	Cal	7	7	.500	20	0	111.2	127	73	70	16	25	51	5.64
1996	Cal	12	11	.522	37	0	189.1	226	126	112	40	67	133	5.32
7 Years		**42**	**54**	**.438**	**184**	**0**	**775.2**	**853**	**462**	**424**	**114**	**262**	**434**	**4.92**

Rico Brogna
Hometown Hero

Born April 18, 1970, in Turners Falls, Massachusetts
6 feet 2, 205 pounds
Position: Infielder
Throws left, bats left
Family: Married to Melissa
1997 Team: Philadelphia Phillies

CAREER HIGHLIGHTS

- Led NL first basemen with .998 fielding percentage (just 3 errors) in 1995
- Had 15-game hitting streak for the Mets in 1994, longest such streak by a Met rookie since 1975
- Went 5-for-5 against St. Louis on July 25, 1994, to become only the third Met rookie ever to accomplish that feat

WARMING UP

During the off-season, Rico Brogna often coaches the freshman boys' basketball team at his old high school. "I think I'd like to coach full-time, either football or basketball, after my baseball career," he says.

FAVORITE BIBLE PASSAGE

"I can do everything through him who gives me strength" (Philippians 4:13).

Rico Brogna

You can't talk to many people in Watertown, Connecticut, without running into someone who wants to discuss their favorite baseball player. That wouldn't be so unusual except that most of the townsfolk have the *same* favorite diamond ace.

At a time when many people no longer hold baseball as dear to their hearts as did the average American in an earlier, more baseball-friendly era, it is surprising to see such devotion. It doesn't seem the norm anymore for towns and villages to have a hometown hero involved in baseball.

Yet in Watertown, the residents have good reason to foster positive feelings and hold in high regard a kid who grew up in their town and sought his fortunes on the baseball field. In fact, it's through mutual love and admiration that Watertown and Rico Brogna have connected. He likes the town as much as the town likes him.

The place to go in Watertown if you want to find out about Rico Brogna is Joe Ro's coffee shop on Main Street. There you can pick up the latest information on Rico, look over memorabilia from his career, and sift through the mounds of clippings and articles that make up the Rico Brogna archives. No matter what current events might be grabbing the headlines on the evening news, Rico Brogna is never far from the hearts and minds of the customers at Joe Ro's.

So why has this town of 20,000 inhabitants—a town Brogna describes as "the kind of place where everyone knows everyone else's business"—fallen for this major league first baseman? Let's start by talking about what he's done for Watertown lately.

New York Mets public relations director Jay Horwitz characterized it best when he described former Met Brogna as "a throwback. He marries his high school sweetheart, buys a house in his hometown, and coaches basketball at his alma mater. You won't find many players like that these days."

The high school sweetheart is the former Melissa Shuhart, whom Rico married in December 1992. When Rico played for the Mets, he could make it to work at Shea Stadium in just an hour and a half from his home in Watertown. And the basketball team he most recently coached was the Watertown High School freshman hoopsters.

Why would a major league baseball player who has established himself as an up-and-coming first baseman spend his off-season trying to help a bunch of fourteen-year-olds learn how to play basketball? "I want to help Watertown win," he says. The team hadn't won much recently, and he wanted to help "turn things around."

For as long as he can remember, Rico Brogna has been a part of the Watertown athletic scene. Although he spent the first seven years of his life in the Boston area, Rico felt at home almost immediately after his parents moved to Watertown.

"The only memories I have of my youth involve athletics," Brogna says. "My dad always coached me—all year 'round." Rico's dad, Joe Brogna, teaches at Taft, a nearby prep school. Joe instilled in his son a love for sports.

"I remember being on the field or in the gym all the time," says Rico. "It was a 24-hour-a-day thing."

In addition, Joe Brogna gave his son a love for his own beloved Boston sports teams. That's why Rico's first memory of major league baseball was the classic 1975 World Series between the Cincinnati Reds and the Red Sox. Rico was just five years old, but he fondly remembers Bernie Carbo's pinch-hit, three-run home run in Game 6.

As Rico grew up in Watertown, playing sports under his

dad's watchful eye, he developed into the town's best athlete. In his junior year, Watertown High's football team won the state championship. Guess who was at quarterback? In his senior year, Brogna was both an all-stater and an All-American in football.

Not surprisingly, the college recruiters made their way to Watertown, frequently stopping at the Brogna household. Clemson was the winner of the recruiting war to nab the well-tooled quarterback. Rico signed a letter of intent to play for the Tigers and had every intention of taking on the Atlantic Coast Conference in the fall of 1988.

"I was set," he says. "Clemson was where I thought I was headed. I didn't really think I was going to play baseball. A lot of scouts told me that the highest I would go in the [baseball] draft would be the fourth or fifth round. I figured that going to school, playing football, and getting an education was the way to go—especially with my dad being an educator."

But then came the surprise of his life. The Detroit Tigers were hurting for power-hitting first basemen, and they heard about this Brogna kid, who was big and strong, with instincts for winning. Consequently, they picked him in the first round of the 1988 draft. Rico expected this about as much as he expected to be drafted into the French Foreign Legion.

But Joe Lewis, a scout in the New England region, had found out about Brogna through some cross-checkers, who are like freelance scouts who attend games and find out who is worth paying attention to. "I must have had a good game at the right time," Brogna says.

At noon on draft day, Rico's parents picked him up from school so he could go home and wait for a phone call. He didn't have to wait long. At 12:30, the Tigers were on the line, telling Rico he was their man.

"I was just shocked!" he recalls. "When I was picked in the first round, it took me totally by surprise. First, I was surprised that the Tigers picked me. I figured that if anyone would choose me, it would be the local teams. Not many scouts take chances in New England."

Suddenly, Brogna had a choice to make. Would he take the

guaranteed first-round bonus money and a shot at first base in Tiger Stadium, or would he settle on the always-risky proposition of trying to be a big-time college quarterback? Either way, one thing was sure: Rico Brogna would be a Tiger. In the end, he decided to wear the navy blue and orange of the Motown Tigers rather than the orange and white of Clemson's striped cats.

"I've never regretted the decision," Brogna says. "There were times when I missed football, but there is no regret at all. I'm very happy with the decision I made. A lot of guys were beginning to do the two-sport thing when I was starting out. I figured that if I was going to pursue baseball, I would go after just that sport."

So the prep hero left home, headed—he hoped—for a fast-track trip to the corner of Michigan and Trumbull in Detroit. After all, if the Tigers needed help at first base right away, surely he could deliver. It wouldn't be long, he figured, until he had worked his way through the system.

What no one knew at the time, though, was that a rather large roadblock would soon be standing squarely in Rico Brogna's way—a guy by the name of Cecil Fielder. Who would have known that this young first baseman, who was a washout with the Toronto Blue Jays and who had gone to Japan to make a living playing ball, would burst onto the scene in 1990 with one of the most prolific home run and RBI years in baseball history? And who would have known he would do it for the Detroit Tigers?

The arrival of Fielder spelled doom for Rico Brogna's future with the club and his dreams of launching missiles into Tiger Stadium's batter-friendly right field seats. And that's when Rico Brogna went into seats a holding pattern over Toledo, with little possibility of landing in Detroit. No matter what kind of success he had in his minor league stops, he couldn't do enough to work his way past Fielder.

Yet for all the bad news that came Brogna's way during his extended trip through the farm system, there was also good news that changed his life. And it was something that helped him tremendously when he was struggling with the Cecil ceiling he kept running into on his way to the big show.

Until Toledo, Brogna's trip through the Tigers' system was rather normal, despite his early dreams of getting there "in a couple of years." His 1988 Rookie League season at Bristol and his 1989 Single A stop in Lakeland were adequate enough to allow him to move along the pipeline to the majors.

But when 1990 came along, Brogna ignited some high expectations among Tiger brass when he led the Eastern League with 21 home runs while playing for London. "That was my breakout year," Brogna says. Still, looming large on the horizon was Fielder, who was enjoying the Mother of All Breakout Years by pounding out 52 home runs.

During Brogna's minor league career, he met a man named Ron Cathey. At the time, Cathey was holding Bible studies and leading chapels for the Tigers during spring training in Lakeland, Florida. Brogna, whose mom had made a habit of taking him to church as a kid in Watertown, was intrigued by this presence of religion in the locker room. "Out of curiosity, I went to the chapels," he recalls.

What he found was a new concept. "I had prayed before," he says, "but I didn't have a relationship with the Lord. I believed in God, but I had never trusted in Jesus Christ."

In June of 1991, three years into his pro career and one year past his desired deadline for reaching the majors, Brogna and Cathey met together to discuss matters of faith. "He led me through the plan of salvation, and he prayed with me as I put my trust in the Lord," Brogna says. "My spiritual growth started at a snail's pace. It's been challenging."

But along the slow journey of faith, he's had mentors such as Cathey who have taught him what it means to live as a Christian. "When I was first saved, Ron was someone I went to when I had questions. I called him, and he would be a listening ear. Whatever was going on in my life, he would be there."

Brogna didn't know it when he turned his life over to Christ, but this was just the kind of help he would soon need. He was spinning his wheels in Toledo, and there seemed to be no way to get unstuck.

That period in Brogna's life is reminiscent of the John Denver song that contains the line, "I spent the longest week of my life one night in Toledo." Rico Brogna could have written that song, except for the fact that he didn't spend just one night in Toledo—he spent three years. The Glass City is a pleasant enough community, but it just wasn't where the young lefty from Watertown wanted to be.

"My time in Toledo was incredibly frustrating," Brogna says. "I totally hit a wall. I struggled big time when I first went up to Triple A. I was trying to get to the big leagues too fast. I had come out of spring training hearing that I was going to be in the big leagues soon, and I believed everything. I just let my head swell up too much."

Rico Brogna's long International League nightmare was just beginning. At Toledo in 1991, Brogna hit a paltry .220 with two home runs in 132 at bats. The Tigers, in no hurry with their future first baseman, sent him back to London to work on his hitting. A .273 average with 13 home runs earned Rico another shot at Toledo for 1992.

The 1992 season proved successful enough at Toledo to earn Brogna that opportunity he had been hoping for since 1988, when he was selected by the Tigers. On August 7, Detroit brought Brogna up to the majors.

The next day, he faced the Toronto Blue Jays' Dave Stieb, one of the toughest right-handers in the league. Brogna promptly slapped a double in his first major league at bat. Three days later, he smacked a two-run homer against the Yankees' Melido Perez for his first big-league round-tripper.

Despite these promising displays of talent, Rico was back in Toledo within two weeks. Those were his only extra base hits, and his .192 average was not what manager Sparky Anderson was looking for. Anderson, known for his hot-and-cold relationships with young players, gave up on Brogna. In fact, one time during the August 1992 call-up, Anderson pinch-hit for Brogna in the *first* inning.

So on August 24, off he went, back down I-75 to contemplate what had gone wrong.

Rico spent the entire 1993 season at Toledo, this time hitting .273 with 11 home runs and 59 RBI. Decent numbers, to be sure, but not good enough to supplant Big Daddy or to impress ol' Sparky.

During those up-and-down years, Detroit had toyed with Brogna's batting style. They figured that if he would become a pull hitter, he would have great success with the Tiger Stadium right field porch, which overhangs the field and snares a lot of fly balls, turning otherwise routine outs into home runs.

But the experiment didn't work. "I was going backward," Brogna says about that time. "My swing broke down mechanically."

When Brogna reported to spring training in 1994, he was not sure what was in store. "There were lots of trade rumors. Cecil was at first, and he wasn't going anywhere. But I didn't put much stock in the rumors. I figured, *Whatever happens, happens.*"

What happened was a trade on March 31 that sent Brogna to the New York Mets for Alan Zinter, another first baseman. While that spelled the end of Zinter's career, it presented a new opportunity and a fresh start for Brogna.

"I was very excited," Brogna says. "I had a great relationship with a lot of people in Detroit, and I was sad to go. But at the same time, I knew I had no future there."

Although the departure from the Tiger organization was none too soon for Brogna's batting career, he still credits the team for helping him with his fielding. Today, playing first base well is one of Brogna's trademarks, and he says he's had to work hard to become a good fielder.

"I think I'm more natural as a hitter. Now my fielding has caught up. I had pretty good instincts, but I didn't have good technique. I really had to concentrate and work on that. I watched the guys with the Tigers, guys like Alan Trammell and Travis Fryman. I worked with them."

So as Brogna moved on to New York, he took with him much more than the frustration of vying for a position that was all but locked up. On the field, he took his sharpened first baseman skills. And, most importantly, he took with him his newfound faith in Jesus Christ.

After the trade, Brogna reported to Norfolk, the Mets' Triple A team in the International League. In one delicious game, Brogna lit up the Toledo Mudhens on June 5 with a 5-for-6 night, including a triple, a home run, and three runs scored. Fifteen days later, he was in Shea Stadium.

The trade to the Mets did a lot of good things for Brogna, but perhaps the best was that it took him back home. "To be going back home was the most exciting thing that had happened to me," he says. "Being able to play in front of my family has been a real highlight the past couple of years."

Between June 20 and the day the strike began in 1994, Rico Brogna turned himself into not only the hero of Watertown, but also a fan favorite in the Big Apple. In the 39 games that remained before the players walked out, Brogna produced like he hadn't since high school: .351 average, 11 doubles, and 7 home runs. Rico was definitely home.

Once the strike was settled and the players went back to work, Brogna took up where he had left off in 1994. His 22 home runs, .273 average, and 77 RBI let everyone know that scout Joe Lewis had been right after all. The kid could, indeed, play in the major leagues. To top off a great year at the plate, Brogna led National League first basemen in fielding.

As a result of his success in 1995, Brogna became the symbol of a young, vibrant Mets team that appeared poised for a return to power in the National League. New York had an exciting young corps of pitchers in Paul Wilson, Jason Isringhausen, and Bill Pulsipher, plus talented position players such as Brogna, shortstop Rey Ordonez, catcher Todd Hundley, and outfielders Bernard Gilkey and Lance Johnson. The 1996 year was picked by many to be a breakthrough year for the Mets.

For Brogna, whose 1995 season meant he had cleared the final hurdle to big-league stardom, it was time to provide leadership for this up-and-coming team.

Yet there would be more hurdles. First, there was off-season surgery on November 8, 1995, to repair torn cartilage in his right knee. That surgery healed, of course, in plenty of time for spring training—and it didn't even slow him down from his duties as a basketball coach.

Then, early in spring training, on March 8, Brogna tore a ligament in his right knee. Although that injury did not require surgery, it put him on the shelf for three weeks. Finally, a couple of months into the season, Rico suffered a partial tear of the labrum in his right shoulder. On July 1, he again had to undergo surgery—this time ending his 1996 season.

For Brogna, and all of the Mets, the year of hope ended in frustration. The Mets finished the season with a disappointing 71–91 record, which landed them in fourth place.

Despite the dark times that 1996 brought to Shea Stadium, Brogna recalls one game as a personal bright spot. Early on, nothing looked bright about this May 11 game between the Mets and the Chicago Cubs at Shea. Tempers flared in the fifth inning, when Cubs reliever Terry Adams threw a pitch behind the head of Mets starting pitcher Pete Harnisch. There had been two other questionable pitches earlier in the game, and home plate umpire Greg Bonin wanted to put a stop to it. He warned both benches after Adams's pitch (meaning the next inside pitch that the ump deemed dangerous would get the pitcher tossed out of the game).

As Bonin was informing the benches of his decision, Harnisch turned and had a few choice words for Cubs catcher Scott Servais. The Mets starter then threw a punch at Servais and both benches and bull pens emptied. After more than fifteen minutes of pushing, shoving, and screaming, the umpires ejected eight players, four from each team, along with Mets bull pen coach Steve Swisher.

"It was a bench-clearing brawl," Brogna recalls. "It was a pretty rough one—pretty violent."

That, of course, was not the bright spot that Brogna remembers. Nor were the bright spots even his two big hits earlier in the game—a triple in the first inning and a home run in the fourth. The big moment for Rico would come later, in the bottom of the ninth. Chicago had stormed back in the top of the inning to tie the game at six runs apiece.

After Brent Mayne had made the first out in the inning, Brogna stepped in against Doug Jones and promptly hit a home run to give the Mets a 7–6 win.

"I had never done that before," Brogna says. "I had never actually hit a home run to win a game in my whole career. When

I hit it and heard the crowd, it gave me chills. I almost started crying, it was so exciting. When you're eight years old, you dream of hitting a home run to win the game in the big leagues. I got a lot of flashbacks that night of the dreams I had as a kid. I was just floating."

Within a few weeks, though, the floating was over. The shoulder problem put an end to another promising year, and Brogna had to settle for a 55-game season.

In November 1996, Brogna got another shock. The Mets traded him to the Philadelphia Phillies for two relief pitchers. Although Brogna was surprised to be moving to a new team, he said he understands that these things are part of the game, and he realized that the Phillies were giving him a chance to play every day.

As depressing as it was to lose another year of his career to injury after toiling so long to prove his abilities, Brogna was able to find something positive about his struggles of 1996. "I learned a lot of patience. It wasn't a productive time for my baseball career, but it was a very productive time for my spiritual walk and my relationship with my wife. The Lord has shown me so much. He's drawn me closer to Him through this time. I've grown more spiritually than I had ever grown before."

Spiritual growth has been a top priority for Brogna ever since his decision to follow Jesus Christ while a Tiger farmhand. Through the program of Baseball Chapel and men such as his 1995 chaplain, George McGovern, he has learned how to trust God in all kinds of circumstances. And he has learned that it is vital to take advantage of ministry opportunities.

In 1996, Brogna and teammate Bobby Jones, a fellow Christian, began working with a youth outreach on Long Island. "We are spokesmen for the ministry," Rico says. "I love working with kids."

So it is no mystery to find Rico Brogna at courtside during the winters back home in Watertown, coaching the young people of his hometown. And it's no mystery that Watertown welcomes Rico and Melissa back home each winter. After all, if you're going to have a hometown hero, you can't do much better than Rico Brogna.

Q & A WITH RICO BROGNA

Q: *You gave up a college career to pursue baseball. Have you had a chance to go to school and work toward a degree?*
Rico: I have taken some accelerated classes and some college classes. I've taken thirty credits over the past seven years. I'd like to continue to take classes while I play so I can teach when I'm done—kind of follow in Dad's footsteps.

Q: *Your fielding is one of your strong points. Has it always been that way?*
Rico: It has taken a lot of work. I had a lot of good hitting coaches, but because I play first base, they don't concentrate on defense as much. They kind of expect you as a first baseman just to be a slugger. I never really got a lot of one-on-one instruction as a first baseman. I've worked the hardest on fielding, trying to improve in that area.

Q: *What do you do to grow spiritually?*
Rico: We go to a church in Watertown that really helps. Also, Melissa and I read the Bible and talk about it, and we read *Our Daily Bread*. The chapel programs in baseball are also very good, so I participate in those.

THE ROAD TO THE MAJORS

• Selected by the Detroit Tigers in the first round of the 1988 draft
• Traded to the New York Mets for Alan Zinter on March 31, 1994
• Traded to the Philadelphia Phillies for Ricardo Jordan and Toby Borland on November 27, 1996

Minor league stops: Bristol, Lakeland, London, Toledo, Norfolk

Minor league highlight: Led the 1991 Toledo Mudhens with 132 hits

Year	Team	G	AB	R	H	2B	3B	HR	RBI	BB	SO	SB	BA	SLG
1992	Det	9	26	3	5	1	0	1	3	3	5	0	.192	.346
1994	NYM	39	131	16	46	11	2	7	20	6	29	1	.351	.626
1995	NYM	134	495	72	143	27	2	22	76	39	111	0	.289	.485
1996	NYM	55	188	18	48	10	1	7	30	19	50	0	.255	.431
4 Years		**237**	**840**	**109**	**242**	**49**	**5**	**37**	**129**	**67**	**195**	**1**	**.288**	**.490**

Brett Butler
Lessons From Adversity

VITAL STATISTICS

Born June 15, 1957, in Los Angeles, California
5 feet 10, 160 pounds
Attended Southeastern Oklahoma State
Position: Outfielder
Throws left, bats left
Family: Wife, Eveline, and four children, Abbi, Stefanie, Katie, and Blake
1997 Team: Los Angeles Dodgers

CAREER HIGHLIGHTS

- Received the 1996 Branch Rickey Award for outstanding community service
- First NL player to lead the league in singles four straight seasons (1992–1995)
- Played in 161 games without committing an error in 1993
- Named to the National League All-Star team in 1991
- Led NL in hits in 1990, with 192; did not hit into a double play all season
- Led AL in runs scored (109) in 1988

WARMING UP

Among the activities that Brett Butler participates in are the Dodgers' 65 Roses Club, which raises money for cystic fibrosis research, the Beat Leukemia Golf Classic in Georgia, the Make-A-Wish Foundation, Professional Athletes Outreach, and the Hollenbeck Youth Center.

FAVORITE BIBLE PASSAGE

"Here I am! I stand at the door and knock. If anyone hears my voice and opens the door, I will come in and eat with him, and he with me" (Revelation 3:20).

Brett Butler

By the time the 1996 baseball season got under way, baseball fans thought they knew Brett Butler fairly well. Since he first set foot on a major league baseball field for the Atlanta Braves in 1981, he had made an undeniable mark on the game. Despite being a 23rd-round draft pick and being told on more than one occasion that he simply did not have the ability to succeed at the big-league level, Butler became one of the game's top players.

Fans knew Butler as a player who had made the most of his skills. Certainly not gifted with great power, Butler capitalized instead on superb bat control and quick feet. As the 1996 season began, he had banged out 2,243 base hits, placing him 118th on baseball's all-time list. He had stolen 535 bases, 24th best in the game's history. He was one of just 26 players in the grand old game who had gotten both 2,000 hits and 500 stolen bases.

Many fans also knew that Brett Butler was a Christian, for he had long been vocal about his faith in Jesus Christ. "I share my faith when the Spirit moves me to share my faith, and that's every day," he says. "The guys [teammates] know my faith. I try to live in a way so that they see it in me."

In addition, fans knew that Brett Butler was a leader—the kind of player who was comfortable as the team's union representative in the midst of tumultuous times. He was a player who relished the leadoff spot in the lineup, not so much for the chance to pick up a few more at bats during the year, but because it gave him the opportunity to get his team going.

Comments such as one made by Dallas Green when Butler signed a contract to play with his New York Mets in the spring of 1995 made fans aware of Butler's ability to lead. Green said, "A winning team has to have the right kind of veteran leadership. Brett will lead by example. He will lead in the clubhouse."

But not all fans who knew about Brett Butler thought of him as someone they *liked*. There were times not long before the 1996 season when Butler was derided by fans for controversial decisions he had made. They knew he had battled with the Los Angeles Dodgers over his contract a year earlier. They recalled that the Dodgers had offered him a huge contract during the strike but had rescinded the offer once the players agreed to get back into uniform. As a result, Butler opted to leave his hometown team to sign with the Mets. He had been called greedy by those who thought they knew his motives but were unaware of what was in his heart.

Some fans also remembered the replacement player fiasco of 1995 in which Butler, who had recently been traded back to L.A., was upset when Mike Busch, who had agreed to be a replacement player during the strike, was called up by the Dodgers to play for the big club. So when Butler made some ill-advised remarks about the Busch situation, fans characterized Butler as unforgiving and hostile. Perhaps they didn't hear when he later apologized, saying, "I regret the way I handled it."

But no matter what any baseball fan thought he or she knew about Brett Butler, new perceptions were surely formed when the 1996 season unfolded and a frightening new chapter opened in Butler's life. Indeed, the crisis that Brett Butler was about to endure led even him to find out new things about himself.

For the then-thirty-eight-year-old outfielder, the prospect of the 1996 season seemed to open up for him a new era of positive hope and promise in Los Angeles. After the ill-fated side trip to Gotham City, he was back where he felt comfortable for what some thought might be his last year in the majors.

He appeared to have his usual positive, upbeat attitude as the Dodgers trained in Vero Beach, even calling the 1996 version of the squad "the best Dodger team I've been on."

What very few people knew, though, was that throughout the entire spring training, Butler was nursing an extremely sore throat—an aggravation that simply would not go away. It would be the beginning of what Butler would later call "a journey we didn't expect."

The journey had begun a few days before spring training while Butler was still home in Atlanta. "It started with a sore throat," he recalls. "One of those things where you tell your wife, 'Hey, babe, my throat's bothering me a little bit.' "

With just five days before he was to report to Vero Beach, Butler visited a friend, Dr. Bob Gadladge, an ear, nose, and throat specialist.

"Bob and I had been friends for about fifteen years," Butler says. "I said, 'Bob, check me out. My throat's bothering me.' He looks in there and starts laughing, and he tells me I have tonsillitis. He says, 'I'll give you antibiotics and a steroid for a few days, and it'll blow over in about ten days. You'll be ready to go.' "

Butler did as the doctor ordered and took off for Vero Beach. As Butler worked through the first days of spring training, the sore throat persisted. Dr. Gadladge ordered more antibiotics, but nothing seemed to alleviate the pain.

Finally, Dr. Gadladge flew to Florida to have another look at Butler's throat. After examining Brett again, he prescribed the strongest antibiotic he could and told the outfielder that if that didn't work, he would have to remove his tonsils.

Soon spring training was over and Butler and the Dodgers headed to L.A. to begin the season. For Butler, though, what could have been a happy return to the scene of some great performances was not turning into an enjoyable experience. "I'd been playing for about a month, and I was fatigued and run-down."

About that time, Butler's wife, Eveline, joined him in Los Angeles. Knowing that Brett was still suffering, she looked in his mouth and did a perfectly good Dr. Mom diagnosis: "This is bad. You need to get your tonsils out."

Soon Butler was visiting a doctor and asking him how long it would take him to get back to the game if he had the surgery. He was told it would take about three weeks for him to heal and return to form. With that in mind, Butler left the team and headed back to Atlanta.

Upon arriving, Butler paid Dr. Gadladge a visit. "He looked in my throat, and he was shocked. He couldn't believe it had tripled in size. In fact, he was not even sure what was causing the problem."

During surgery on May 3, Dr. Gadladge discovered that the problem was much more serious than chronically inflamed tonsils. He found a golf-ball-sized growth behind Butler's tonsil.

Although Dr. Gadladge was not greatly alarmed initially, a few days later he knew he had cause to be concerned. On Monday, May 9, he stopped by the Butler house to deliver the news himself. He looked at his longtime friend and said, "Brett, you have cancer."

Brett Butler, star baseball player, was gravely ill.

That diagnosis was the starting point on an unexpected journey for Butler during the 1996 baseball season—one that thousands of Americans watched closely.

"When he first told me that I had cancer, it was still on the back burner of my thought process. My first thought was to get through the pain. For eight days after the tonsillectomy, I was in the worst pain that I could possibly be in. Every swallow was agonizing. I was more worried about getting rid of the pain of the tonsillectomy than the cancer itself. After eight or nine days, the pain subsided, and I was able to reach in and analyze what was happening.

"The first thing you think about when someone says *cancer* is death," Butler says. "*I have cancer? I'm going to die.* If it hits someone else, you don't think about it a whole lot. But when it hits close to home, then you think, *Wow! Cancer. Death.*

"My first reaction was to be mad at God. I told Him, 'Only thirty-eight years, Lord? That's it? You know how I've loved You.'"

Next, Butler says, his attention turned toward Eveline and their four children. "I began to wonder what was going to happen to them," Butler recalls. If cancer meant death, then he must learn to face the possibilities that would follow.

Yet Butler's initial reactions were soon replaced by hope and trust. "In the quietness of my heart, God revealed to me, 'Hey, I'm God. Who are you to question Me? Look what I've done for you thus far. In life or in death, I'm in control. And I love your family more than you could. So just relax and let Me show you what mighty things I can do in your life.'

"I learned that I was able to have the peace to understand that there's a bigger picture than just Brett Butler having cancer. God was going to work out some things, not only in my life, but through my teammates and people throughout major league baseball and throughout the country who are going to get some kind of teaching from what God has to say when we're in the pits and valleys in life. They are going to see that when we step out with childlike faith, He's going to direct us."

The first thing Butler had to face in his new walk of faith was more surgery. Because doctors performing the tonsillectomy discovered that the growth in his neck was cancerous, they scheduled a new operation to remove lymph nodes from Butler's neck. On May 21, Dr. William Grist removed fifty nodes, later discovering that one of them was malignant and the other forty-nine were benign.

To begin what Butler called a "mopping up" procedure that would thwart any further cancerous growth, he was scheduled for a battery of radiation treatments. Determined to defeat the disease and return to baseball, Butler had a difficult road ahead: He would have to recover from his second operation, undergo radiation, recover from that, and get back into playing shape. It would take a miracle, it seemed, for him to play again in 1996.

For the next four months, baseball fans watched to see what would happen with this player everyone thought they knew. Would he be able to come back to the game he loved? Would the cancer reappear? Would the Dodgers stay in the race long enough to give him an incentive to return? Would he continue to trust God even after life had taken this terrible detour?

Along the way, several issues would appear in Butler's life—issues that would not have come up if he hadn't contracted cancer. They were issues that would test his faith.

Like many people who suffer serious illnesses, Butler struggled with questions such as: "Why me? Why now? Why did I, a man of faith and a healthy athlete, get cancer?" Early reports tried to pinpoint two possible tangible reasons for his cancer. First, about fifteen years earlier, Butler had used smokeless tobacco for a couple of seasons. Second, his parents smoked when he was a child, so secondhand smoke may have caused the disease.

During the time when Butler was on radiation, he had a discussion about this with his spiritual mentor, Tim Cash. Tim referred to the Scripture passage in John 9:2 in which Jesus was asked whose sin caused the man to be born blind—his or his parents. Then Tim told Brett that Jesus' answer had been that it was the fault of neither; instead, it had happened so God's work could be displayed.

"The cancer," Tim told him, "was not a punishment because your parents smoked or because of some stint with smokeless tobacco early in your career, but it was that God might be glorified."

For Butler, that was much-needed reassurance that his suffering would not be in vain. His illness had a purpose.

The second issue Butler wrestled with was whether the disease might end his life. As disheartening as it was to realize he might never play baseball again, that was nothing compared with the looming specter of death. Despite this fear, Butler took courage from the fact that his type of cancer had a recovery rate of 85 percent.

Even more encouraging were assurances from fellow Christians that God had told them Butler would not succumb to his disease.

"Things happened that were signs, in my opinion, from God that said, 'Hey, I haven't turned My back on you. I'm here, and you've trusted Me this far. You can continue to trust Me. All you have to do is be still, step out with childlike faith, and I'll do some powerful things.'

"I had a friend tell me God had revealed to her that I wasn't going to die. She said she had this peace only two other times in her life, and it had been true both times.

"Another friend brought his pastor to see me," Butler continues. "The pastor told me he had been praying, 'How can I console this gentleman who has cancer?' He said God revealed to him that I was a minister who played baseball and that my ministry was not over."

Throughout his questions and concerns about the future, Butler drew strength from Eveline's faith. "What helped me the most was the peace God gave my wife. When this whole thing came about, she could have broken down, but she went to prayer. God gave her a real peace. She was my strength to get me through this."

As his radiation therapy progressed, Butler began to consider his return to baseball. He wondered if he could overcome the effects of his illness and treatment to again roam center field at Dodger Stadium. He also wondered if his shoulder was damaged when the lymph nodes were removed.

Early indications were that his body was responding better than had been expected to the trauma it had undergone. "God spared me a lot of pain," Butler says. "The doctors told me that after eight or nine days of radiation, I wouldn't be able to eat any solid food, that I'd be on a liquid diet." With just three days left in his radiation treatments, though, Butler was proud to proclaim that for breakfast he had "Eggo waffles with my kids. Sure, it hurt some, but I did pretty well."

Other complications, such as the loss of his saliva glands and the inability to sleep, were also predicted, but Butler suffered much less from those side effects than many others who have had the same treatment. What's more, with therapy and exercise, he was able to rebuild his shoulder muscles.

Along with the support of family and friends, and his swift progress toward recovery, something else spurred Butler's return to baseball—the outpouring of love he received from thousands of people all over the country.

"You wonder how you touch people's lives," Butler says.

"God has allowed me to step back and observe. Any good that I've been able to do in my life and in the sixteen years I've played major league baseball has come back to me a hundredfold through the love, cards, prayers, and phone calls. It's been an overwhelming experience."

What was truly overwhelming was what happened on September 6, 1996. After four months and five days, after two operations and thirty-two radiation sessions, after millions of prayers and hundreds of hours of treatment and physical therapy, Brett Butler was announced as the starting center fielder for the Los Angeles Dodgers.

The uniform that had hung in his locker and that his teammates had carried with them on road trips since he had left the team in May was again worn by the man they called Bugsy. A standing-room-only crowd had come to Chavez Ravine to see a spectacle that rarely happens in sports—an athlete returning from cancer surgery to play again.

Valiant men such as Dave Dravecky and Mario Lemieux had done it before, and now Brett Butler would join that elite group of athletes who fought back from serious illness to take up their sport once again. Heightening the drama was the fact that the Dodgers were embroiled in a pennant race, battling San Diego for a division title and Montreal for a wild-card slot in the play-offs.

The Dodgers were looking for a miracle September, and Brett Butler wanted to be part of it. "No way I would have tried this if we didn't have a chance to win a world championship," Butler said at the time. "To me, the whole thing is a miracle."

When Butler stepped back into the lineup against the Pittsburgh Pirates that September night, he showed that he could still do what he had always done—manufacture runs. Although he did not reach base his first two times up, in the fifth inning, he singled for his first hit in ninety-eight days.

In the eighth inning, he demonstrated his scrappy style of play, which has drawn admiration throughout his career. First, he received a base on balls from Marc Wilkins. Then, as he had done so many times before, he promptly stole second, went to third on a throwing error, and raced home on a sacrifice fly by

Eric Karros, punctuating his run by sliding across the plate and jumping up to clap his hands together. His teammates mobbed him when he reached the dugout.

Final score: Dodgers 2, Pirates 1. Winning run: Brett Butler. Just like old times.

"It means more to me than any game I've ever been in," Butler said after that comeback game.

And why not? Most people would have guessed his season, if not his career, had ended in early May on an Atlanta operating room table.

Dodger manager Bill Russell observed, "If you don't believe in miracles, you better. Brett just did one tonight."

But Brett Butler ran out of miracles less than a week later.

Baseball had seen it before when Dave Dravecky returned in triumph from cancer surgery only to be sidelined by injury soon afterward. For Butler, the bubble burst on September 11. While attempting to bunt against Cincinnati Reds pitcher Giovanni Carrara, Butler was hit on his throwing hand, breaking the fifth metacarpal bone. His season was finished for good this time.

It was not the ending anyone expected for that dramatic season. There would be no play-offs. No shot at the World Series. No more miracles.

The roller-coaster ride that had characterized the 1996 season had come to a stop.

So what did it all mean? What lessons did this remarkable year teach the man who had nearly come to the end of a fantastic baseball career?

For one thing, it has taught him more about God than he could have learned any other way. "God has given me a purpose that can be accomplished through both the good and the bad," he says. "I've learned that if we are going to accept the good God gives us, we have to be willing to accept the bad. Also, we have to trust that His perfect will is going to be done.

"I know now that I'm able to stand on the rock of God's character," he continues. "God is all-loving, He's kind, and more than that, He's trustworthy. What we have to do is step out with a trusting faith. If Brett Butler lives another fifty or sixty years, or Brett Butler dies tomorrow, God's perfect plan will be accomplished, and I can have peace and contentment. God didn't go to sleep and wake up one day and say, 'Uh-oh, Brett Butler has cancer. I shouldn't have gone to sleep.' God has His eye on each one of us."

It's clear that Butler's experience with cancer gave him a new understanding of God's sovereignty. "Before, I felt like I had control of my life. I had accepted Christ as my Savior, and God was directing my life, to a degree. But still, I thought I had control. My cancer made me realize that I don't have any control. God has control, and He can do what He wants with you, with me, with my family, with our friends. We have to go with that trusting faith, and we have to go with God's will, whatever it is."

Brett Butler seems to know himself and his God better than ever. He has faced the possibility of mortality and has put his life squarely in the hands of the Master of immortality.

What else does anyone need to know about Brett Butler?

Q & A WITH BRETT BUTLER

Q: *What encouragement can you give others because of the illness you went through?*
Brett: God is longing to love us with a father's love. He wants us to step over that line and say, "I trust You." I've developed a deeper and more loving relationship with God, and He wants to do that with all of His children. As human beings, we can love only so much, but with God, love is infinite and without depth or width or length. It's unbelievable. It's a love that cannot be measured. He is standing there with open arms, saying, "Trust Me."

Q: *What's one good thing that has resulted from your cancer?*
Brett: To be able to share with people who have come to me and said, "I'm praying for you." Many of these people aren't churchgoers and have no idea about Jesus Christ. I've been able to talk with them. This has opened up the door for them to receive Jesus as their Savior somewhere down the line.

Q: *How should a Christian handle the great sums of money he earns as a baseball player?*

Brett: It's not the money itself that's the problem; it's the *love* of money that gets people into trouble. You have to take a step back and look at it from a distance. You have to evaluate and reevaluate to make sure you don't get caught up in the same trap as King Solomon. Here was a man who was so rich that eventually the money took over. To me, the money isn't mine; it's God's. And it's my obligation to be a good steward of His money and do things that will benefit Him and the kingdom of God.

THE ROAD TO THE MAJORS

- Selected by the Atlanta Braves in the 23rd round of the June 1979 draft
- Traded to the Cleveland Indians on October 21, 1983
- Signed as a free agent by the San Francisco Giants on December 1, 1987
- Signed as a free agent by the Los Angeles Dodgers on December 15, 1990
- Signed as a free agent by the New York Mets on April 11, 1995
- Traded to the Dodgers on August 18, 1995

Minor league stops: Bradenton, Greenwood, Anderson, Durham, Richmond

Minor league highlight: In 1981, while playing for Richmond, Butler was named the International League Most Valuable Player

Year	Team	G	AB	R	H	2B	3B	HR	RBI	BB	SO	SB	BA	SLG
1981	Atl	40	126	17	32	2	3	0	4	19	17	9	.254	.317
1982	Atl	89	240	35	52	2	0	0	7	25	35	21	.217	.225
1983	Atl	151	549	84	154	21	13	5	37	54	56	39	.281	.393
1984	Cle	159	602	108	162	25	9	3	49	86	62	52	.269	.355
1985	Cle	152	591	106	184	28	14	5	50	63	42	47	.311	.431
1986	Cle	161	587	92	163	17	14	4	51	70	65	32	.278	.375
1987	Cle	137	522	91	154	25	8	9	41	91	55	33	.295	.425
1988	SF	157	568	109	163	27	9	6	43	97	64	43	.287	.398
1989	SF	154	594	100	168	22	4	4	36	59	69	31	.283	.354
1990	SF	160	622	108	192	20	9	3	44	90	62	51	.309	.384
1991	LA	161	615	112	182	13	5	2	38	108	79	38	.296	.343
1992	LA	157	553	86	171	14	11	3	39	95	67	41	.309	.391
1993	LA	156	607	80	181	21	10	1	42	86	69	39	.298	.371
1994	LA	111	417	79	131	13	9	8	33	68	52	27	.314	.446
1995	NYN	90	367	54	114	13	7	1	25	43	42	21	.311	.392
	LA	39	146	24	40	5	2	0	13	24	9	11	.274	.336
1996	LA	34	131	22	35	1	1	0	8	9	22	8	.267	.290
16 Years		2108	7837	1307	2278	269	128	54	560	1087	867	543	.291	.378

Chad Curtis
A Dream Fulfilled

VITAL STATISTICS

Born: November 6, 1968, in Marion, Indiana
5 feet 10, 185 pounds
Attended Grand Canyon College
Position: Outfielder
Throws right, bats right
Family: Wife, Candace, and two children, Corazon and Cassidy
1997 Team: Cleveland Indians

- Played in every game for the Tigers in 1995
- Led Angels in games played, at bats, doubles, triples, and stolen bases in 1994
- Stole forty-eight bases (fifth in the league) in 1993
- Led American League outfielders with sixteen assists in 1992
- Stole forty-three bases in his rookie season with the Angels in 1992

WARMING UP

In early 1996, Chad Curtis had spoken at chapel for the students at Grand Rapids (Michigan) Baptist High School. Later, after the season began, Curtis was on a road trip for the Tigers, playing in Minnesota. While the Tigers were in town, the Dayspring Chorale from Grand Rapids Baptist was also in the Twin Cities on a singing tour, and they decided to go to a Tigers-Twins game. When the scoreboard flashed a message that the group was at the game, Curtis happened to see it and noticed the kids in the upper deck, cheering wildly. From his center field position, he turned and waved to the students—which, of course, made their day.

FAVORITE BIBLE PASSAGE

"As for me and my household, we will serve the Lord" (Joshua 24:15).

Chad Curtis

I f you had worked as hard as Chad Curtis did to become a professional baseball player, you would probably be willing to get married in your baseball uniform too. He can be allowed that one extravagance.

After all, playing pro baseball was a dream he had nurtured since he was five years old, when he announced to his grandmother that he was going to be a big leaguer when he grew up. Like so many people who would follow after her, Grandma wasn't buying it. "She shook her head and told me I was setting my goals too high," Curtis recalls.

Even at that early age, Curtis had begun developing his skills under the tutelage of his father. And he had already chosen a set of stars to whom he could hook his dream wagon. Tiger Stadium—the playground of stars like Alan Trammell, Lou Whitaker, and Kirk Gibson—was a two-hour drive from his home in Middleville, Michigan. It was those three Tigers in particular who would serve as Chad's baseball role models. "If I was role-playing in the backyard," he recalls, "I was always Alan Trammell."

But becoming Alan Trammell's peer as a major leaguer would be an incredibly difficult challenge for Curtis. No matter how well he would perform in future years, it seemed he had a tough time proving he was for real.

When he was eleven, his family moved to Benson, Arizona, near Tucson. Although that move probably seemed insignificant in baseball terms at the time, it would eventually have serious implications for Curtis.

At Benson Union High School, Curtis's athletic career flourished. He participated in baseball, basketball, football, and track, with baseball looking like a third-place finisher (and track running last). "I was more of a football player than a baseball player," says the former two-time All-State quarterback. What's more, Curtis's track coach allowed him to play baseball and run in the track meets on the days he didn't have a game. During his senior year, the baseball team lost early in the tournament, allowing him to run in the district and state track competition.

When it came time to decide which college to attend, Curtis had a simple choice. He could go to either a school that was offering him a football scholarship or one *not* offering him a baseball scholarship. "I didn't have any baseball scholarship offers," he says. "I had quite a few football offers from universities out west. I had contact with the University of Arizona and some smaller schools."

It's been the story of Chad's life in baseball. An All-Stater on the diamond as well as the gridiron, he couldn't convince anyone that he was good enough to play college-level baseball.

Why not take Arizona up on that scholarship and pursue football? Ironically, the reason he didn't stay with football is the same reason he couldn't get anyone to pay attention to him in baseball—his size. Chad's mom, Carol, says, "He just evaluated things and figured that he had a better shot in baseball because of his lack of size."

So, undrafted by pro baseball teams and unrecruited by colleges, Curtis had no choice but to carve out his own baseball career. He had some things to prove in the game he loved if he was ever going to get to Tiger Stadium as a player. Curtis's snub by college baseball scouts wouldn't be the last time so-called experts would doubt his ability to produce in baseball. And it wouldn't be the last time they would be wrong.

Curtis took his love for baseball, his drive to succeed, and his less-than-ideal-for-an-outfielder body and went to Yavapai Community College in Prescott, Arizona. As a walk-on. That was far from the path to the big leagues taken by his boyhood heroes, Trammell and Gibson.

"I wasn't expected to make that team," Curtis recalls. "So I said to myself, *Look, if I'm not going to achieve my goals, it's going to be because I'm not good enough, not because I didn't put everything I had into it.*"

He did make the Yavapai team and played there a year before switching to Cochise Community College for his second year of college ball. It was a breakthrough year for the young infielder-outfielder.

"Cochise was my first real taste of baseball success," he explains. "I was an honorable mention junior college All-American. More important, we ended up playing in the junior college World Series. Getting the taste of winning baseball and overcoming obstacles as a team was a big thrill."

New thrills were just ahead as Curtis transferred again—this time to Grand Canyon College in Phoenix, a school that was then a member of the National Association of Intercollegiate Athletics (NAIA), an organization made up of small colleges.

But to play there, Chad again had some convincing to do. Despite his great year at Cochise, he was still a walk-on at Grand Canyon. No one doubted that the Antelopes had a good program behind coach Gil Stafford. But surely by then some-one would have noticed that Curtis could play! Nobody may have taken his abilities seriously up to that point, but Curtis was about to make people take note.

From an outsider's perspective, the indirect route Chad was taking to fulfill that prophecy he proclaimed as a five-year-old may have seemed like a waste of time. After all, by the time Curtis was trying out for his third college team in three years, many baseball players his age had already moved up a couple of rungs on the minor league ladder. But there was more at stake in Curtis's life than baseball. His slow rise to professional baseball allowed him a chance to make changes in another area of his life, changes that were sorely needed *before* he headed for the pros.

His faith in Jesus Christ had taken root when he was a nine-year-old in Michigan; but as he grew older, his commitment wavered. "I had accepted the Lord when I was in my hometown church—First Baptist of Middleville," he recalls. "I had a really good youth program with Awana and things like that. I got to know the Scriptures and a lot of characters of the Bible. But after we moved, there were periods of time when I just wasn't living for the Lord. I had drifted away from my faith a little bit through high school and my first couple of years of college.

"God gave me the opportunity to go to Grand Canyon, which is a Christian school, to get me back to Him and to show me that I was putting baseball and other things before Him. God showed me that I needed to put Him as my top priority."

In addition to getting reacquainted with God while at Grand Canyon, Chad also met a baseball player who would influence him and become a link between amateur and pro baseball. This player would have all the tools that baseball experts thought Curtis didn't have. He was an outfielder with size and power. Standing 6 feet 3 inches tall and weighing 220 pounds, Tim Salmon *looked* like an outfielder.

Curtis, on the other hand, looked more like a second baseman.

Yet their statistics at Grand Canyon made them both look like candidates for the next step—professional baseball. In 1989, Curtis hit .369, smashed 19 home runs, and knocked in 83 runs. He also stole 36 bases. The other leader of the number-one-ranked team was Salmon, who batted .356, pounded out 19 home runs, and tallied 63 RBIs.

During that season, Curtis realized his teammate might boost his chances of playing pro ball. Chad had told his mom, "The big league scouts will come to watch Tim play, but they're going to see me too."

In addition, the third member of the Antelope outfield, Paul Swingle, was a player who was attracting the scouts' attention.

When draft day came along, though, it was Salmon who got the high draft pick. The Angels nabbed him in the third round. That left Curtis to wait. And wait. And wait.

Finally, he got the call. "My coach at Grand Canyon had told me I had a good enough season to be drafted high, and projections had me going somewhere in round ten of the draft. It turned out that I didn't get a call for four or five days. I found out I was drafted [by the Angels] in the 45th round. I was pretty disappointed. I felt I did what I needed to do in college to get drafted in a higher spot. I think the scouts thought that with my college numbers, I was playing all the way up to my potential. They didn't see room for improvement."

After the initial disappointment wore off, Curtis made a decision about his draft status that would spur him on. "I realized that I got what I wanted—an opportunity to play," he says. "All I wanted was a shot. I'm in the same spot as everyone else."

Curtis set out to show all doubters that he had the ability and drive to go far in baseball. After thirty-two games at Mesa in the Rookie League, where he hit .303 and proved that he could hit with a wooden bat, he moved on to Single A Quad City. This team would prove to be a memorable stop on the Chad Curtis "I Told You I Can Play This Game" Tour. For one thing, the 1990 Quad City team was outstanding. For Curtis, it was a reminder of the success he had enjoyed in college.

"It was a great team to play for," he says. "Our coach, Donnie Long, was a discipline-oriented coach, and he expected his players to do things right. That was what I was used to, coming out of college. He had a good rapport with his players. We were a team—like we were at Grand Canyon." Long was named Midwest League Manager of the Year as he guided his team to an 81–59 mark and the league championship.

The second reason Quad City stands out in Chad Curtis's mind relates to a girl he had met several years earlier in Benson. When he was a sophomore playing baseball for Benson Union, an eighth-grader named Candace Reynolds and her mother stopped by the baseball field to watch a game. "We talked a little bit after the game," Chad recalls. "But I really didn't know who she was. She and her mom just liked watching baseball games. Soon, I took an interest in her, and she took an interest in me. We were just friends for a couple of years, and then we started dating."

In the spring of 1990, Chad and Candace got engaged and decided to get married in November—after the baseball season.

"Right before I left for spring training," says Curtis, "I decided I didn't want to be out in Iowa all by myself. So I called Candace and said, 'Why don't you fly out here to Iowa and we'll get married.'"

So Candace and her mom made the trip from Arizona to Iowa.

"We went to the justice of the peace at 10:00 A.M. He said, 'You can start the paperwork today, and three days later you can get married.' Her mom wasn't going to be in Iowa that long, so we talked him into marrying us at 1:30 that day."

Just one problem: Chad had a baseball game that afternoon. So he put on his baseball uniform, took Candace and her mom back to the courthouse, and got married. He made it back to the field before the first pitch.

Several years earlier, Candace's mother had seen her future son-in-law in a baseball uniform. She probably never dreamed that someday he would be standing at the altar, dressed the same way, marrying her daughter. Chad puts it into perspective, though: "It was probably the best-looking suit I had."

In November, at about the time Chad and Candace had originally planned to marry, they held a reception for friends and family. Chad did not wear his baseball uniform to that event.

Playing in the low minors is a notoriously poor-paying job, but for Chad and Candace, it didn't matter. "We never sat down and said, 'Can we afford to get married?' We wanted to get married, and we figured things would work themselves out. We were trusting God, and we were getting married before Him. We asked Him to take care of us, and we figured He would provide. We didn't have a lot of money or anything, but we look back on those times as some of the best we ever had together."

One reason the newlyweds enjoyed Quad City was that they were befriended by some fellow Christians. "The Lord led us to a family in Iowa. We got to know them really well, and we still stay in touch. It really had a grounding effect on us and made us a part of the community."

On the field for Quad City that summer, Curtis continued to prove that he was a legitimate major league prospect. He batted .307 with 14 home runs and 65 runs batted in. He made the Midwest League All-Star team while leading the league in hits (151), total bases (223), and on-base percentage (.390).

The Angels were finally convinced they had something.

In 1991, they moved him up from Single A Quad City to Triple A Edmonton, where he again turned in a strong performance, batting .316, leading the league in hits with 151, making the All-Star team, and earning a shot at the big club for 1992.

Despite an outstanding season at Edmonton, Curtis found his stay there disconcerting at times. "When you're in Triple A, you're one step from the big leagues," he says. "Players are thinking a little more about themselves. They're thinking, *What can I do to make it to the next level, to get to the big leagues?* That was hard for me. That's not the way I had always played. I guess I got spoiled at Quad City."

Sure, Curtis had something to prove at Edmonton. He was still making his way to the majors. But to him, the team was most important. "If you look at teams that win, they're ones that have a lot of fun together. One of the things that may be wrong with the game at the professional level is that it's a job, a business. It leads to being a little more individual-oriented as opposed to team-oriented."

Chad Curtis had one more stop before he would finally live out his major league dream: La Guarira, Venezuela. He and Candace went there so he could play in the Venezuelan Winter League, a final tune-up for the big time. All Chad did there was bat .338, hit sixteen doubles and eight triples, and win the league MVP award.

In addition to the opportunity to hone his athletic skills, the time in Venezuela strengthened Curtis's marriage. "Candace and I look at that trip as one of the most fulfilling times we spent together, because we were so dependent on each other." They both learned a bit of Spanish, and they still look forward to going back to Venezuela for a visit.

The Angels invited Curtis to spring training in February 1992, but manager Buck Rodgers didn't give Curtis much of a chance to make the team. Nevertheless, he made the most of every opportunity to prove himself, and he ended up winning a spot on the roster. Finally, after a lifetime of struggling against people who didn't believe in him, Chad Curtis was wearing a big league uniform in a major league park. Now it was up to him to show that he belonged there—and demonstrate once and for all that he had not set his goals too high.

It was April 8, 1992. The Angels were starting the season at home, and their rookie outfielder was leading off for them. In the stands were Ted and Carol Curtis, watching as their son, wearing number 30, stepped in to face Greg Hibbard of the Chicago White Sox. Hibbard took the sign, went into his windup, and fired the first major league pitch Chad had ever seen. He swung and lined the ball right back where it came from—up the middle and out into center field for his first major league hit.

The kid with the less-than-prototypical body was standing on first base with a major league career batting average of 1.000.

"People ask me what is my major league highlight, and I would say that's it," he says. "It was the culmination of all the time and effort that I had put into baseball—from the time my dad and I began when I was four years old to when I was twenty-three years old. My fantasy changed to reality with that game. I never thought of doing anything else. In my mind, I was going to be a major league player, and no one was going to tell me I couldn't."

But Chad Curtis was not done driving himself.

Now that he had arrived on the scene, he determined to establish himself as a quality major leaguer. In three years as a California Angel, he did that and more. During his rookie season, Curtis stole 43 bases, the second-best total ever by an Angels rookie. In the outfield, he led the American League with 16 assists, which tied a club record. And he was in the majors full-time a year earlier than his more highly touted college friend, Tim Salmon.

The numbers improved in 1993 as he successfully avoided the dreaded sophomore slump. His average soared to .285 and he stole 48 bases while again putting together a stellar performance in the outfield. Even after such a fine season, though, Curtis was not completely satisfied. He knew he could do even better.

In 1994, Curtis began to add a new element to his game— the element people had long thought could not be there. He began to belt home runs. In the strike-shortened season, he pounded out 11 homers in 114 games. His best previous power performance was his rookie year when he'd posted 10 in 139 games. In every sense of the word, he was a complete major league player.

Another milestone in Curtis's big league journey occurred on April 13, 1995, when he was traded from the California Angels to the Detroit Tigers. Even though he was thrilled at the chance to play ball in his home state, he had mixed emotions when he learned of the trade. "My first thoughts were my relationships with my teammates on the Angels. *I'm going to miss those guys.* But still I thought, *If you're going to get traded and have to uproot, it's probably good to go to a place you're familiar with."*

The best thing about returning to Michigan was that he would be sharing the clubhouse with his heroes. "I'm going to be playing with all three of my favorite baseball players of all time: Alan Trammell, Lou Whitaker, and Kirk Gibson," he said at the time. "Those guys were young players who gave everything they had when I was at a very impressionable age."

Throughout Chad's first year in Detroit, it appeared that he had indeed found a home. His power numbers continued to rise, as he hit 21 home runs and knocked in 67 runs—both career highs. Yet the team around him was disintegrating. Gibson and Whitaker both retired. Trammell was on the verge of hanging up his glove. And the pitching was a nightmare. Even legendary manager Sparky Anderson, the heart and soul of the Tigers for many years, had seen enough. He retired after the 1995 season.

As all new seasons do, 1996 began with an element of hope. There was a new manager in town as Buddy Bell moved over from a coaching position with Cleveland. But it was not long until hope was replaced by despair in Detroit. Clearly, this was not a good baseball team. Only Curtis, Travis Fryman, and Cecil Fielder were legitimate major league stars, and they were surrounded by a host of players no one had heard of.

Soon, the negativity was affecting Curtis. Going into the season, he had not missed a game for the Tigers. But when he began to struggle at the plate early on, Bell sat him out. It was for Chad the beginning of the end for what could have been a grand career in Detroit.

"Buddy lost confidence in me," Curtis explains. "I was playing on a team that was on pace to be the worst in the history of baseball. My personality is such that I looked at it as my fault and I had to do something about it. I put so much pressure on myself to try to get the team going that I began struggling. Buddy saw that. I don't know if he knew why I was struggling, but he decided to put somebody else out there. That hit my confidence even more. I felt like I was bailing out. But that's the last thing I wanted to do. It was my team, and if my team was sinking, I wanted to stay with it."

Despite his resolve to hang in there with the team, the Tigers did not stay with Chad. When Brett Butler was diagnosed with cancer, the Los Angeles Dodgers knew they needed help in center field, so they traded for Curtis. His Tiger career, for the time being, at least, was over.

Although he hated to leave the favorite team of his youth, Curtis found the move to L.A. beneficial. "It really rejuvenated me. I never really experienced a pennant race until I had a chance to play for the Dodgers. The game is a lot of fun when you're going out there winning and doing the things you're supposed to do."

In December of 1996, Curtis signed as a free agent with the Cleveland Indians, a team that will surely have him in the thick of other pennant races should he stay with them.

The 1996 season, with its bittersweet moments, was an educational experience for Chad. "I realized something important: for several years I've looked at myself the same way other people look at me—and that is as Chad Curtis, the baseball player. I even asked one of my friends, 'If you were going to introduce me to someone, what would you say?' He said, 'I'd say, "This is Chad Curtis. He plays baseball."'

"That's what I've been thinking for a long time—I'm a worthwhile person because I'm a baseball player. When I was playing for a poor team and playing poorly myself, I felt I wasn't worthwhile. All of a sudden the thing that I've been saying gives me value I'm not doing well at. But does that make me not a worthwhile person? I really struggled with that.

"I was reading my Bible a lot and praying and talking to my Christian friends. I was talking to my wife, and we came to the conclusion that I needed to quit looking at myself that way. I had to think about why God sees me as worthwhile. The only reason God sees me as worthwhile is because I have a relationship with Him through Jesus Christ. I still can't say I've got a real good grip on that, but I think realizing that got me going in the right direction."

For Chad Curtis, his lifelong dream had come true. He was a major league player. Yet he discovered, as most people do, that even fulfilled dreams do not come without disappointments and difficult lessons. And he has learned that fulfilling dreams is a much better experience if you have others who live those dreams with you.

Chad Curtis plays baseball with a lot of heart. He's worked hard to get where he is. And he still wants to get better. "I want to be the best," he says. No one deserves it more.

Q & A WITH CHAD CURTIS

Q: *Who was the most influential person for you growing up?*
Chad: My father was an exceptional role model. He always let me know that the most important thing was faith. That made a big impact on me. I went through some times when I wasn't necessarily following the Lord, but I came back because I had a godly role model.

Q: *What is something about major league baseball that bothers you when compared to the minor leagues and amateur ball?*
Chad: I got to the big leagues, and I noticed the political decisions. This guy's going to play because he was drafted higher

or this guy's going to play because we have money invested in him. And sometimes things in the game itself bother me. You can't steal a base because you might offend the other team. Or you can't swing at a certain pitch because there's something going on with the guy batting behind you. I just want to go out and play.

Q: *When you analyze what went wrong in Detroit that led to your being traded, what do you think was the problem?*
Chad: There's something about baseball that some people don't understand. Baseball is not a game of prototypes like football. We can take a guy who is 6 feet 7 and 320 pounds and say, "That guy's going to be a good lineman." But in baseball, I think sometimes people look at a guy and say he's a fast 6 foot 1, 180-pound switch-hitter, so he must be a center fielder. I think that's the direction the Tigers were looking at. They wanted a prototype player for each position. When you do that, you don't look at the intangibles—the drive and the desire.

Q: *How do you stay strong spiritually?*
Chad: I try to start my day by reading the Bible and praying. That keeps my mind focused on what is important. I also enjoy Christian fellowship, either on my team or at church.

THE ROAD TO THE MAJORS

• Selected by the California Angels
• Traded to the Detroit Tigers for Tony Phillips on April 13, 1995
• Traded to the Los Angeles Dodgers for Joey Eischen and John Cummings on July 31, 1996
• Signed by the Cleveland Indians on December 18, 1996

Minor league stops: Mesa, Quad City, Edmonton

Minor league highlight: Selected to the Triple A All-Star team in 1991 while playing at Edmonton, where he stole 46 bases and hit .316

THE CURTIS FILE

Year	Team	G	AB	R	H	2B	3B	HR	RBI	BB	SO	SB	BA	SLG
1992	Cal	139	441	59	114	16	2	10	46	51	71	43	.259	.372
1993	Cal	152	583	94	166	25	3	6	59	70	89	48	.285	.369
1994	Cal	114	453	67	116	23	4	11	50	37	69	25	.256	.397
1995	Det	144	586	96	157	29	3	21	67	70	93	27	.268	.435
1996	Det	104	400	65	105	20	1	10	37	53	73	16	.263	.393
	LA	43	104	20	22	5	0	2	9	17	15	2	.212	.317
5 Years		**696**	**2567**	**401**	**680**	**118**	**13**	**60**	**268**	**298**	**410**	**161**	**.265**	**.391**

Mark Dewey
It's What's Inside that Counts

VITAL STATISTICS

Born January 2, 1965, in Grand Rapids, Michigan
6 feet, 216 pounds
Attended Grand Valley State University
Position: Relief pitcher
Throws right, bats right
Family: Wife, Monique, and two children, Caleb and Seth
1997 Team: Milwaukee Brewers

- Pitched in 78 games in 1996
- Held right-handed batters to a 9.195 batting average in 1995
- Surrendered no runs in first five major league appearances

WARMING UP

When it comes to baseball, all Mark Dewey wants is a chance to pitch. He doesn't want a lot of hoopla. He doesn't need anyone to stroke his ego. That's why he has appreciated the managers he's played for along the way: Jim Leyland, Jeff Torborg, Roger Craig, and Dusty Baker. He says they simply told him, "Here's the ball. Go get 'em." As Mark says, "I don't need a shoulder to cry on when I do poorly, and I don't need anyone to pat me on the back when I do well. Just keep giving me the ball."

FAVORITE BIBLE PASSAGE

True to form, Mark Dewey doesn't have a specific Scripture passage that is his favorite. Instead, he has a favorite *theme*. "My favorite theme in Scripture is that God does all things according to His good pleasure," he says. "The sovereignty of God and the fact that He is a holy, righteous God who can do what He wills—that is the most comforting theme in the Bible."

Mark Dewey

In one sense, appearances are not important to Mark Dewey.

That could be a problem for Dewey, because as a relief pitcher, his lifeblood is appearances. In fact, he made a bunch of them in 1996. Fifty-nine times he came out of the bull pen to attempt to frustrate opposing batters and help the San Francisco Giants secure a win.

Appearances of another kind are also in Dewey's best interest, because they are the kind that provide opportunities for him to tell others about his faith in Jesus Christ. These appearances include speaking engagements and working with young people at God's Garage, a ministry built around sports in his hometown of Grand Rapids, Michigan.

Those two kinds of appearances, then, are perfectly acceptable to the right-hander, who has been in professional baseball since 1987 and in the majors since 1990.

It's a third kind of appearance that Mark Dewey doesn't care for—the outward appearances many people put on to impress others. Dewey is a man who thrives on what is on the inside—both spiritually and intellectually. He understands how easily and how often our words and actions fail to reflect what is going on internally—not always because we are trying to be deceitful, but because we sometimes don't understand what is right and true.

Mark learned that firsthand in regard to the Christian faith, but it took him almost thirty years to experience it. Growing up in a strongly religious community, he had heard the story of Jesus Christ from the time he was little. Yet he knows now that he never brought that truth inside. He never let it move from his head to his heart.

"I was brought up going to church, but it wasn't until I was an adult and out of the church that I became a Christian," he says. "I remember going to Sunday school and vacation Bible school, but I don't recall how much we did or didn't study the Bible. I knew the gospel intellectually, but it never took root.

"When you grow up in a community like I did, where virtually everybody went to church, a lot of people *thought* they were Christians. That is the biggest deception to overcome— that you're a Christian because you believe certain things intellectually and that you've gone to church. There are many people who have a lot of head knowledge, but they've never given their lives to Jesus."

For Dewey, the journey to discovering this truth would take him through his high school years at Jenison High School in Michigan, through a successful career in the classroom and on the diamond at Grand Valley State University, and through his first few years of minor league baseball. Thinking he was a Christian but not giving it much thought since a Sunday job at age sixteen had put an end to his habit of attending church, Dewey pushed forward through life.

Taking advantage of a community that had a good Little League system and a successful high school program, Dewey pursued his first love, baseball. In fact, Dewey's junior varsity coach at Jenison High, Reed Johnson, gave Mark the kind of compliment that can keep a kid going for a long time.

"After I pitched a game as a sophomore, Johnson called me in and told me he thought I had the ability to be a very good pitcher in college and maybe beyond. It never really dawned on me the extent of what that comment meant, nor do I think anyone else would have thought of that while I was in high school. But it stuck in my mind. And it proved to be right."

At the time, that comment seemed ironic, since Dewey thought he was never the best pitcher on his high school team and that, in fact, he was a better position player than a pitcher.

"When I graduated high school," he says, "I intended not to pitch anymore. I intended to play right field because of my arm. Plus, I liked to hit."

After a successful senior year in which the Jenison Wildcats captured their first league championship in baseball, Dewey took his baseball skills just a few miles away to Grand Valley State University, a Division II college that boasted a former major leaguer—Phil Regan—as its baseball coach.

Yet before Dewey matriculated at GVSU, the Vulture, as Regan was called during his days as a relief pitcher for the Los Angeles Dodgers, migrated west to be a coach for the Seattle Mariners. So instead of playing for a former big leaguer, Dewey again was coached by his old mentor Reed Johnson, who took the coaching job at Grand Valley.

Dewey, who did not fulfill his wishes of playing right field, set several school records for the Lakers. Those included most appearances (54), most innings pitched (258.2), most wins (20), and most strikeouts (185). To top it off, Dewey fired a no-hitter on March 28, 1987, against Butler University.

The San Francisco Giants nabbed Dewey in the later rounds of the 1987 draft, fulfilling the prophecy of Reed Johnson from several years before and surprising the young pitcher himself.

"I thought the Dodgers were going to draft me," Dewey says. "A Dodger scout had showed the most interest in me. Actually, there were probably eight teams that had shown considerable interest in me, not counting San Francisco. All the Giants did was send a scout who came to one game, and it wasn't a good performance at that. It was my third game in five days, so I didn't have a lot of stuff on my fastball."

On draft day, though, it was San Francisco who called. "When I got the phone call, I was shocked," Mark says. He was so surprised that when Herman Hannah, the scout who had recommended him to the Giants, came to his home for the signing, Dewey asked him, "Why in the world did you draft me? You saw me pitch only once, and I didn't have anything that day."

Hannah told Dewey, "I saw that you had good movement on your fastball." But there was more. There was an intangible that has already been mentioned that marks the life of this baseball player. According to the Giants' scouting report on Dewey, Hannah reported, "May not have the best stuff, but you can't see what's inside of him."

Once more, what's inside won out over appearances. The scout could tell that below the surface burned a fire of determination that is necessary for any prospect to turn potential into a profitable career. He signed Dewey for his heart as much as for his arm.

Having earned his bachelor's degree, Dewey was ready to face the daunting challenge of starting at the bottom rung of baseball's ladder. As a 23rd-round pick, he was not slated for a fast track to the majors, so he steeled himself for the long haul.

At the outset of his minor league sojourn, Dewey split his duties between starting and relieving. At Class A Everett in the Northwest League, Dewey started 10 games, relieved in 9, and finished the year with a 7–3 record while helping his team win the league's Western Division title. That earned him a trip to the Midwest League, Clinton, another Class A team, where he fashioned a 1.43 ERA and a 10–4 record. His role was changing, as he started just seven games in his 37 mound appearances. That was the last year Dewey would ever start a game; he was being groomed for a relief role at Candlestick Park.

His success and the Giants' excitement with him led Dewey to believe he should be moving up the ladder. Yet in 1989, he spent the year with the Single A San Jose club. "I was pitching very well, and I was given an indication that they'd probably bring me up to Double A. But I stayed the whole year in San Jose, and that was really kind of disappointing."

Dewey pitched so well in 1989 that he was named the team's Most Valuable Player on the basis of his 30 saves. As good as that sounds, it was bittersweet for Dewey, since he would soon turn twenty-five years old and still be pitching in Class A. The window of opportunity was beginning to slide shut.

He thought that on the strength of his good years with the club, the Giants would shoot him right past Double A and send him to their Triple A team in Phoenix. Nothing doing. His orders were to go to Shreveport.

Why in the world am I going to Double A ball? Dewey recalls thinking. Before long, he would find out, and it had very little to do with baseball. Instead, it had to do with a young woman named Monique.

One of the weirdest phenomena in baseball has to do with baseball players and the women of Shreveport. According to Dewey, "You don't want to play in the Texas League if you want to stay single, because if you go through Shreveport, you'll get married. There's probably ten guys who I played baseball with who married someone from Shreveport. It's amazing."

Two examples are Scott Garrelts, who played for the Giants between 1982 and 1991; and 1996 World Series hero John Wetteland, whom was with the Dodgers when he met his wife-to-be in the land of the bayous.

Dewey met Monique, who lived in a suburb of Shreveport, and started dating. Soon, however, they had to part ways—she went to college in Alabama, and he finally moved up to the Phoenix farm club.

If Dewey was worried about his slow movement in the system, 1990 changed that worry into exultation. Within the space of five months, he played at three levels—starting in Shreveport in April, moving to Phoenix in June, and arriving in San Francisco on August 24.

Dewey's progress was accelerated by the owners' lockout in the spring of 1990. Because Dewey was in a minor league camp, he kept playing even as the major leaguers took an extended vacation. That gave the Giants' bigwigs a chance to see him pitch. Manager Roger Craig, pitching coach Norm Sherry, and general manager Al Rosen all went to the minor league camp and saw Dewey and his colleagues in action. Later, when it was time to consider bringing him up, the brass knew what kind of player they had in Dewey.

In late August, twenty-year-old rookie Mark Dewey took the mound at Candlestick Park for his long-awaited baptism into major league baseball. Reed Johnson's prediction from ten years earlier had come true—and beyond.

In the opposing dugout that day were the Philadelphia Phillies. As Dewey threw his warm-up pitches, standing in to eye the new kid on the block was Phils' catcher Darren Daulton. Daulton was just coming into his own as a hitter and made for a menacing challenge. Dewey describes what happened.

"He hit the first pitch to center field for an out," Dewey recalls. "Matt Williams was playing third, and as he tossed the ball back to me, he said, 'It's easy up here, isn't it?'"

Getting Darren Daulton out was nice, and so was retiring the side in that inning without allowing a run, but Dewey had another goal in mind.

"I just wanted to face Dale Murphy. I didn't care what he did. I just wanted to pitch to him." The slugger, a fixture in the major leagues for many years, was in the waning years of his career, but he was still a threat to take anyone, especially an awestruck rookie, deep.

Dewey got his wish. Dale Murphy stood in against Dewey and struck out. The great hitter became the rookie's first big-league strikeout. In Dewey's fourteen appearances in 1990, he carved out an impressive 2.78 ERA. Yet it would be the last time in a long time that he would pitch for the Giants. As Dewey was soon to find out, making it to the top rung of baseball's ladder does not necessarily mean you get to stay there. For Dewey, big changes were still on the horizon.

During his short stay with the Giants, Mark Dewey had given every appearance that he was a Christian. In fact, he had even spoken publicly about his faith a few times. "I remember speaking in the off-season and talking about the Lord, yet I wasn't saved. I was the full-blown example of calling out, 'Lord, Lord,' and His saying, 'Depart from me; I never knew you.'"

Even his teammate Brett Butler had been impressed, and he offered to pay for Mark to attend the Professional Athletes Outreach conference in November. "I said that would be great. I was pretty gung ho religiously," Dewey recalls.

Accompanying him to the conference was his girlfriend, Monique. "One night someone presented the gospel, and they asked for people to raise their hand if they wanted information about being saved. Monique raised her hand. I kind of looked at her and said, 'What are you raising your hand for?' She thought she was a Christian, and I thought I was a Christian, but neither of us was. So at the PAO conference, she trusted Christ."

For Dewey, though, it wasn't that easy. It would be six more months before he would turn his life over to Jesus Christ and stop just appearing to do so. And it had been a journey that had started at least two years before.

"In 1989, I was playing in San Jose. We had a Baseball Chapel meeting in Visalia, California, and they handed out pocket-sized New Testaments that also included Psalms and Proverbs. Being an athlete, I was big at that time into the positive-thinking, self-help books. I had devoured them over the previous two years. As I read the Bible for the first time as an adult, though, it started hitting me how relevant it was to life today.

"The following year I started reading the Norman Vincent Peale- and Robert Schuller-type books, so I kind of made the shift from the positive-thinking, performance-enhancing thing to the so-called Christian positive thinking. I went through that, but it was the next year, 1991, when I realized that you could think positive all you want, but you're a sinner and you need a Savior. It really hit me for the first time.

"One night in late April 1991, the Lord showed me who I actually was and that I had absolutely no righteousness on my own. It was at that point that I truly understood what it means to trust Jesus as your Lord and Savior.

"I think I always understood what Jesus did. My problem was the same as the Pharisees'. It wasn't the lack of knowledge; it was the belief that there was something in me that was pretty good, something that merited favor from God. I had never understood my total depravity. I had never understood that I was indeed a sinner and that all my righteousness was like filthy rags. That never hit me until that night, and when it did, that's when I was saved."

Other changes were in store for Dewey in 1991. Not only did he enter into a redemptive relationship with Jesus Christ, but he also entered into a marriage relationship with Monique that year. It was, Dewey says, "a very enjoyable season," even though he spent the entire year in the minor leagues. After a short stay with Phoenix, Dewey was placed on waivers by the

Giants and claimed by the Mets. That turned out to be a bonus, for the Tidewater team for whom he played that summer had a large contingent of Christian players. It was a great place for a baby Christian who wanted to grow.

The next few years would be up and down for Dewey. The 1992 season was marked by the birth of the Deweys' first son, but it was also a time of stress. Mark was riding the shuttle between Tidewater and the Mets, which made it tough on Monique and Caleb.

"It would always work out that I would be on a road trip with Tidewater for nine days or so, and then the Mets would call me up, and I'd go to New York. There was one time when I went about a month without seeing my wife and son back in Tidewater. That was tough."

The 1993 season saw the Dewey family splitting their time between two other teams, Buffalo and its major league parent, the Pittsburgh Pirates. Dewey spent two years with the Pirates, coming away with great appreciation for the coaching staff. At the time, Jim Leyland was at the helm, and Ray Miller was his pitching coach. "They were quality people and easy to play for."

But when an opportunity arose to return to San Francisco after the 1994 season, Dewey jumped at the chance. "I wanted to go somewhere where people knew me," he says.

The return paid off in 1996, as Dewey had his best year in the majors. Although Dewey says, "I don't base my season on statistics," he can look back on that year knowing that he was one of the Giants' key players. He appeared in 59 games and compiled a 4–2 record and a 3.75 ERA.

What Dewey does use to gauge his success is this: "I pray that I will concentrate, be intense, and use the ability God has blessed me with. I also base my success on how I've enhanced the chances of the team winning. I've never had a year any- where where I think my value to the team has been greater than it was that season."

In the years since Dewey trusted Jesus Christ as Savior, he has sought to grow spiritually and follow God's leading in his life. He makes decisions based on prayer and guidance from the Bible. In the summer of 1996, while putting together a highly successful year on the mound, his penchant for doing things according to biblical standards caused him some trouble.

On July 31, the Giants held an "Until There's a Cure" day at Candlestick Park. It was an AIDS awareness event that Dewey felt had ramifications on the issue of homosexuality. He declined to participate. What's more, each player was issued a ribbon to wear during the game—a ribbon that symbolized AIDS awareness. Dewey felt that the ribbon stood for ideas he was opposed to biblically, so he turned it sideways to resemble the Christian fish symbol.

As might be expected, there was a powerful backlash against Dewey's actions from the media and others in the San Francisco area. For standing up for his beliefs, Dewey took a verbal beating from many fronts.

"The most vicious articles about me were written by people who never spoke to me about what happened that day," he says. "Of all the people who wrote about me, only one talked to me in depth enough to know what I was thinking. So I experienced something I knew as a college broadcasting major and through working with the media for the past ten years: You'd better be wary of believing what you read."

Again, people who thought they knew Dewey were judging by outward appearances. If they had gone to the trouble to find out what is inside Mark Dewey, they would have been in for a refreshing look at a man who is solidly convinced of his faith, who loves to think deeply about life, and who is not happy with superficial answers.

He's a man who prefers old-time Christian literature (Spurgeon, John Bunyan, Calvin, Moody) to the new. He's a man who thinks we have too much teaching on how to be a good plumber, father, or whatever, and not enough on how to be an obedient follower of God. He's a man who values the accountability of friends who teach each other—who enjoy being iron that sharpens iron.

Whether he's quietly standing against something he thinks is wrong or diligently studying to know more about his Savior, Mark Dewey represents more than whatever you perceive from a distance. Unless you see his heart, you don't know where he stands. With his heart, he pitches. With his heart, he loves his God. With his heart, he cares for his family. With his heart, he stands up for his beliefs.

Don't just look at Mark Dewey. Listen to him. He'll tell you it's what's inside that counts.

Q & A WITH MARK DEWEY

Q: *You enjoy reading some of the classical Christian writers. What is it about them that stands out?*

Mark: When you read Spurgeon and Calvin, you see men whose goal was to know God. They knew that if they came closer to God, everything else would fall into place. Also, Spurgeon observed during the 1800s that there was not as much contained in a *paragraph* then as there was in a *sentence* a hundred years before. There is so much depth in their writing.

Q: *Was there anything positive that came out of the incident at Candlestick Park this summer when you did not participate in the AIDS day?*

Mark: I received more than five hundred pieces of fan mail concerning that. All but ten were extremely encouraging and supportive. I heard from a lot of Christians who said it meant to them that we have to stand for what's right regardless of the circumstances. Some people have tried to make me out to be a hero, but I don't see it that way. I simply did what I thought was right.

Q: *What has being a father for the past few years taught you?*

Mark: Disciplining my children gives me a better look at my heavenly Father. I've also discovered that if I would be as patient with everyone as I am with my children, I'd be a better man. I really give my children the benefit of the doubt, and I should do that with everyone else.

Q: *What's your advice for a kid who wants to be a pitcher?*

Mark: Throw your fastball, and throw it a lot. People talk about the curveball or slider hurting your arm, and that may be true if you throw it incorrectly. But the problem I see more often is that if you don't throw a lot of fastballs, you're not going to develop the kind of arm strength you need in the higher levels of baseball. Be able to throw your fastball for strikes, but not down the middle.

THE ROAD TO THE MAJORS

• Selected by the San Francisco Giants, 23rd round of 1987 draft
• Claimed on waivers by New York Mets, May 9, 1991
• Claimed on waivers by Pittsburgh Pirates, May 11, 1993
• Signed as free agent by San Francisco Giants, October 28, 1994

Minor league stops: Everett, Clinton, San Jose, Shreveport, Phoenix, Tidewater, Buffalo

Minor league highlight: Named MVP of the San Jose Giants in 1989 while setting a California League record with thirty saves

Year	Team	W	L	PCT	G	SV	IP	H	R	ER	HR	TBB	SO	ERA
1990	SF	1	1	.500	14	0	22.2	22	7	7	1	5	11	2.78
1992	NYN	1	0	1.000	20	0	33.1	37	16	16	2	10	24	4.32
1993	Pit	1	2	.333	21	7	26.2	14	8	7	0	10	14	2.36
1994	Pit	2	1	.667	45	1	51.1	61	22	21	4	19	30	3.68
1995	SF	1	0	1.000	27	0	31.2	30	12	11	2	17	32	3.13
1996	SF	6	3	.667	78	0	83.1	79	40	39	9	41	57	4.21
6 Years		**12**	**7**	**.632**	**205**	**8**	**249**	**243**	**105**	**101**	**18**	**102**	**168**	**3.65**

Travis Fryman
Leader of a New Generation

VITAL STATISTICS

Born March 25, 1969
6 feet 1, 195 pounds
Position: Infielder
Throws right, bats right
Family: Married to Kathleen
1997 Team: Detroit Tigers

CAREER HIGHLIGHTS

- Named to All-Star team four times (1992–1994, 1996)
- Belted two grand slam home runs and had five 4-hit games in 1995
- Led Tigers in games, hits, total bases, and at bats in 1992
- Slugged a home run for his first major league hit in 1990

WARMING UP

Travis Fryman lists four keys to making sure you handle the pressures of everyday life, whether you're a baseball player or a kid who works at McDonald's: (1) Read the Bible each day; (2) spend lots of time praying; (3) develop friendships with Christians and grow and learn with them; and (4) take a stand for what you know is right.

FAVORITE BIBLE PASSAGE

"Do not think of yourself more highly than you ought, but rather think of yourself with sober judgment, in accordance with the measure of faith God has given you" (Romans 12:3).

Travis says, "What that says to me is not to get caught up in my successes or failures. When I look in the mirror each day, I should look at myself in terms of where my relationship is with God—how much I'm trusting Him and leaning on Him."

Travis Fryman

What happened to Travis Fryman in 1996 shouldn't happen to anybody. Through no fault of his own, he became the best player on the worst team in baseball.

The Detroit Tigers, who failed to regroup when their stars from the late 1980s started to retire or leave, sat back and watched as one by one the old guard drifted away. They watched as Lance Parrish's back failed him, Jack Morris went off to help someone else win the Series, Alan Trammell and Lou Whitaker finally showed their age, Kirk Gibson lost his touch, Cecil Fielder started to panic, and Sparky Anderson grew weary of going out to the mound to try to rescue his wayward pitchers from another shellacking.

They all drifted away, leaving behind an assortment of youngsters with big dreams, considerable potential, and minimal major league experience. The new breed of Tiger had names like Tony Clark, Bobby Higginson, Justin Thompson, and Melvin Nieves—and they were led into battle by Buddy Bell.

After the remodeling dust had settled and the new team was ready to be unveiled, only one familiar name remained. Only one player was left to link the Tigers of the twenty-first century with the popular team that had opened the '90s with anticipation, only to self-destruct by mid-decade. Only Travis

Fryman stood as a symbol of past successes *and* future hopes.

Some call Travis Fryman a throwback player—someone who recalls the names of baseball's glory years with his indomitable spirit, quiet demeanor, and unyielding work ethic. For Tiger old-timers, he reflects the spirit of Al Kaline. Indeed, Fryman's early career stats were reminiscent of the Hall of Fame outfielder's. For instance, in 1991, Fryman was the youngest Tiger to rap at least 20 home runs and drive in at least 90 runs since Kaline had done so as a twenty-year-old in 1955. In addition, when Fryman slammed 22 home runs in 1993, he joined Kaline as one of only two Tigers ever with three straight 20-home run and 90-RBI seasons before his twenty-fifth birthday.

But there is another way to look at this talented infielder from Florida. He's not just a throwback to the past; he is a *link* to the past—or at least a link to the early '70s.

Because of his name, some people assume that the link between Travis Fryman and the '70s is that his dad was a pitcher during that era for the Braves and the Reds. But that is just not the case. There was a pitcher named Woody Fryman on the scene back then—a pitcher from the same commonwealth in which Travis was born: Kentucky. Problem is, Woody was not Travis's dad.

People who should know better have made that mistake, Travis says. "A reporter in New York a few years ago came up to me and said, 'I can remember when you used to run around the clubhouse.'" The reporter was mistaking Travis for Woody Fryman's son.

The link between Travis Fryman and that era of baseball's history does have a Kentucky connection, though. Travis's dad, who has been an athletic director for many years at Travis's alma mater, Tate High School in Pensacola, Florida, grew up in Kentucky. For him—as with many people whose childhoods are spent in Kentucky—the baseball team of choice was the Cincinnati Reds. Even after the family moved to Florida when Travis was two years old, the Fryman family retained their loyalty to Cincinnati.

"It was my dad's favorite team, so it was pretty natural that it was the team I grew up wanting to play for," says Travis.

His heroes on the Big Red Machine were Pete Rose, Johnny Bench, and "because he played shortstop," Davey Concepcion. "Any Cincinnati Red was pretty neat to me."

There was another man in the red and white uniform who captured Travis's attention—a man who would later have a huge impact on his career: Sparky Anderson. Sparky, of course, was the skipper of the Big Red Machine, the brains behind the team's dominance. In 1990, Anderson would become Fryman's first major league manager, completing the Reds-to-Tigers cycle.

That cycle almost came to fruition for Fryman in a different way.

As a student at Tate High School, Fryman had a variety of opportunities open up to him. First, because he was a good student (3.7 GPA), he attracted the attention of West Point. "As I began to get recruiting letters from colleges around the country, I got letters from West Point as well," Fryman recalls. "There was a time when I thought I wanted to pursue a career in the military, so I returned their questionnaires. They followed up my interest with a one-on-one interview and a physical exam. The opportunity was there."

But the timing wasn't. The folks from Annapolis wanted Travis's name on the dotted line by the second week of March during his senior year. That, however, was during baseball season, and Fryman had other things on his mind besides platoons, drill sergeants, and artillery lessons.

His visions related more to teams, baseball managers, and batting instructions. He was playing on one of the best high school baseball teams in the country. He was the successor at shortstop to future major leaguer Jay Bell, and the previous year, the team had been state champions. Fryman was on his way to an All-State and All-American season as a slick-fielding middle infielder.

So when West Point asked for his signature, he decided to save it for what he felt was a likely pro baseball contract. He did sign up with another educational institution, Georgia Tech—but that letter of intent would not bind him if he became a high draft pick, as the contract with West Point would have.

"If I didn't get drafted high enough—if baseball didn't look like it would work out—then I could still play for Georgia Tech and go to college," Travis says.

When the baseball draft took place in the spring, though, it was fairly certain that it would be a baseball and not the books that Fryman would be hitting. The question was, would it be his favorite team, the Cincinnati Reds, or someone else who would secure his services?

"I felt like I would be drafted in the top three rounds, and really, I expected to go in the second," Travis says, recalling that day. "The only team I thought might take a chance on me in the first round was the Tigers."

In fact, even though the Reds and the Mets showed the most interest in him, he really wanted to go to the team that needed him the most—whoever it was.

"My dad and I had taken the time to look at the minor league systems of a few of the teams who might draft me at the highest level. We wanted to see what obstacles were in the way—if they had any young shortstop prospects. The best organization in that regard was the Detroit Tigers, and it worked out that they drafted me."

The Tigers chose the eighteen-year-old shortstop as the 30th pick overall in a supplemental round between the first and second rounds. The Fryman family was happy, because he had the opportunity to progress swiftly through the system. "If I didn't make it," Travis says, "it would only be because I couldn't cut it. There were no promising shortstops in the way. You can be a great player and be stuck in the minor leagues behind a guy like Barry Larkin. That's a nightmare. Opportunity is half the battle, and the opportunity was going to be there in the Tiger system."

Besides his considerable skills, Fryman would take with him to his first minor league destination a Christian faith that was still very much in the formative stage. "I had accepted Christ as a young boy. My parents are both Christian people, and I grew up in a churchgoing family. I have committed Christian grandparents, and we have a strong, religious, moral fiber in our family. I understood what I did when I accepted Christ as a boy, but I didn't know how to make Him Lord of my life. I struggled with that through most of my teen years and into my young adult years."

Assured of his salvation but immature in his spiritual growth, Fryman's primary focus was getting to the major leagues. The first two years of Fryman's pro career demonstrated that he was a talented infielder who had a lot to learn at the plate. At Bristol in the Rookie League and then at Fayetteville in Class A, Fryman hit .234, hardly the kind of average that impresses the major league brass. In 188 games at those levels, Travis had hit just two home runs. "I was not a strong offensive player," Fryman says now. "A lot of it had to do with physical maturity. I was tall and lanky. I was a solid defensive player coming out of high school, but I just lacked physical strength."

After the second season of being a good-field, no-hit shortstop, Fryman got some much-needed assistance. Ken "Parker, a major league scout who lived in Pensacola, approached Travis after his second season in the pros and offered to throw batting practice for him during the winter. When Travis got home to Florida, they went to work.

"He threw me batting practice five days a week from the first of November till the day I left for spring training," Travis says. "And I got on a weight program, I was lifting weights six days a week, and I basically didn't do anything that entire winter but play baseball. I got stronger physically, and I made a lot of progress hitting through Parker's instruction. That next season was the first successful offensive season I had ever had."

Playing at Double A London, Fryman pounded out 40 extra base hits in 118 games, compared with 21 in 122 games the year before. Most dramatic was the increase in his slugging percentage, which went from .294 in Fayetteville to .403 in London.

The next season, 1990, it took Fryman just eighty-seven games at Triple A Toledo to show the Tigers that he was ready. On July 7 of that year, Fryman was called up to the big club at age twenty-one. To prove his transformation from a light hitter to a power hitter, Fryman made his first major league hit a memorable one—a three-run home run off Kansas City's Jeff Montgomery on July 8. He's been a regular in the Tiger lineup ever since.

On the field, there was another transformation that Fryman would have to make. When Fryman arrived with the Tigers, his manager was the skipper he had grown up admiring as the leader of the Cincinnati Reds. Sparky may or may not have known about that connection, but what mattered to him was how to get the most out of this talented young player.

As Fryman and his dad had suspected, he hadn't had any problems sailing through the farm system with no other short-stop prospects in his way. Yet when he got to the big club, it was a different story. There at short, as he had been since 1977, was Alan Trammell. How Sparky, Trammell, and Fryman would handle this squeeze play would have a lasting effect on all concerned.

As long as Travis Fryman had been involved in baseball, he had never played any other position besides shortstop. And as long as Alan Trammell and Lou Whitaker had been playing ball together since the mid-'70s, they had been together at short and second. What would Sparky do? He moved the rookie to third base.

"My first game in the majors, I played shortstop," Fryman recalls. "But the next day I played third base. I tell people that I always prayed for an opportunity to play in the big leagues, but I wasn't specific enough with my prayer life. I needed to specify which position."

Instead of moaning and complaining, Fryman simply moved over to third and showed everyone he could make the transition. "You can gripe and say, 'I don't know how to play there,' or you can buckle down and get out there and do your best." Fryman did just that and attracted the admiration of people throughout baseball.

Today, Fryman credits the two other principals in this minidrama with being extremely instrumental in his success as a baseball player. The first was the shortstop who prompted Travis's move to third. "What helped me with that transition was the character of Alan Trammell. Here's a guy with a great reputation in baseball, and here I am a young guy. Although I played third base at first, I was sometimes moved to short. He and I have been flip-flopped since I've been in the majors. But it really hasn't bothered him because of his professionalism. The best piece of advice Sparky ever gave me was this: 'Watch Alan Trammell. Do what he does, and you'll be all right.'"

It is Anderson who was the other person to help Fryman through the transition. "I don't think I could have come under anyone at that time who could have been any better for me than Sparky Anderson. He's taken criticism for not being good with young players, but I just did not see that. He spent time with me. He corrected me when I made mistakes. He let me play and make mistakes. He showed confidence in me. I treated him with respect at all times and listened to what he had to say. I think of Sparky Anderson in the highest regard."

As the strike season of 1994 unfolded, Fryman should have been one of the most secure young men in America. His development as a ballplayer was proceeding well. He was in the first year of a five-year contract that would pay him $25 million. He had already been on three All-Star teams at the age of twenty-four. But inside, something was gnawing at him.

"I got to a point in my life where on the outside everything was great. I had signed a lucrative contract, I had a beautiful wife, my career was going well, and I was having the best season of my career. Yet I simply was not happy." And he knew why. "I was becoming more and more consumed by baseball, and I was missing the point of what God had for my life.

"I've been real fortunate since I've been in the major leagues to play with some solid Christian men, such as Frank Tanana. I watched those men and learned how to handle adversity. I've always struggled, as do a lot of athletes whose sport has been the lord of their life. I was that way, and I defined myself by my successes and failures as a baseball player.

"The problem was that I was a child of God and I had accepted Christ and I had the Holy Spirit dwelling within me. The Holy Spirit was trying to say, 'Hey, you're not using baseball the way you're supposed to be using it.' So basically I had a tug-of-war going on inside of me. As a Christian, you'll never experience peace and joy unless you're in line with what God wants you to do. I wasn't there."

As Fryman had observed Tanana, Tiger chapel leader Jeff

Totten, and others, he noticed they had a consistency that he was missing. "I saw struggles in their spiritual walks, but seeing how they dealt with those struggles spoke to me and began to convict me that I wasn't dealing with shortcomings the way they should be dealt with. I was basically dodging the bullet. I was living only half the verse in 1 Corinthians 13 that says, 'When I was a child, I talked like a child, I thought like a child, I reasoned like a child. When I became a man, I put childish things behind me.' I knew I needed to put away childish things, so I rededicated my life to Christ."

While the players were on strike and everyone in baseball was bemoaning the loss of what promised to be a remarkable season, Travis Fryman was doing something far more important than slugging home runs. He was doing business with God, promising to make a relationship with Him his top priority.

Earlier, Travis's wife, Kathy, had made her own decision to follow Jesus. While sitting in a car in the parking lot at Tiger Stadium, Cathy Tanana, Frank's wife, had led Kathy to Christ.

"My wife was one of the most moral people I had ever met when we dated," Travis says. "She grew up in a strong Irish-Catholic family, but she had never understood what a personal relationship with Christ was all about. Cathy Tanana also grew up Catholic, so the Lord really worked there and used their friendship to help answer Kathy's questions and let her see what she was missing."

So after Kathy's new decision to follow Jesus and Travis's renewed commitment, the Fryman family began to attend church regularly and study the Bible together—all in preparation for their life of service and dedication to God. Thus, when the strike ended and the 1995 season began, it was a brand-new Travis Fryman who was leading the charge for the Tigers.

No one knew it at the time, but it was the beginning of some hard times for Detroit. Even as late as July 9, the Tigers still showed signs of being a decent team. At that point, their record was 37–33, which was better than most people had predicted. Perhaps the team could rebuild piece by piece and still retain some semblance of respectability.

But it didn't happen. For the remainder of the season, the

Tigers were 23–51 as they settled quietly near the bottom of the American League East. Had not the Toronto Blue Jays fallen even farther, the Tigers would have finished dead last.

Still, it was the next season that would test the hearts and souls of Tiger players and fans. In 1996 there was no hopeful .500 mark at the All-Star break. There was just one miserable thrashing after another. The Tigers endured one of the worst seasons in baseball history, losing 109 games.

In the middle of it all, Fryman described it as "a very difficult year. It's been a real challenge personally and spiritually. It's been a real help to have some good Christian guys on the club. We try to help keep each other in line during this difficult season and keep our eyes focused on what they should be focused on. It's been tough, but God has revealed some areas in our lives that we haven't totally turned over to Him, and He's dealing with those."

As the Detroit Tigers set out to rebuild their team, Travis Fryman found himself in an unusual situation. As the team looked to rebuild for the future, he found that he was the elder statesman on the team. Still in his twenties, he was looked to for leadership on and off the field. He had learned from the old master, Sparky Anderson; he had listened to the old pro, Alan Trammell; and he had turned his life over wholeheartedly to the Savior. He was ready to be the leader the team needed.

"Because we have such young players, that presents some opportunities as far as my witness is concerned," he says. "The younger players watch carefully, and it gives me opportunities to be more outspoken. This is a role that I've been preparing for for six or seven years. You have to be careful, because people are looking at you as a teammate and as a spiritual leader.

"I'm also our chapel leader. It's a good situation for me because I am the elder statesman, but my age is not one that comes between the younger players and myself."

At an age when some players are just getting their first taste of the majors, Travis Fryman is taking on the roles he saw his old heroes on the Cincinnati Reds handle with relish. And if the Tigers can keep their nucleus together as the Reds did during their wonder years, maybe the young infielder will be the part of a team that a whole new generation of fans will look up to. Maybe someday he can be the best player on the best team in baseball.

Q & A WITH TRAVIS FRYMAN

Q: *What is the danger in making your faith known to your team-mates?*
Travis: One slip or one moment when you take your eyes off God, and you lose focus. Maybe something happens during the game and you give in. Maybe you fling your helmet or use language that's not becoming. Other players watch that. As you become more outspoken about your faith, you're subjected to much more scrutiny.

Q: *You were influenced greatly by Frank Tanana. What was one key lesson he taught you?*
Travis: One thing about Frank that always touched me was that any time he did not perform well, he was always friendly and outspoken. He was even-tempered and always had lots of self-control. It always seemed that he was in a good mood and had a lot of joy in life.

Q: *Your hometown of Pensacola has produced a lot of great athletes, hasn't it?*
Travis: We've had quite a few major league baseball players, most notably Don Sutton. Also, Jay Bell, Mark Whitten, Greg Litton, and me. Our town has a good Little League program and a lot of community involvement. We can also claim Emmitt Smith. The only run-in I had with Emmitt was in middle school basketball. I think he bloodied my lip to reject a layup I was trying.

Q: *You've been studying the Bible diligently since 1994. What kinds of things are you interested in?*
Travis: Man has been trying to make the Bible easier to understand, but the Holy Spirit is supposed to help you understand it. When you read the King James Version, you may not understand right away. You're forced to slow down, ask questions,

and pray for understanding. So I'm really challenged to spend more time in my King James Bible and to do some digging. This all started when I read the Lord's Prayer in another version and there were some parts of it left out. So it's challenged me to study my King James Bible.

THE ROAD TO THE MAJORS

• Selected by the Detroit Tigers in the third round of the 1987 draft

Minor league stops: Bristol, Fayetteville, London, Toledo

Minor league highlight: Selected to All-Star teams while at both London and Toledo. With Toledo, was picked to play in Triple A Alliance All-Star game but was called up to the Tigers three days before the game.

THE FRYMAN FILE

Year	Team	G	AB	R	H	2B	3B	HR	RBI	BB	SO	SB	BA	SLG
1990	Det	66	232	32	69	11	1	9	27	17	51	3	.297	.470
1991	Det	149	557	65	144	36	3	21	91	40	149	12	.259	.447
1992	Det	161	659	87	175	31	4	20	96	45	144	8	.266	.416
1993	Det	151	607	98	182	37	5	22	97	77	128	9	.300	.486
1994	Det	114	464	66	122	34	5	18	85	45	128	2	.263	.474
1995	Det	144	567	79	156	21	5	15	81	63	100	4	.275	.409
1996	Det	157	616	90	165	32	3	22	100	57	118	4	.268	.437
7 Years		**942**	**3702**	**517**	**1013**	**202**	**26**	**127**	**577**	**344**	**818**	**42**	**.274**	**.445**

Joe Girardi
Just Plain Joe

VITAL STATISTICS

Born October 14, 1964, in Peoria, Illinois
5 feet 11, 195 pounds
College: Northwestern University
Position: Catcher
Throws right, bats right
Family: Married to Kim
1997 Team: New York Yankees

CAREER HIGHLIGHTS

- Batted .294 and led Yankees with 11 sacrifice bunts in 1996
- Led the Rockies and tied for fifth in NL with 12 sacrifice bunts in 1995
- Hit a 2-run home run in first-ever pinch-hitting role in 1991
- Stole 8 bases in 1990, most for a Cubs catcher since 1924
- In 1989, became first Cub rookie catcher to start on Opening Day since Randy Hundley in 1966
- Hit a single in first major league at bat in 1989

WARMING UP

Joe Girardi depends heavily on his wife, Kim, in every area of his life, and he has learned the importance of sharing his heart with her. "I'm learning that the worst thing I can do to my marriage is never to be vulnerable to my wife," he says. "Through Christ, I realize that there's no shame in sharing with your wife that you're hurting." Part of the appreciation Joe has for Kim results from a 1993 car accident in which the truck she was driving went out of control and rolled over twice before hitting a tree. "I think that brought us closer together, knowing that we are vulnerable as people and we are not invincible. God really took care of her."

FAVORITE BIBLE PASSAGE

"Consider it pure joy, my brothers, whenever you face trials of many kinds, because you know that the testing of your faith develops perseverance" (James 1:2–3).

Joe Girardi

Joe Girardi sure knows how to pick his spots.

On October 27, 1996, the New York Yankees catcher had the game of his life in the best possible situation. It was Game 6 of the World Series, which turned out to be a stunning display of resiliency by a team full of players who had learned from experience that being down does not mean being out.

Having battled back from a 2-games-to-0 deficit, the Yanks went into the sixth game at home with a 3-games-to-2 lead and an eagerness to put a stop to any thoughts the Braves had about mounting a comeback of their own.

Before that game, Joe Girardi had been relatively silent in the series. Platooning with the Yankees' other catcher, Jim Leyritz, Girardi had played in Games 2, 3, and 4, but was 0–7 at the plate in those contests. Clearly, there was pressure on him to perform, especially since Leyritz had hit a heroic three-run home run in Game 4. It was time for Girardi to contribute.

It didn't take him long to remind Yankee fans that they had *two* fine catchers. In the first inning, Terry Pendleton tried to steal second and was gunned down by Girardi. Then, in the third, with the game still scoreless, Paul O'Neill doubled and went to third on a ground out. Up stepped Girardi. Not noted for his power, the Yankee backstop had just twenty-seven extra-base hits during the entire regular season. But he climbed all over a Greg Maddux pitch and belted a triple to the center field wall to start the scoring for New York. Rookie sensation Derek Jeter then slapped a single past the Braves' drawn-in infield, and Girardi coasted home.

But Girardi was far from done. In the Braves' half of the fifth inning, with the score 2–1, Marquis Grissom singled. On an ensuing pitch to the next hitter, the ball got away from Girardi. Grissom streaked toward second while Girardi pounced on the elusive ball and rocketed a strike toward second.

"Out!" signaled umpire Terry Tata.

Grissom screamed his disapproval, and Braves manager Bobby Cox flew out of the Atlanta dugout to protest. He protested too much for third-base umpire Tim Welke, who relieved Cox of his managerial duties for the evening. Girardi's quick action had cost the Braves a base runner and their manager.

In the fifth inning, Girardi picked up his second hit of the game, a single to left. The inning ended, though, when Girardi was erased on the front end of a double play grounder off the bat of Jeter.

His hitting heroics over, Girardi remained behind the plate as the Yankees held on to their 3–1 lead. In the ninth, the Braves got another run back when they scored off John Wetteland, but the big right-hander was not about to give up the lead. After Wetteland came into the game to replace Mariano Rivera, he struck out Andruw Jones, gave up an infield single to Ryan Klesko and a single to right to Terry Pendleton, and struck out Luis Polonia. With two out, Wetteland was touched for a single to right by Grissom, scoring Klesko.

Now there was a runner on second with two outs. Only Mark Lemke, a player with a remarkable history of postseason heroics, stood between the Yankees and their first World Series title since 1977. With enough drama hanging on every pitch to make even a New York cop nervous (especially the dozens of them who were waiting to ride horseback onto the field to discourage any mayhem should the Yanks win), Wetteland finally coerced Lemke to hit a lazy pop-up to third baseman Charlie Hayes.

Joe Girardi raced to the mound to meet his good friend and

batterymate John Wetteland in a victory embrace. That image—of Wetteland with his still-gloved hand around Girardi's neck, his pitching hand raised heavenward, and his mouth open in exultation while teammates raced to add their ecstasy to the celebration—was splashed on newspapers and magazines and sports highlight programs around the world. *Sports Illustrated* recorded it for the ages. So did *The Sporting News*.

Suddenly, the whole sporting world knew about Joe Girardi.

After eight years of admirable work for the Chicago Cubs, the Colorado Rockies, and the Yankees, Joe Girardi had, in one evening of outstanding play, become what every kid who ever kicked the dirt of a Little League field dreams of becoming: a World Series hero. It was an appropriate payoff for one of the truly good people in baseball.

In an era when many athletes have egos that wouldn't fit inside the Superdome, Joe Girardi is a refreshing exception. Need proof? Listen in on a conversation that occurred when Joe was asked this question: "Could you describe Joe Girardi to someone who doesn't know him?"

A long silence.

Joe: "Hmm. I wish my wife were here."

Hearing her nearby, he calls, "Kim!" He explains the question.

Kim: "That's a tough question."

Joe, a graduate of Northwestern University with a degree in industrial engineering, says, "She's the smart one. She'll know what to say."

Kim: "What I've heard you say a lot is that your biggest desire is to be a godly man and husband."

Joe: "That's something that John Wetteland has tried to teach me—that, as a husband, I'm responsible for my wife and kids and their walk with the Lord. We're supposed to be leaders in the home. I guess I'm a man who struggles just like every other man who is trying to become more Christlike."

Kim: "You're a team player."

Joe: "I don't like a lot of attention. I just want to be treated like a man. I don't like people looking at me like I'm a spectacle.

Sometimes I feel like I'm a gorilla."

The exchange ends as Joe says simply, "I want to be real."

Who can ask for anything more?

In a sense, it's no surprise that Joe Girardi is who he is. He is Mr. Middle America. He grew up in Peoria, Illinois, the center of the Midwest, and the city that is often cited as the litmus test city for American values. His parents were hardworking people. Joe's dad, Gerald, was a salesman who also ran a restaurant. His mom, Angela, was a child psychologist. They had five children, of whom Joe was the fourth. And as one would suspect in such a family, it was Joe's parents who were his biggest influence.

"The major impact in my life was my parents," Joe recalls. "They did everything they could to give me an opportunity to succeed. They were really supportive of anything I did, and they really pushed education."

In addition, they emphasized sports. "Everyone was pretty athletic," Girardi says of his three brothers and sister. "My dad's best sport was basketball, but we mostly played baseball and football."

For Joe, it was a toss-up between those two sports, but he admits he liked football better. "There is something about playing once a week on Friday nights," he says about his career as a high school quarterback. "You build up that emotion. And I liked the contact, too."

But he excelled at baseball. "For baseball, speed and size wasn't such a big factor." And at under six feet tall, he lacked the size for big-time football.

He received offers to play both sports in college, but only small schools recruited him to play football. As an All-State baseball player, though, there was considerably more interest in his baseball skills by larger colleges.

"I thought I had a better chance for a career in baseball," he recalls. "We played in a high school tournament, and there was a scout there who asked me if I would be willing to sign if I was drafted. That gave me an idea that I would have a possibility—at least a chance to play minor league baseball."

Girardi's post-high school career was decided on the basis

of a game he played in the state tournament. Northwestern University coach Ron Wellman was at the game, and he was impressed by what he saw in the young catcher. Ironically, the effort Wellman witnessed that afternoon would be a bit of foreshadowing of another key game later in Girardi's career. Explaining what may have attracted Wellman's attention, Joe says nonchalantly that he "got a couple of hits and threw out a couple of guys." Sounds a lot like a late-evening performance he put on fourteen years later in the World Series. Standard operating procedure for a good catcher: getting a couple of hits and throwing out a couple of guys.

When Joe told his parents that Northwestern was interested in him, he says, "Their eyes lit up." They liked the idea because "they had always stressed education." Northwestern is noted for its high academic standards.

"I didn't know an awful lot about Northwestern," Girardi says. "But I wanted to play pro ball. That was my goal. Yet I knew something was right when their eyes lit up."

Girardi successfully combined both pursuits while in Evanston, Illinois, the home of Northwestern. He was twice named All-Big Ten, and he was named an academic All-American three times. Plus, he stayed all four years and earned his degree.

During Girardi's time at Northwestern, though, he faced every son's nightmare. When he was nineteen years old, his mother died of cancer. He didn't realize it at the time, but Angela Girardi's death would help drive him toward a spiritual decision four years later.

Another significant event—this one much happier—occurred when he met, Kim, a fellow student, during his senior year of college. She too would play a valuable role in that upcoming decision.

After graduation, Girardi did what all college students set out to do. He used what he learned in college on his first job. In this case, though, he didn't use what he learned in the classroom. He didn't sign up to design a manufacturing plant for his favorite corporation. Instead, he used what he learned on the baseball field. He signed up to do what he could to help his favorite baseball team.

"I was a huge Cubs fan growing up," he says. "The players I liked were Ron Santo and Jose Cardenal." In 1986, the Cubs made him a part of their lore by drafting him in the fifth round and putting him on the road to Wrigley Field. "I had an idea they were going to draft me. There was a scout, John Hennesy, who was around a lot when we played. He pretty much lived at our ballpark."

So what did they see in Girardi? "I think they liked the way I played the game. My hustle, my intensity. I'm not the type of player whose offensive power is going to stand out—hitting bombs and stuff like that."

In Girardi's first year as a Cub minor leaguer, he got a bonus that does not happen often. He got to play for his hometown team—Peoria. Playing in the Midwest League that summer, he found that his game still played well in Peoria, hitting .309, best in the Midwest among catchers. That success was rewarded by a promotion to the Cubs' Winston-Salem farm team for the 1987 season. It would be another stellar season on the field for Girardi. He was named to the Carolina League All-Star team on the basis of a season in which he batted .280, hit eight home runs, and threw out 44 percent of the runners who tried to steal on him.

But it was not on the field that Girardi's most important highlight occurred that season. This highlight was influenced by the memory of his mother and the advice of Kim. "I was in Winston-Salem and hitting over .300, but I didn't know why I was playing. I used to think I was playing to keep my mom alive."

Now that she was gone, Girardi was left to find a new reason to continue, a new purpose to perform. That's when Kim came to the rescue. "She set me straight on why I was playing. I was playing because God gave me talents."

Yet that was not a complete answer for Girardi. After all, he did not know God personally through a relationship with Jesus Christ. Kim, however, was a Christian, and she had begun to influence his thinking.

"She had introduced me to some good friends of hers who were Christians. I knew there was something different about them, but I didn't know what."

Later, Kim told him what the difference was. "Kim explained to me about having a personal relationship with Jesus Christ. That was really what I wanted to do. I was struggling. My mom had died three and a half years earlier, and I had never really dealt with it."

So during that All-Star season in Winston-Salem, Joe Girardi prayed to receive Jesus Christ. It was the first step of his Christian life, which would steadily grow deeper and deeper over the following years.

After another year of preparation on the field, Girardi was given a shot with the Cubs as the season opened in 1989. The first game of his major league career was also the first game of the season, as Girardi became the only Cub rookie in twenty-three years to start on Opening Day. Providing the opposition on that afternoon at Wrigley Field were the Philadelphia Phillies.

"The moment I remember most about that day was when Mike Schmidt walked to the plate," Joe recalls. "That was when I knew I had really made it. I remembered watching him play as a kid and later hen I was at Northwestern. I knew he was a Cub killer. I remember his having so many wonderful days at Wrigley Field with the wind blowing out."

How does a brand-new catcher respond when a legend comes to the plate? Does he politely welcome him and wish him well? Does he stay cool and just watch? Or does he stare?

"I was pretty amazed that we were in the same little circle," Girardi says. "I just stared at him for a long time. I had this anger toward him for ruining so many of my days as a teenager."

When it was Girardi's turn to step in to hit, he did some damage of his own, getting a single off the Phils' Floyd Youmans. In his next 11 at bats, Girardi got five more hits and was hitting .500 after the first few games.

"I started off hot," Joe says. "I think part of it was the excitement. Also, when you first come into the big leagues, the pitchers don't know you, and they haven't seen you. Once you get around the league once, the advance scouts send their reports, and that's probably why you cool off and you have to make the adjustments."

Unfortunately, Girardi failed to make the necessary adjustments, and his batting average plummeted. He was sent back down to Iowa after just one month. "I was crushed. I remember telling Kim that I didn't ever think I would make it back. I was absolutely crushed and crying on her shoulder. And she said, 'Don't worry. You'll be back.'"

Of course, she was right. On June 13, the Cubs summoned Girardi again. "I was never so happy as when I got called up the second time," he says.

Having survived the minors to taste the good living in the majors, Girardi knew the difference. Except for two rehabilitation stints (1991 in Iowa and 1993 in Colorado Springs), his minor league career was ended with the second call-up.

"You play minor league baseball, and it's just a wonderful time and you're on top of the world. You don't realize how much better it is in the big leagues until you get there."

But he would not be staying with the Cubs. After two admirable seasons in the Windy City (1990 and 1992) and one disastrous season that was marked by a serious back injury and a broken nose (1991), Girardi found himself unprotected by the Cubs in the expansion draft. Rosters for two new teams, the Florida Marlins and the Colorado Rockies, had to be stocked, and Girardi was made available.

For the first time in his life, he would not be based in Illinois. Even when he traveled the minor league roads as a part of the Cubs organization, he knew he was still connected to Chicago. But now he was headed to Denver.

"I was excited and nervous at the same time," he says. "I was leaving a situation where I was comfortable. I had to make all new friends and find a new place to live. Kim and I were married by then, and she had to give up her job. At the time, I don't think my faith was nearly as strong as it is now. I had to find out about trusting in the Lord and how He can take a situation that seems so bad and make it good. I'm less worried now about where I'm going to be. I know that God is going to take care of me."

While a member of the upstart Colorado Rockies, Girardi put together three good seasons both at bat and behind the plate. His .274 batting average and his usual sparkling play as a catcher made him a valuable member of the emerging team.

Yet an incident that occurred in 1995 during the baseball strike probably spelled the end of the road for Girardi in Colorado. In March, as teams tried to put replacement teams together while the regular players were out on the work stoppage, the Rockies offered to pay minor league players $150 for every game they played in.

Girardi, who was the Rockies' union representative, spoke out about the practice, saying that he felt the Colorado team was not acting like a model organization by doing that. That seemed to anger Bob Gebhard, the team's general manager, and he told reporters to "consider the source."

Immediately, Girardi felt bad about the incident. He said, "I made a mistake. I was wrong in my statements, and I'm man enough to admit it." Later, he apologized to the Rockies.

Girardi considers that event the lowlight of his stay in Colorado, but he also feels that it was a growing time for him. "That incident brought me closer to my wife because she was on my side. Also, at the time I found James 1 to be a comfort. I went through a lot of trials and tough times, but God made it turn out for the best. That was a huge faith-builder for me."

After the 1995 season, the Rockies shipped Girardi to New York. How would the Big Apple taste to a guy from Peoria? It had to be on his mind as he and Kim moved again. Now, instead of being part of a team just building a history, he would be a member of the team with the richest legacy in American team sports. He would be occupying the spot once filled by Bill Dickey, Yogi Berra, Elston Howard, and Thurman Munson. And he would be playing before fans who have been known to be tough on friend and foe alike.

Besides, it wouldn't be all October celebrations and jumping into a pile of happy Yankees. There were times when Girardi wondered what God was doing.

That's when Kim came to the rescue again.

"It was amazing what Kim did for me during my first year in New York," he says. "We had times when I really struggled. She always seemed to pick me up and let me know that God had me there for a reason. 'Don't give up,' she would say. 'Fight this through. If you do, you'll see later in your life that God put you here for a reason.' For a while, I kept saying, 'Yeah, sure!' But she was right. I'm very blessed to have her in my corner every day. She's a very strong Christian."

And Girardi proved to be the strong catcher the Yankees thought they were getting. A model of consistency at the plate, he hit .293 before the All-Star Game and .294 after the break. Joe Torre called on Girardi to start 110 games during the regular season, and he excelled behind the plate.

Girardi won rave reviews from the Yankees' pitchers for his ability to handle them and adjust to their various styles, and his teammates marveled at his relentless hustle and inspiring attitude. As he had done with the Rockies, he became a clubhouse leader with the Yankees.

This was a Yankees team that seemed far different from past editions of the Bronx Bombers. Their stories of courage and heart made even coldhearted baseball writers squeeze out words of praise. For Girardi, the team was outstanding because it had "a lot of wonderful stories about perseverance. Guys had gone through so many trials, but they persevered. Guys were at the bottom, and they rose to the top."

Among those people was Dwight Gooden. After undergoing rehabilitation for a life-threatening drug problem, he came back to pitch well for the Yankees. His performance on May 14 typified the comeback spirit of this team. On that day, with Joe Girardi calling the pitches sixty feet away, he threw his first major league no-hitter. For one glorious day, Doc Gooden had conquered his enemy. After the game, Girardi said that catching Gooden's no-no was the highlight of his major league career.

Little did he know that a little more than five months later he would be jumping into the arms of another pitcher, this time celebrating another new all-time highlight—a World Championship.

One year. Two remarkable highlights. To be followed by proclamations of greatness? To be punctuated by grandiose claims and boastful remarks? Not from Joe Girardi. He may have an unusual ability to pick his spots—knowing just when to shine the brightest as a player—but he lets his playing do the talking.

"People ask how it feels to win the World Series, and I don't like to talk about it. I'm just uncomfortable. I think we're called to be humble. I was just there doing what God gave me the gifts to do. I was just given a wonderful opportunity."

There's hope for baseball after all.

Q & A WITH JOE GIRARDI

Q: *How have you changed spiritually as a result of your World Series success?*

Joe: I think the biggest change for me was to see how important it is to win souls for God. I got a letter from a Christian association, and they wanted me to speak at a breakfast. I had never done that. I was nervous. I had spoken to Christians one-on-one, and I was comfortable with that. But Kim encouraged me to do it. She said, "You really need to give back. God has blessed you with this, and you need to do it." At first, I said, "I can't do this." But after she talked to me, I said, "OK. I have no fear of doing this—speaking to a large group." And I think this is one reason God sent us to New York—to prepare to go out and win souls.

Q: *What might be waiting for you after baseball?*

Joe: We'll just see where God wants us to go. Kim and I have talked about it, and my next goal besides being a player might be becoming a general manager. That's not the easiest place to get to, but if God creates that avenue, I would love to take it.

Q: *How do you handle the things in baseball that can cause a player to get angry and upset?*

Joe: It's difficult for a lot of players to handle emotions and anger. I try not to show anger in public because I don't think it's a good example. Once in a while I snap, and when I do, I ask the Lord to forgive me, and I hope fans don't take something bad from it.

THE ROAD TO THE MAJORS

- Selected by the Chicago Cubs in the fifth round of the 1986 draft
- Selected by the Colorado Rockies as 10th pick of the first round of the 1992 expansion draft
- Traded to the New York Yankees on November 20, 1995, for Mike DeJean and Steve Shoemaker
- Signed a two-year contract with the New York Yankees, December 2, 1996

Minor league stops: Peoria, Winston-Salem, Pittsfield, Iowa, Colorado Springs

Minor league highlight: Played in the Eastern League All-Star game in 1988, a season during which Girardi led the league's catchers in fielding percentage, putouts, assists, and total chances

THE GIRARDI FILE

Year	Team	G	AB	R	H	2B	3B	HR	RBI	BB	SO	SB	BA	SLG
1989	ChiC	59	157	15	39	10	0	1	14	11	26	2	.248	.331
1990	ChiC	133	419	36	113	24	2	1	38	17	50	8	.270	.344
1991	ChiC	21	47	3	9	2	0	0	6	6	6	0	.191	.234
1992	ChiC	91	270	19	73	3	1	1	12	19	38	0	.270	.300
1993	Col	86	310	35	90	14	5	3	31	24	41	6	.290	.397
1994	Col	93	330	47	91	9	4	4	34	21	48	3	.276	.364
1995	Col	125	462	63	121	17	2	8	55	29	76	3	.262	.359
1996	NYY	124	422	55	124	22	3	2	45	30	55	13	.294	.374
8 Years		**732**	**2417**	**273**	**660**	**101**	**17**	**20**	**235**	**157**	**340**	**35**	**.273**	**.354**

Sterling Hitchcock
East Coast, West Coast

VITAL STATISTICS

Born April 29, 1971, in Fayetteville, North Carolina
6 feet 1, 192 pounds
Position: Pitcher
Throws left, bats left
Family: Wife, Carrey, and one child, Calyn
1997 Team: San Diego Padres

CAREER HIGHLIGHTS

- Won a career-high thirteen games for the Mariners in 1996
- Beat Toronto 6–1 to clinch the Yankees' wild card play-off spot in 1995
- Had a record of 3–0 in his five starts as a Yankee in 1994
- In 1992, was the youngest pitcher in the AL at age twenty-one

WARMING UP

Sterling and Carrey Hitchcock entered a new era of their lives on November 22, 1996, when their first child, Calyn, was born. For the Hitchcocks, it would mean a whole new lifestyle. Previously, Carrey enjoyed joining Sterling on road trips, but as they faced the prospect of hauling all of their new little girl's paraphernalia around the National League, they wondered how different life would be as a threesome.

FAVORITE BIBLE PASSAGE

"If you confess with your mouth, 'Jesus is Lord,' and believe in your heart that God raised him from the dead, you will be saved. For it is with your heart that you believe and are justified, and it is with your mouth that you confess and are saved. As the Scripture says, 'Anyone who trusts in him will never be put to shame.' For there is no difference between Jew and Gentile—the same Lord is Lord of all and richly blesses all who call on him, for, 'Everyone who calls on the name of the Lord will be saved.'" Sterling puts the Scripture reference, Romans 10:9–13, below every autograph he signs.

Sterling Hitchcock

Let's say you played for a baseball team. You had been a part of that team's organization for seven years. That team had given you your first opportunity to play by drafting you right out of high school. Then that team moved you along the minor league pipeline until you came out in the majors.

Then let's say you played admirably for this team, but they traded you to a team far away—a team with much less tradition than your team, a team that had never been to the World Series. And then the team that traded you proceeded to appear in the World Series the very next year. In fact, they didn't just *go* to the Fall Classic, they won it.

And you were left with no championship ring.

Wouldn't you be jumping-up-and-down mad? Wouldn't you be so angry with that ungrateful other team that you'd like to stomp on anything left in the house that had their logo on it?

Not if you're Sterling Hitchcock, you wouldn't.

The above scenario happened to Sterling Hitchcock, and he is not the least bit upset about it. In fact, he is ecstatic that the Yankees shipped him to Seattle in December of 1995.

"It was a total blessing for my wife, Carrey, and me," Hitchcock says. "In New York, I never got the opportunity to pitch, and I don't think I ever would have."

The Yankees had slated Hitchcock to come out of the bull pen in 1996 if he had remained, which would have surely meant middle relief. The Yanks already had Mariano Rivera and John Wetteland as closers. That would have left Hitchcock in relief pitchers' no-man's-land. So the best opportunity for Hitchcock was the trade.

But what about the tradition of Yankee Stadium and those famous uniforms with the classy pinstripes?

"Polyester is polyester," Hitchcock told a reporter.

And what about playing in the media capital of the world? Anything there to miss?

"Do I miss the media?" he responded to another reporter's question. "Sure—like I miss shoulder surgery."

Don't get the idea that Hitchcock is ungrateful for what the Yankees gave him. He's not. It's just that it was not his kind of town.

Indeed, Hitchcock is grateful for a number of things that came his way because of the Yankees. For one, he was glad to have been a part of the game that sealed for the Yankees their wild card appearance in the 1995 postseason. As the season wound down, Hitchcock seemed to get stronger. He won five of his last six starts in 1995, his first full season in the majors. Included in that streak of successes was his 6–1 victory over the Toronto Blue Jays on September 30, the win that landed the Yankees in the play-offs.

Yet it wasn't his own play-off possibilities that made Hitchcock the happiest after that game; it was his vicarious joy for teammate Don Mattingly. "Seeing the look on Mattingly's face when we got into the play-offs, that's something I'll never forget," he says.

Hitchcock was also grateful to have been a Yankee because of something that happened to him early in 1994. The team was in Fort Lauderdale for spring training. One day after practice, Kevin Maas asked Sterling if he and Carrey could join him and his wife that evening for a get-together.

"Kevin said there was going to be a potter there. I told him we didn't have anything else to do, so, yeah, we could go."

What Sterling and Carrey discovered when they arrived

was that the potter was a Christian. As he spun the wheel and created a piece of pottery, he explained the gospel of Jesus Christ.

"The message he gave that night was just what Carrey and I needed," Sterling says. "We had been searching. We knew all along that we wanted to get started in church, but we never took the first step."

That night, Sterling and Carrey accepted Jesus Christ as their Savior. "It turned out to be a perfect night," Hitchcock says of his encounter with the potter.

On March 29, not long after that milestone evening, Kevin Maas was released by the Yankees. Just in time, he had made an eternal impact on Sterling and Carrey Hitchcock.

There's another reason Sterling is grateful to have been a Yankee, and it is the most basic baseball reason of all. The Yankees gave him the opportunity to play pro ball. It was the Yanks who had drafted him right out of high school in 1989. That was significant because there wasn't much in Sterling Hitchcock's background to suggest he might one day stand on the mound at Yankee Stadium.

Growing up in Seffner, Florida, as the son of a retired Air Force man and the second of three boys, Sterling had little familial influence toward baseball. "My older brother was six years older and was into sports when he was younger, but then he got into cars and things like that. My younger brother is a bookworm, so he didn't have any interest in sports."

So as the only athlete in the family, Sterling turned his attention to sandlot football and Little League baseball. His favorite pitcher as a kid was Roger Clemens, which may make Mr. Clemens feel old if he knew about it, but it didn't do much for Sterling's game. In fact, Sterling claims that he was not a good pitcher as a kid.

"In Little League, I was all right but nothing special. I didn't throw hard. I didn't do anything special."

Therefore, he says that when he got older and started observing Roger the Rocket, "I looked at Clemens and all the talent he had, and I knew I'd never be able to pitch like him. So I didn't try. I didn't model myself after him or anything." But then, how many pitchers in the history of baseball can even come close to Roger Clemens?

It wasn't until Hitchcock's junior year in high school that he finally began to progress as a pitcher. One boost to his improvement came when major leaguers Jody Reed and Jeff Gray of the Red Sox came to Armwood High School to work out with the team. "Gray was a pitcher," Sterling says, "and he helped me a lot. He really got me started."

Another reason for his development was a growth spurt in his junior year. "I got a lot bigger and stronger," he says. As he began to find his groove as a pitcher, he started to attract the attention of college recruiters.

Interest from colleges also had a ripple effect on his activity in the classroom. "I had no direction as a student before then. I was pretty smart, but I never really thought much about going to college. When the colleges started coming to see me pitch, I thought I might get a free education. So I thought it was time to correct the ship and start getting better grades."

Surprisingly, during Hitchcock's senior year at Armwood, he discovered that there might be some interest in him at an even higher level. Most of that attention came as the result of one game. "We had a big winter All-Star game, and at that game basically every college in the Southeast was represented. Also, a lot of major league scouts were there. I happened to pitch very well that night."

In fact, he had been pitching very well for a while. In his three years at Armwood, he compiled a 13–6 record with a 1.32 ERA. In 143 innings, he struck out 209 batters, and he set school records in ERA, innings pitched, and strikeouts.

That was good enough for Yankee scout Jack Gillis. On the day of the 1989 draft, he told Hitchcock, "We can take you in the fourth round, but there's another guy we would like to take now. We'll hold off until later rounds for you, but we'll still take care of you as if we had taken you in an earlier round."

This arrangement was fine with Sterling, as long as the Yankees kept their end of the bargain. The Yanks selected Hitchcock in the ninth round of the 1989 draft. He became the first athlete in the history of Armwood High School to turn pro.

Minor league rookies can be sent any number of places to get their first experience in baseball, but for Sterling there could have been no better place than Sarasota in the Gulf Coast League. First, he would be competing against players his age, and he was confident he could do well. Second, it was close to home. "The big benefit was that I could come home on weekends and see my girlfriend and family."

Even better, Hitchcock's pitching performance picked up where it had left off in high school. Despite the short Gulf Coast schedule (58 games), Hitchcock had 13 starts to lead the league. He finished the year with a 9–1 record, a 1.64 ERA, and a league-leading 98 strikeouts. *Baseball America* magazine called Hitchcock the best major league prospect in the league. For a young man who claims that he "basically stunk as a pitcher" in Little League, he had come a long way.

Hitchcock's great rookie league season earned him a promotion to Single A Greensboro. Eager to continue his success, he nevertheless ran into a roadblock—himself. "I was just awful," he says of his first few outings with the Hornets. "My pitching coach, Dave Jorn, sat me down and said, 'Look, someone considers you a prospect in this organization. It's my job to get you figured out and headed in the right direction.'"

Jorn, along with the manager of the Hornets, former major league pitcher Tony Cloninger, saw a new Sterling Hitchcock the rest of the season. With their help, the young lefty says, "That's the best ball I threw in my entire career."

On July 7, pitching against Sumter, Hitchcock hurled a 1–0 no-hitter. In his next start, he limited Savannah to just three hits. For the year, Hitchcock threw five shutouts and allowed opposing hitters to hit just .171 off his slants. He was not yet twenty years old.

Two years later, he was the youngest pitcher in the American League.

What followed for Sterling and Carrey Hitchcock would not be the storybook ending one would hope for such a nice young couple. Instead of being able to establish themselves in New York, they would ride the Steinbrenner Shuttle for the next

3 years. Look at their itinerary during those seasons:

September 8, 1992	New York Yankees
April 3, 1993	Columbus Clippers
August 26, 1993	New York Yankees
August 31, 1993	Prince William
September 5, 1993	New York Yankees
April 3, 1994	New York Yankees
April 16, 1994	Columbus Clippers
May 3, 1994	New York Yankees
July 3, 1994	Columbus Clippers
July 10, 1994	Albany Yankees
July 18, 1994	New York Yankees
August 9, 1994	Columbus Clippers

Those were difficult times for Hitchcock; it seemed as if he spent more time packing and unpacking than he did pitching. "When you're trying to get established in the major leagues, but you go up and down, up and down, up and down, it's tough. Sometimes there is no reason other than they want to send you down. Sometimes it has nothing to do with how you're play-ing—other than they just have something in mind. That was very frustrating, not only for me but for my wife as well. She had to go through it with me."

Mercifully, Hitchcock was allowed to take a break from the shuttle trips during the 1995 season, and he spent the complete campaign with the big club. And, as mentioned earlier, he pitched well for the Yankees.

Yet when the play-offs came against the Mariners, it didn't seem to matter that he had been exclusively a starter during the season. His two appearances in the Divisional Champi-onship came in relief. The die was apparently cast. The Yankees wanted him to come out of the bull pen in 1996. But then came the trade. He would pack and head for the West Coast and a new lease on baseball life.

In Seattle, Hitchcock was assured, he would be an integral part of the starting rotation. "I knew I would start every fifth day. As a pitcher, that's all you can ask for—just the opportunity." What he didn't know was that Randy Johnson would miss almost the entire season, meaning that Hitchcock, in effect, was the staff ace.

It was the chance he wanted, but it was a learning situation just the same. "As I look back on that first year in Seattle," he recalls, "I may have been putting too much pressure on myself. Instead of just going out and pitching, I may have had higher expectations than I should have had. Also, at the end of the season when I started getting tired, I had to learn to get through it. But just being able to answer the call thirty-five times during the season was a highlight of 1996."

Part of Hitchcock's education as a pitcher came from the opportunity to observe and learn from one of the game's top moundsmen. "Randy Johnson pulled me aside in spring training, and we talked about pitching. You see a guy who is 6 feet 10 inches tall and throws the ball ninety-eight miles an hour, and you don't think there's a lot of knowledge that goes into it. But he's a really intelligent pitcher, and he's relayed a little bit of that to me."

Still another benefit of moving to Seattle was the spiritual assistance the Hitchcocks receive during the season from Chuck and Barb Snyder, a couple who have a ministry to professional athletes in Seattle. "During the season, we attended a Bible study with the Snyders. They are special people, and they have been special to Carrey and me. It was awesome being around them and their influence."

Being in Seattle also opened up a new avenue of ministry for Sterling. During the season, he worked with a foster child organization called Tree House. "I helped them to keep their warehouse open. It provides food and other things for foster children."

With that outreach and others, Hitchcock says, "I'm just trying to make people aware of others' needs. As I do, I realize that I need to portray an image of Christ to everybody around me. That speaks more than saying, 'Hey, look at me. I'm a Christian.' It's more important that people see I'm a Christian by the way I live."

Sterling Hitchcock went from one coast to the other with

his December 1995 trade to the Mariners. For him, the move brightened a career that seemed destined to turn dark if he had stayed in New York. His future seemed to glow with new possibilities as he pitched in Seattle.

And 364 days after the first trade, on December 7, 1996, when the Mariners sent him down the West Coast to San Diego, to another team on the verge of the play-offs and looking for a talented young lefty to take them there, the future got even better. It's so bright, in fact, it looks—well, Sterling.

Q & A WITH STERLING HITCHCOCK

Q: *Was there any special reason your parents gave you the name Sterling? Was it a family name?*
Sterling: No, I think they just picked it out of the air.

Q: *You liked Roger Clemens as a teenager. Does this mean you were a Red Sox fan?*
Sterling: I was a Mets fan in the early '80s. I liked guys like Darryl Strawberry.

Q: *What do you do to stay strong spiritually?*
Sterling: One thing we really enjoyed in 1995 was attending the Pro Athletes Outreach conference after the season. It was a terrific time. It was a week of the most spiritually filling meetings I've ever been to. Unfortunately, we couldn't attend in 1996 because of the baby. We also attend church in Florida during the off-season.

Q: *Who is the toughest hitter you have had to face?*
Sterling: It's hard to single out one hitter. Frank Thomas is at the top of my list. Also, Rafael Palmiero is very tough. Kevin Seitzer is one of the most underrated hitters. He is a tough out.

Q: *What was your reaction to the trade that sent you from Seattle to San Diego?*
Sterling: Carrey and I were both really surprised about it. We didn't know I was being shopped around by the Mariners. But

we were optimistic about it and happy to be going to San Diego.

THE ROAD TO THE MAJORS

- Selected by the New York Yankees in the ninth round of the 1989 draft
- Traded to Seattle with Russ Davis for Tino Martinez, Jeff Nelson, and Jim Mecir on December 7, 1995
- Traded to the San Diego Padres for Scott Sanders on December 7, 1996

Minor league stops: Sarasota, Greensboro, Prince William, Albany-Colonie, Columbus

Minor league highlight: After his first year in the minors with Sarasota in the Gulf Coast League, Hitchcock was named by *Baseball America* as the top major league prospect in the league. He was 9–1 with a 1.64 ERA that season.

THE HITCHCOCK FILE

Year	Team	W	L	PCT	G	SV	IP	H	R	ER	HR	TBB	SO	ERA
1992	NYY	0	2	.000	3	0	13.0	23	12	12	2	6	6	8.31
1993	NY	1	2	.333	6	0	31.0	32	18	16	4	14	26	4.65
1994	NY	4	1	.800	23	2	49.1	48	24	23	3	29	37	4.20
1995	NY	11	10	.524	27	0	168.1	155	91	88	22	68	121	4.70
1996	Sea	13	9	.591	35	0	196.2	245	131	117	27	73	132	5.26
5 Years		**29**	**24**	**.547**	**94**	**2**	**458.1**	**503**	**276**	**256**	**58**	**190**	**322**	**5.03**

Todd Hollandsworth
Rookie of the Year—Finally

VITAL STATISTICS

Born April 20, 1973, in Dayton, Ohio
6 feet 2, 193 pounds
Position: Outfielder
Throws left, bats left
Family: Unmarried
1997 Team: Los Angeles Dodgers

CAREER HIGHLIGHTS

- Named National League Rookie of the Year in 1996
- Had three hits in first major league game (1995), three more than opposing team (teammate Ramon Martinez pitched a no-hitter against the Marlins)

WARMING UP

Watching Todd Hollandsworth play baseball is a reminder of how the game should be played—flat-out, 100 percent, no-holds-barred. That's why when he is asked if there is anything about being a major leaguer he doesn't like, he has a hard time thinking of something. "I can't say there is. I love playing ball." When pressed, though, he finally reveals that the travel does cause a bit of a strain. "When the season is over," he says, "you don't want to go near another airplane." Probably because you can't play baseball in a 747.

FAVORITE BIBLE PASSAGE

"There are so many things I learn that it's hard to pick one verse [or passage]. . . . I find a verse and I say, 'This is my favorite,' and I'll open the Bible the next day and find another verse that is just as meaningful."

Todd Hollandsworth

Todd Hollandsworth was having an absolutely miserable
first year as a member of the Los Angeles Dodgers in 1995.

Oh, he started off just fine, going three for four in his first
major league start against the Florida Marlins on July 14, 1995.
Four days later, he hit his first major league home run off Shane
Reynolds in the second inning of a game against the Astros and
then belted another one off Reynolds in the seventh inning.
And soon after that, he knocked in four runs in a game at Joe
Robbie Stadium, again against the Marlins.

In addition to those fine initial encounters against National
League pitching, Hollandsworth had six multi-hit games, four
multi-RBI games, and a six-game hitting streak. It wasn't because
he was having trouble hitting that his rookie year seemed to be
giving him trouble—it was that he kept getting hurt.

On May 3, he was placed on the fifteen-day disabled list for
a broken hamate bone in his right hand. Surgery on May 9 kept
him out of action until July 7. Then, on August 10, he was back
on the DL, this time suffering from a broken right thumb he had
incurred while sliding into third on August 8. That injury sidelined him until September 12.

All told, Hollandsworth's injuries left him with just 41 games
played, 103 plate appearances, and little chance to put up the

numbers that were expected of him. His .233 batting average was his worst ever in pro ball.

Meanwhile, a first-year teammate of Todd's was the sensation of baseball. Hideo Nomo, hardly a fresh-faced rookie at age twenty-six, was barnstorming the National League, creating Nomomania and showing the world that a star in the Japanese League could get out North American major leaguers. Nomo had already won the Japanese Rookie of the Year award in 1990 while pitching for Kintetsu, and now he was clearly the top choice to win the National League version. His 13–6 record, 2.54 ERA, and 236 strikeouts made him a shoo-in for the award.

Despite Hollandsworth's fine minor league career, despite the fact that he was named 1994's seventh-best major league prospect in the Pacific Coast League, and despite the fact that he had been touted as the top import in the Dominican Winter League between the 1994 and 1995 seasons, his rookie year was not turning out the way everyone had hoped.

The string of Los Angeles Dodger Rookie of the Year Awards would remain intact, but he would not be the 1995 recipient, that was for sure. The succession would be Eric Karros (1992), Mike Piazza (1993), Raul Mondesi (1994), and Hideo Nomo (1995). There would be no such award on Todd Hollandsworth's trophy shelf.

Or so Todd thought.

The frustration of the 1995 season wore heavily on Hollandsworth. Not because he wouldn't win an award—that wasn't his biggest concern. Instead, his up-and-down year caused him to rethink his purpose in the game of baseball.

"It was a turmoil-filled season," he recalls. "I was asking God, 'Am I not supposed to be playing baseball? Is there something else you want me to pursue? Am I not fulfilling something you want me to do, Lord?'"

His checkered season had him asking questions about his role with the Dodgers as well. "I went through that whole season not understanding what I was supposed to do. Am I supposed to be a backup player? Am I going to be a fourth or fifth outfielder?"

Todd Hollandsworth is not a player to sit back and watch

the world go by. He's a take-charge player—a run-through-the-wall kind of guy. He would just as soon take the extra base as look at it. If the ball is in the vicinity, he'll catch up to it or dive trying. Many who have seen him play call him a throwback player—someone who reminds them of the good old days of baseball, when players wore flannels, small gloves, and marks all over their bodies from going full tilt toward victory.

That's why the 1995 summer of injuries was eating away at him so much. That's why the questions bombarded his mind. And that's why an innocent statement by an astute sportswriter turned Hollandsworth's thinking around in late 1995. At the end of the season, the scribe mentioned to Todd that he had not accumulated enough playing time during the 1995 season to jeopardize his rookie status. Technically, he would be a rookie again in 1996.

Hideo Nomo could have his grand entrance into American baseball and celebrate with the Rookie of the Year trophy. Todd Hollandsworth would get a brand-new start in 1996.

"When the reporter said that," he says, "I looked up at the sky and said, 'God, this is just amazing.' It was almost like I felt it was my destiny."

Hollandsworth had been including God in his daily life since he was a teenager. He had grown up in a Christian home and trusted Christ at an early age, but it wasn't until high school that he realized his faith should be evident all week, not just on Sundays.

"I didn't really understand what Christ meant in my life until I was about fifteen or sixteen years old," he recalls. "I was so into athletics that I didn't understand how God could work in my life until I was a sophomore or junior in high school. It was a matter of maturing. I had always taken my Bible to church on Sunday, but when I would come home, I would just put it down and pick it up again the next Sunday. But then I started reading it regularly, and I started understanding that God is a factor in my life, in everything I did. I discovered that in all my words and in all my deeds, I needed to honor the Lord. Until then, I didn't realize that my faith was a total, daily commitment."

Hollandsworth's early commitments were mostly to sports. Growing up as the son of a management-level employee of United Parcel Service, Hollandsworth took his athletic skills all over the country. The family lived in Ohio, New Jersey, Montana, and Washington, as Todd's dad was transferred to various UPS offices. When they finally settled in Bellevue, Washington, Todd was a freshman in high school.

At Newport High School in Bellevue, a community near Seattle, Todd competed in football, baseball, and basketball. "I was best at football," he says. That skill, combined with his baseball prowess, opened the way for him to receive several offers to play both sports in college. "A lot of colleges were in favor of doing a joint scholarship, so I could pull money from both the baseball and football programs." The Pac 10 schools were especially interested, including Arizona, Arizona State, Washington, and Washington State.

In the classroom, Hollandsworth was a 3.4 GPA student who now feels he could have done even better if he'd had to. "I was so focused on athletics and succeeding there that it took away from my academics. I knew how the system worked. The system, especially in high school, is that if you are a good student and a great athlete, you'll be able to go to college wherever you want. I had the grades to get into the school of my choice."

That choice never had to be made, however, for the Los Angeles Dodgers came along in 1991 and drafted him. Amazingly, though, the Dodgers weren't in any hurry to inform their third-round pick that he had been chosen.

"The draft started on Monday," Todd recalls. "When I was drafted in 1991, there were 60 rounds. The first 10 rounds were on the first day, and 11–25 were on the second. Then 26–60 were on the third."

After the third day passed without a phone call, Hollandsworth thought he hadn't been drafted.

"I thought, *Well, I guess I'm going to college.* It was confusing. The way I had been approached by several teams before the draft, I thought sure I was going to get an outstanding offer. But nobody called."

Finally, after the draft had ended, the Los Angeles Dodgers

called and told Hollandsworth they had picked him. "I hadn't heard about it on the news because the newspeople were waiting to hear from me."

The phone call was startling not only for its lateness, but also because of the team. "I had absolutely no idea the Dodgers were going to draft me. I would say they were at the bottom of my list, because I had not talked to them much at all. A lot of other organizations told me they were interested."

As Hollandsworth headed for his first experiences in the minor leagues with his surprising new team, he had a built-in advantage. His nomadic lifestyle as a youngster readied him for the frequent uprooting that occurs in professional baseball.

"What God had our family do by moving around helped me put things into perspective in baseball," he says. "Baseball is a lot like our family was. You may not be in the same city for a long time. In the minor leagues, I went all the way across the country and back in three and a half years years. I had a short tour of duty in the minor leagues, but I still did a lot of moving. I played in the Midwest League, the Texas League, the California League, and the Pacific Coast League.

"My moving around at a young age prepared me for moving around as a ballplayer. When I look back on it now, it amazes me how God had those things incorporated in my life. As a kid, you don't know how you're going to handle all those moves, but now it's a blessing. As much as I hated moving, going to three different high schools in three different parts of the country, I look back on it now and see that the new friends I had to make and the adjusting I had to do helped me in baseball."

After stops in Yakima (1991) and Bakersfield (1992), Hollandsworth moved to the Double A San Antonio Missions in 1993. There he was named the ninth-best major league prospect in the Texas League and L.A.'s second-best Dodger-to-be. That year, he pounded out 17 home runs and led the league in triples with 9.

In 1994, he put together a monster season for the Albuquerque Dukes, the Dodgers' Triple A affiliate. His home run total grew to 19 and he knocked in 91 runs in just 132 games, easily putting him on the fast track to Chavez Ravine. But first, he stopped off in the Dominican Republic, where he batted .320 in the Winter League and earned a spot on the All-Star team.

The stage was set for The Year of the Disabled List—a year that began with promise, ended in despair, yet was brightened with the hope of a new beginning in 1996.

If a player might seem a bit pretentious to even think about earning the Rookie of the Year Award, then he probably doesn't play for the Los Angeles Dodgers. For upcoming Dodgers, the award might seem like a birthright. Look at the list of players in team history who had been named the National League's best rookie prior to the 1996 season:

Jackie Robinson	1947	Steve Howe	1980
Don Newcombe	1949	Fernando Valenzuela	1981
Joe Black	1952	Steve Sax	1982
Jim Gilliam	1953	Eric Karros	1992
Frank Howard	1960	Mike Piazza	1993
Jim Lefebvre	1965	Raul Mondesi	1994
Ted Sizemore	1969	Hideo Nomo	1995
Rick Sutcliffe	1979		

No other team was even close in the rookie race. When Derek Jeter copped the award in the American League in 1996, the runner-up Yankees took their eighth such prize.

Although Hollandsworth ended the 1995 season feeling he'd been given a second chance to earn the top-rookie honor, he began 1996 with little hope of fulfilling that destiny. In fact, he had added just one point to his 1995 batting average through the end of April, hitting just .234. Then some encouraging words from one of the Dodgers' former Rookie of the Year winners, Eric Karros, gave Hollandsworth a boost. He told Todd to hang in there, and the young outfielder did.

But it was more than a teammate's platitude that got Hollandsworth going. "I got off to a slow start, but I had a totally different approach," he says. "In 1995, I was questioning my purpose. In 1996, I said, 'Father, if this is meant to be, it's in your hands. If I'm going to be Rookie of the Year, I'm going to go out there every day and give it everything I've got. I'm going to be smart, and I'm going to play as hard as I can. I'm going to do my homework on these pitchers, and I'm going to be as ready as I possibly can. If it works, it does; if it doesn't, my life is in your hands. If it's not meant for me to play baseball, I'll move on. If it is, allow me to continue.'"

And continue he did.

Improving throughout the season, Hollandsworth proved his worth to the Dodgers when he took over the leadoff spot in the batting order for cancer-stricken Brett Butler. Hollandsworth thought this move indicated that the Dodgers were looking at him in a new way—a way that appealed to him.

"You go through your rookie season knowing that organizations are going to say, 'We're going to try to get out of him what we can. We don't expect as much.' I didn't like that. I wanted them to expect something of me. I wanted them to say, 'We need this guy to succeed.' When they put me into the leadoff position, that's when it occurred."

In August, manager Bill Russell sat down with Hollandsworth and told him, "We need you to lead off. We need you to be a spark on this team. We need you to get on base. We need you to help us get into the play-offs."

That was like offering a steak to a bulldog.

"That's when I really started to thrive," Hollandsworth says. "The challenge is to be depended on. When you're batting sixth or seventh, you don't feel nearly as important. But when I was moved to leadoff, I had to come to the field every day ready to play. Not that I wasn't ready before, but I felt my importance was increased, and that helped my development."

Leading off was a new experience for Hollandsworth, but not one that scared him. After all, here was a player whose childhood baseball heroes were three of the most fearless players in the game: Kirk Gibson, Mike Schmidt, and Andy Van Slyke.

"I took on the challenge of leading off, and I said, 'I'm going to have fun.' Bill Russell told me, 'We're not expecting you to change your game. You've never done this before. We don't expect you to go up there and take first-pitch fastballs down the middle. Keep doing what you've been doing. Keep whack-ing the ball. Keep hitting your doubles and your extra-base hits. Keep stealing bases. Keep doing what you were doing at the bottom of the order and do it at the top.'"

Russell picked the right guy for the job. As the season went on to become a dogfight with the Padres for the NL West title, Hollandsworth continued to improve. During the twenty-nine games he led off, he batted .316 with eight doubles, two triples, five home runs, and seventeen RBIs.

In addition to his new role as a dependable leadoff hitter, Hollandsworth also convinced the team that he was an every-day player, moving out of a platooning role on August 28 and becoming the regular left fielder.

When the season finally ended, Hollandsworth had com-piled a .291 batting average with 12 home runs and 59 RBIs. He led National League rookies in hits, doubles, home runs, RBIs, stolen bases, and fewest errors. And when the Baseball Writ-ers' Association of America cast their ballots, Hollandsworth had 15 first-place votes and 105 points for Rookie of the Year, outpolling Florida shortstop Edgar Reneria (84) and Pittsburgh catcher Jason Kendall (30).

"It's a great honor in my eyes to be [the Dodgers'] fifth in a row," Hollandsworth said at a news conference after being named the Rookie of the Year in November 1996. "I believe it's just a beginning and something to build on. That's what the year was all about—a start."

A successful major league career wasn't the only thing Todd Hollandsworth started in 1996. This time it was some-thing more personal than professional.

It all started in June when the Dodgers visited Atlanta for a four-game series against the Braves. At the time, Butler was in the middle of recuperation from his cancer surgery about six weeks earlier, but he was well enough to host a get-together for his friends at his Atlanta home. Players and their wives were invited, but Todd Hollandsworth was single. Therefore, Eveline and Brett Butler made arrangements for Clare Harris, a single friend of theirs, to be present. They told Todd, "We have this great girl we want you to meet."

"I said, 'Let whatever happens, happen.'"

What happened was rather typical of blind dates. "It was kind of an awkward situation for people," Todd says of the mixture of teammates, wives, and this blind-date couple. "Neither of us had been in that kind of situation. For an hour or so, we just kind of walked around. But then things died down and people started to go home. The next thing I knew, it was 11:30 and we had been talking for five hours."

They're still talking. In November 1996, the same month Hollandsworth won the big baseball award, he became engaged to Clare. As the 1997 season was about to unfold, the couple was planning a November wedding.

It was nothing short of an incredible year for Todd Hollandsworth in 1996.

"The older you get, the more you sit back in amazement," he says. "God has worked so many miracles in my life. It blows my mind to see how God works in my life—and to see how important He has become to me."

Q & A WITH TODD HOLLANDSWORTH

Q: *A lot of people wonder about sports agents and what kind of relationship a player has with his agent. What is your player-agent relationship like?*

Todd: I like my agent, Tracy Codd, a lot. People say, "Why don't you sign with someone with a bigger name?" But Tracy has helped me very much. He helped me when I was just a peon in Class A ball, and he treats me the same now as he did then. I respect him for that. I owe a lot to him.

Q: *How does it make you feel when people compare you to Kirk Gibson?*

Todd: It's funny—people want to make those comparisons, but I can't believe it because he was such an incredible athlete. I'm not even close to him. I just never envision myself being the caliber athlete he was, but I try to play as hard. It makes me feel great to have people say that, and I feel that if I have the career he had, I'll be very fortunate.

Q: *What did you learn from Brett Butler in 1996?*
Todd: I've been learning from Brett from the day I met him. In 1996, with what he went through, I learned to understand how strong his faith is. Even with all he went through, his faith was not going to falter, and that's the sign of a rock, a soldier for Christ. That's what I want to be. He said, "I'm going to get through this. I'm going to fight this." I told Brett, "This isn't God making this happen. This may be an outside force trying to tear you down because you are such a strong soldier, but God has you in His hands, and He is going to take care of you."

THE ROAD TO THE MAJORS

• Selected by the Los Angeles Dodgers in the third round of the 1991 draft

Minor league stops: Yakima, Bakersfield, San Antonio, Albuquerque, San Bernardino

Minor league highlight: Led the Pacific Coast champion Albuquerque Dukes in games played (132) while hitting .285 with 19 home runs and 91 runs batted in

THE HOLLANDSWORTH FILE

Year	Team	G	AB	R	H	2B	3B	HR	RBI	BB	SO	SB	BA	SLG
1995	LA	41	103	16	24	2	0	5	13	10	29	2	.233	.398
1996	LA	149	478	64	139	26	4	12	59	41	93	21	.291	.437
2 Years		**190**	**581**	**80**	**163**	**28**	**4**	**17**	**72**	**51**	**122**	**23**	**.281**	**.430**

Rex Hudler
Not What You Think

VITAL STATISTICS

Born September 2, 1960, in Tempe, Arizona
6 feet, 195 pounds
Position: Infielder
Throws right, bats right
Family: Wife, Jennifer, and two children, Alyssa and Cade
1997 Team: Philadelphia Phillies

- Hit a career-best .311 for the Angels in 1996
- Was 12 for 12 in stolen base attempts in 1995
- Started at four different positions for Angels (first base, second base, third base, left field) in 1994
- Stole nineteen consecutive bases in first nineteen attempts for Montreal in 1988

WARMING UP

In the June 1978 free agent draft, Rex Hudler was selected ahead of Cal Ripken, Jr. The two struck up a friendship when Hudler played for the Orioles organization in 1986 and 1987. In 1995, when the Angels were in Baltimore during the record-breaking game of Ripken's consecutive-game streak, Hud and Rip got together. Ripken gave Hudler a signed bat that night—one of two he signed. The other went to the President of the United States.

FAVORITE BIBLE PASSAGE

"Whatever you do, work at it with all your heart, as working for the Lord, not for men" Colossians 3:23.

Rex Hudler

The 1996 baseball season was something of a coming out year for Rex Hudler. Although Rex had been around professional baseball almost as long as Atlanta's twenty-year-old rookie Andruw Jones had been alive, he never seemed to attract much attention until this season.

Suddenly, he was everywhere.

There were the frequent references to "Wonder Dog" on ESPN.

There were funny articles in national magazines about Rex and some of the bizarre things he has done in his career. (For instance, that bug he ate on a dare from his teammates. We won't talk about that, since his wife, Jennifer, has told Rex she's not too fond of hearing about that anymore.)

There was Rex in the listings of top hitters, as he had a career year at the plate.

But behind it all, there seemed to be the impression being left by all these reports that Rex Hudler was a bit unusual . . . that he hoed a row that was in somebody else's field . . . that he enjoyed the weird, wild, and wacky reputation that accompanies being a bug-eating baseball player with his switch stuck on "go." Having the name Rex is all part of the fun.

As entertaining as those portrayals might be, though, they don't give a complete picture of the man. They promote a caricature, overemphasizing some points while neglecting others.

Although Rex Hudler probably cares little about things turning out that way (at least not as much as Jennifer does), it seems only right to set the record straight. It's not fair to have people left with the impression that Rex Hudler is nothing more than a guy who likes to goof around.

Rex Hudler's goal in life goes far beyond being a very good baseball player. It transcends being a popular sports figure with some, let's say, unusual characteristics. It encompasses something much more important than a few highlight appearances and an article or two in *Sports Illustrated*.

The most important thing this former first-round draft pick from Fresno wants people to know is that he loves Jesus Christ. That devotion to Christ began when Hudler was eight years old.

"I remember walking the aisle with my mom at a Baptist church and inviting Jesus into my life," he says. "I was raised in a Christian family, so I had the opportunity to understand the gospel at a young age."

And that devotion to Jesus has guided him through all of the worthwhile endeavors he has enjoyed in life.

As the middle male offspring in Marlyn and Ann Hudler's five-person household, Rex Hudler was something of a model son. It's something he credits to a decision he made because of his two brothers. As he observed his older and younger brothers, he noticed that their behavior sometimes caused their parents quite a bit of grief. "It seems like they made Mom cry all the time," he recalls.

For Rex, that was not acceptable. "I told myself I didn't want that. I was schooled in the Bible at a young age, and I remembered that Ephesians 6 says, 'Children, obey your parents, for this is one of God's top commands, and you'll have a long life full of blessing'" (at least that's Hudler's translation). Young Rex set out to prove the truth of that verse.

"I kept thinking, *I want to make my parents happy.* I'd clean house for my mom and try to do the little things right. I saw the pain and grief my brothers put my parents through. I had a soft spot for my mom and dad."

So if growing up trying to please one's parents leads to people thinking a kid is a bit different, then Rex wouldn't mind being considered unusual.

"I wasn't a perfect child by any means," he admits. "But I had an idea that if I would get along with my parents and listen to them, they would actually help me. And they sure enough did."

One of the ways Rex received help from his dad was with sports. "My dad was always there for us. He got off work at five o'clock, and he always made time for us. I remember my dad would come home and practice with us for the pitch, hit, and throw competition [a national competition in basic baseball skills]. There was a school yard behind our back fence, and we would go there and my dad would work with us. He also helped us with punt, pass, and kick [a similar competition in football]."

Just when you think you have Rex Hudler figured out, he throws a curve. It would be easy to assume that because he has played pro ball since 1978 that baseball was his favorite sport as a kid. Then again, since he was recruited by major colleges to play football, it wouldn't seem too far-fetched to think *that* was his preferred childhood sport.

Wrong on both counts. "Soccer was my favorite sport," Hudler says. "I loved soccer. I started playing it when I was seven or eight years old. I loved to run. I think it developed my legs, my speed, and my competitiveness. I played all through high school up until my senior year."

So if soccer was his favorite, why did he stop? Not surprisingly, it was because of something his parents told him.

"In high school, I played every sport I could. I wanted to play all of them. As I got to my senior year, I was doing pretty well in baseball and football. My folks made a suggestion. They said that there's not much future as a pro athlete in soccer and that I might be wise to drop it and concentrate on baseball and football."

Today, kids can look ahead and see the success of Major League Soccer as a possible avenue of pursuit. But back then it was a dead-end street, even for a successful inside striker like Hudler. Still, the two avenues that were open to Hudler held great promise.

As a star infielder at Bullard High School and as a fan of the Big Red Machine, the Cincinnati Reds, Hudler dreamt of being a baseball hero like Pete Rose. And as a star flanker and defensive back for Bullard and as a fan of the Dallas Cowboys, he dreamt of being an NFL star like his football hero, Roger Staubach.

If Hudler wanted to pursue a future on the gridiron, he was assured of some big-time exposure. His two biggest pursuers when he was a high school senior were Notre Dame and Michigan State. Both schools coveted him as their next star wide receiver. In fact, in what must have been an incredible experience for a high school kid, he visited both colleges on the same recruiting trip.

"That they would let me get out of school to do that was really something!" he says of his trip. "To go to Notre Dame and see the golden dome and the great memorabilia! They had their highlight film narrated by Lindsey Nelson. It was so professional! I was thinking, *Wow!*"

Even more impressive was Hudler's host on the recruiting trip—a quarterback who would go on to do some rather spectacular things in his career. A kid by the name of Joe Montana.

"Then Dan Devine [Irish head coach] sat behind his desk and said, 'Son, we have a scholarship for you.' I was so flattered and humbled. God's grace was with me. I told Mr. Devine that I would love to come, but I would have to talk to my folks."

He also had another visit to make. "Then I got on a plane and went to Michigan State. Kirk Gibson met me at the airport and took me around campus. They knew I had just come from Notre Dame, so they rolled out the red carpet for me. It was a neat feeling to be wanted and to realize that because I had listened to my parents and did the things as a young kid that I should have done, it was paying off. I had no idea how it would pay off in the future, but the immediate satisfaction I gained from listening to my parents made me feel great."

Returning to Fresno, Hudler made his decision—he signed a letter of intent to become a member of the Fighting Irish football team. "Everybody in Fresno knew it," he says of his decision. "It was in the headlines. It was big news."

Local star Rex Hudler would be going to Notre Dame.

But that's before he gave much thought to baseball.

"Baseball was the last sport of my high school career, and I said, 'I'm going to play and have fun and not worry about anything.'"

The next thing he knew, he was having a terrific year as the Bullard High shortstop, and the major league scouts were flocking to see him play. "It was exciting to see all the scouts at the game with their clipboards," he says. And soon, they were on the phone.

"They would call and tell my mom and dad, 'Your kid has the chance to be one of the top picks in the draft.'"

Not to worry. Ann Hudler, proud mother of a soon-to-be college student, would take care of those pesky scouts.

"Mom would tell them, 'Don't waste your pick. Don't draft Rex, because he's going to college. He's going to Notre Dame.'"

Yet a Triple Crown season in his conference (he led the league in home runs, RBIs, and batting average) had the scouts drooling. "I remember that rumors were flying around about the draft. A couple of teams had come in and worked me out. It was getting exciting."

Finally, draft day arrived, and Rex came rushing home from school to see if his name had been called.

"Mom! Did anybody call?" Rex yelled to his mom as he walked in the door.

"Yes, the Yankees drafted you," she told him.

"Really! That's a great team!" Rex replied.

"Well, I told them they wasted their pick and that you're going to college."

"Way to go, Mom. Way to blow them off. That could have been my future there!"

"Son, they'll come back if they want you. They'll be back."

By that time, Hudler had grown fond of the idea of going to the pros to play baseball instead of going to Notre Dame to play football. But what could he do? He had grown up obeying his parents and trusting that they knew what they were doing.

But this was the New York Yankees!

"I told Mom, 'If we can work out a deal, let's do it.' I felt like baseball would be a lot easier on my body in the long run. It would give me an opportunity at age seventeen to start paying my dues. Two weeks later, New York called. That was a long two weeks."

The Yankees arranged a meeting in Fresno with the Hudlers. Yankee general manager Al Rosen and director of player development Jack Butterfield visited the Hudler home. They told Rex and his parents, "Whatever he wants as a signing bonus, we'll give him."

"They knew I had the scholarship, and my mom had been playing hardball, so they knew they had to come up with some money to get me. When they started talking about money, though, my mom made me leave the room. She sent me out to get a hot dog."

When Rex Hudler came back into the room, he was a New York Yankee. And he was $125,000 richer.

"When it came right down to choosing my colleges and choosing between baseball and football, there was a lot of prayer involved. A lot of Scripture reading. I knew that God carried my future, and I remember trying to find verses that could help me make my decisions. I wanted His will to be done in my life."

It seemed to be the ideal situation for a young man who had grown up living by the standards of the Bible, seeking God, and obeying his parents. As a first-round pick, he seemed to have an open road to Yankee Stadium. Soon, it seemed, Rex Hudler would be a bright light for God in Gotham City.

Sadly, though, there would be no quick and easy ride to the big time. And there would not be a consistent testimony for Jesus in Rex Hudler's immediate future. In fact, Hudler's baseball life seemed to be one that attracted detours.

"My struggles occurred when I signed with pro baseball and when I got on my own," Hudler says honestly. "I began doing my own thing. I was stubborn. I tried to live my life the way I wanted to. I forgot the great things God had done for me."

The first signs of trouble began right away. His first pro assignment sent him across the country to Florida. "I was out there searching," he recalls. "I was getting into things I shouldn't have. I experienced drugs and alcohol."

Looking back, Hudler feels that God was holding him back from the big leagues while he was going through his "wild oats" period. At the time, Rex was trying to get back on track. He would read James 1 and tell God, "In your time." Yet he was not willing to commit himself to a sold-out Christian life.

"One of the big sin areas of my life was women," he says. "I knew that was not pleasing to God and the Holy Spirit." So he prayed for three years that God would bring him a wife—that He would handpick somebody.

By now, Hudler had spent several years in the Yankees organization, and he had worked his way up to the Triple A Columbus team.

It was in Columbus that his prayer for a wife would be answered—but not without some obstacles to overcome. Her name was Jennifer Myers, and at first she didn't much like the idea of dating Rex.

"She was afraid of a baseball player," Rex recalls. "When she found out that I played ball, she was nervous. She had heard about the lifestyle of players. And, of course, I was living that lifestyle at the time."

Hudler knew she was a Christian, so he told her that he was a believer too, and that he wanted to live for Christ. "That attracted her to me, she told me later," Hudler says.

Yet all was not right in Hudlerville. He may have promised Jennifer that he was going to live God's way, but he wasn't really doing so. And he was beginning to lead Jennifer down the wrong path as well.

The two ended up getting engaged, but they were not demonstrating Christian principles with their relationship. "After the 1987 baseball season," Hudler says, "I wanted her to come out to Fresno to live with me during the off-season so she could get to know my family. I was really excited about her coming out there with me. We got a little apartment, and I was going to my old church.

"It was the worst off-season of my life. I accepted a job working for my dad. He was in the steel business, and I was his purchasing agent. I made a lot of mistakes. At the same time, I was coming off a career-threatening stress fracture. Well, my dad's business went bankrupt, and my older brother was doing drugs. He kept showing up at my doorstep physically and emotionally spent."

Rex Hudler's life was not following the straight-to-the-big-time path it seemed it would take ten years earlier. His major league career so far consisted of forty-three games. He seemed to be a perennial minor leaguer who would have to be content with an occasional cup of coffee in the bigs. And he was still rebelling against God's standards for his life.

"All this was going on," Hudler recalls, "and I could hear God speaking through this. I would pray and say to Him, 'I'm just dating one woman. Look at all this turmoil. I don't understand.'"

Hudler would get a response from God that to him sounded like this: "Hud"—he's convinced God calls him "Hud"—"you are not right with Me. You aren't married to Jennifer."

"I got some counseling on that, and a good friend told me, 'Hud, you probably need to go your separate ways.' I wanted to honor God. I wanted to honor my relationship with Jennifer— and our upcoming marriage."

So Rex told Jennifer that it was time to stop their live-in situation. He told her, "We have such a long life ahead. Why not make a sacrifice for a short time? You go your way, and I'll go mine."

Jennifer replied, "Honey, that sounds good. He'll bless us for that. He'll honor us for lifting Him up."

From Hudler's perspective, when he finally turned this last vestige of his rebellious lifestyle over to God, his life got back on track.

"Jennifer went back to Ohio, and I signed with a new team, the Expos, for 1988. Their Triple A team was in Indianapolis, so I got to see Jennifer once in a while. I got promoted to the major leagues halfway through that year. I stole eighteen straight bases and hit .270 and had a really good year.

"Jennifer and I got married after the season. We rededicated our lives to doing things God's way. We told Him we'd try not to ever fall into that other life again and that we would stay committed to Him."

Rex Hudler has not spent another day in the minor leagues since.

Some athletes would be bitter about having to travel the tedious minor league roads for so long—wondering why their younger years were spent toiling in places like Greensboro, Fort Lauderdale, and Rochester. Some would have buried their careers in self-pity and sulked off to wonder about what might have been. But Rex Hudler stuck to his dream, and he never doubted God's goodness in making him wait. In fact, to Hud's way of thinking, his marathon minor league career was his own fault.

"It seems that the bottom line is that God wanted obedience from me. He knew that I was grounded in Him and that I was never going to turn away from Him forever. I would leave Him for little bits of time, but He had to break me and bring me to my knees. It wasn't like me praying, 'If you let me play, I'll do this.' It was a much bigger picture than that. It was for life."

As for Jennifer, Hudler seems ready to pinch himself to make sure he's not dreaming. "It wasn't an accident that we got together and got married. I prayed for her for three years. I prayed that God would bring somebody compatible to me. Jennifer is very talented. I had no idea that God would hook me up with someone who is so skilled—who has a beautiful voice and wants to sing for Him." In fact, Jennifer has designs on a singing career, but for now has put her plans on hold to raise their daughter, Alyssa, and their newest addition, Cade, who was born in November 1996.

Since Hudler has become a fixture in the major leagues, he has spent time with the Expos (1988–90), the St. Louis Cardinals (1990–92), and the California Angels since 1994. If you look carefully, you'll notice a year—1993—missing from that list. That was the year of the Yakult Swallows.

Rex Hudler calls his season in Japanese baseball as a member of the Swallows, the year "God took me to Japan and worked me over." He and Jennifer see this unusual pilgrimage to the Land of the Rising Sun as another of the growing, maturing times in their Christian life.

Hudler says it took great faith just to go to Japan in the first place. When the Hudlers sensed God leading them to Japan, their first worry was their house in St. Louis. A slow real estate market in the area caused Hudler to fear their home wouldn't sell. Rex recalls how God explained His feeling on the subject. "He seemed to say, 'Hud, don't worry about the house. I put the mountains together, and you're worried about Me selling your house?'" In fact, the house sold in a matter of days.

But the house was just the beginning of faith-stretching experiences. During the first three or four months of the season, Hudler's Japanese manager threatened to send him home several times. They said he was playing shabby defense and was costing them ball games.

"God took me through that process," he says. "I kept smiling and accepting it and told the boss, 'Look, stay with me, and I'll be a good player for you.'"

Still the conflict continued. The manager would go so far as to tell Hudler that when they lost, he was the main culprit.

"He went right to the core," Hudler recalls, "but it wasn't the truth. I was hitting. But I didn't give in. I didn't blast him. I just said, 'I'm going to practice harder, and I'll be better when you put me out there.' God gave me that attitude."

It paid off. As the season wore on, Rex Hudler became the Swallows' go-to guy. "I was making the double plays, hitting home runs, doing all the right things to help us win."

When the season was over, the Yakult Swallows were the champions of the Japanese Baseball League. "After winning that seventh game, I was weeping like a small child. God kept His promise. He said, 'I'm going to put you on a winner, and I'm going to mold your character.' It was a blessed summer to play in Japan."

That happy ending to the Hudlers' Japanese experience was not repeated the following spring, though, when Hudler showed up at the San Francisco Giants' spring training site. "I was excited about coming back to America and playing—especially being raised in Fresno and getting to play for the Giants.

"I showed up and worked hard. But then all of a sudden, I had a foot injury. It was a painful injury, but I felt that God wanted me to show up every day and play hard. I battled this thing. I'd hit a double, and I'd limp into second. But I did it with a smile. I tried to be an encouragement."

Hudler expected that he would make the team that spring. He could play seven positions and pinch-hit. But it wasn't enough. The Giants called him into the office after a month of spring training and said, "Rex, we're sorry. We have to release you."

Hudler was devastated. He was sure this was where he was supposed to be. Hudler took a deep breath and said to the Giants' brass, including manager Dusty Baker, "Thank you for having me. What a wonderful opportunity to be here for thirty days and play for you. Dusty, I think you're a great manager. I got to play with some of the greatest baseball players, and I got to meet Willie Mays and Willie McCovey—some of my great all-time heroes. I'm better for being here. Thank you very much."

If you want to think Rex Hudler is unusual, do so because of the unusual faith he possesses and how he has learned to live it out. "The Holy Spirit was in my heart and shining brightly," Hudler says.

With his release from the Giants came new questions: Was he through with baseball? Could he hook up with another team? Would it be the end?

Actually, two beginnings were about to occur for Hudler and his wife. First, in late March 1994, Jennifer gave birth to Alyssa, who was, Hudler proudly proclaims, "Made in Japan."

Then, while Hudler was at the hospital with his wife and child, the California Angels caught up with him and offered him a spot on their roster. He went home from the hospital with a new daughter and a new lease on his baseball career. Alyssa was born on March 25; Hudler's new career with the Angels began on the 28th when he signed his contract.

Buck Rodgers, the Angels' manager, was in Montreal when Hudler played with the Expos, and he liked what he had seen. Rodgers told Hudler, "You're going to platoon and hit against left-handed pitching." It was the opportunity Hudler was looking for.

"God told me, 'Hud, you were in the right state but not the right city. I wanted you in L.A., not in San Francisco.'"

Indeed, the California Angels turned out to be a perfect fit for Hudler. His great attitude and competitive fire blended nicely with the young talent the Angels had assembled. In 1995, the team made a run at the Western Division title, only to see their hopes fade in the closing weeks of the season. And in 1996, while the team never realized the high expectations many observers had for them, Hudler turned in his best year ever.

At age thirty-six—eighteen years after he was first drafted—Hudler hit .311, stole fourteen bases, and pounded out sixteen home runs for the Angels. And he attracted a lot of attention.

"God chose to lift me up that summer," Hudler says. "It was the greatest summer of my career personally, statistically, and as far as coverage goes. It was unbelievable. Apparently, my work is not done in baseball."

And it's a good thing. There aren't many people around like Rex Hudler: fun-loving yet with a serious heart for God; talented yet humble; intense yet generous.

"I just absolutely love the game of baseball," he says. "I don't want to waste any opportunities, so I play with the pedal to the metal."

Baseball needs a few dozen more people just like Rex Hudler.

Q & A WITH REX HUDLER

Q: *Who is the toughest pitcher you've ever faced?*
Rex: I had all kinds of trouble with left-hander Terry Mulholland when I was in the National League and he pitched for Philadelphia. I think I was 1 for 25 against him. And Dwight Gooden in his prime was tough.

Q: *What do you plan to do once your playing career is over?*
Rex: Managing a team would be appealing to me because I love to motivate. I like to encourage young people. It would be a great challenge. But the ultimate picture is what God wants me to do. When I'm retired, I'm going to ask Him what to do. He's going to put me in a place where He wants me to be.

Q: *What did you learn about Japanese baseball in your year in Japan?*
Rex: It's a different game. The fields are smaller, and the home

run distances are marked in meters, not feet. Also, the ball-strike call is reversed. If the count is full, you have a 2–3 count. The season is thirty-five games shorter than it is in North America. That gave Jennifer and me more off-days for sightseeing.

Q: *Since you grew up playing soccer, do you still follow the game today?*

Rex: I follow the pro league a little, and I probably follow it more each year. During the World Cup in 1994, I saw a game at Stanford Stadium between Russia and Cameroon. The Russian guys broke a record. One guy scored five goals. It was awesome. There were more than 100,000 people there.

THE ROAD TO THE MAJORS

- Selected by the New York Yankees in the first round of the 1978 draft
- Traded to the Baltimore Orioles with Rich Bordi for Gary Roenicke and Leo Hernandez on December 12, 1985
- Granted free agency on October 15, 1987
- Signed by the Montreal Expos' Indianapolis minor league team on December 18, 1987
- Traded to the St. Louis Cardinals for John Costello on April 23, 1990
- Released by St. Louis on December 7, 1992
- Signed by Yakult Swallows of the Japan Central League for the 1993 season
- Signed as a free agent by the San Francisco Giants on December 20, 1993
- Released by San Francisco on March 22, 1994
- Signed by the California Angels on March 28, 1994
- Signed by the Philadelphia Phillies as a free agent on November 21, 1996

Minor league stops: Oneonta, New York, Fort Lauderdale, Greensboro, Nashville, Columbus, Rochester, Indianapolis

Minor league highlight: In 1986, hit .419 for Rochester in International League postseason play-offs

Year	Team	G	AB	R	H	2B	3B	HR	RBI	BB	SO	SB	BA	SLG
1984	NYY	9	7	2	1	1	0	0	0	1	5	0	.143	.286
1985	NYY	20	51	4	8	0	1	0	1	1	9	0	.157	.196
1986	Bal	14	1	1	0	0	0	0	0	0	0	1	.000	.000
1988	Mon	77	216	38	59	14	2	4	14	10	34	29	.273	.412
1989	Mon	92	155	21	38	7	0	6	13	6	23	15	.245	.406
1990	Mon	4	3	1	1	0	0	0	0	0	1	0	.333	.333
	StL	89	217	30	61	11	2	7	22	12	31	18	.281	.447
1991	StL	101	207	21	47	10	2	1	15	10	29	12	.227	.309
1992	StL	61	98	17	24	4	0	3	5	2	23	2	.245	.378
1994	Cal	56	124	17	37	8	0	8	20	6	28	2	.298	.556
1995	Cal	84	223	30	59	16	0	6	27	10	48	13	.265	.417
1996	Cal	92	302	60	94	20	3	16	40	9	54	14	.311	.556
11 Years		**699**	**1604**	**242**	**429**	**91**	**10**	**51**	**157**	**67**	**285**	**106**	**.267**	**.432**

Scott Karl
No Fear

VITAL STATISTICS

Born August 9, 1971, in Fontana, California
6 feet 3, 205 pounds
Attended the University of Hawaii
Position: Pitcher
Throws left, bats left
Family: Unmarried
1997 Team: Milwaukee Brewers

CAREER HIGHLIGHTS

- Won 13 games for the Brewers in 1996
- Pitched at least 6 innings in 14 of his last 18 starts as a rookie in 1995
- Picked up first career complete game versus Boston on last day of the season in 1995

WARMING UP

On the back of a baseball card Scott had printed to share his Christian testimony, he lists his hobby as scuba diving and his favorite musical group as the Dakota Motor Company.

FAVORITE BIBLE PASSAGE

"Trust in the Lord with all your heart and lean not on your own understanding; in all your ways acknowledge him, and he will make your paths straight" (Proverbs 3:5–6). Scott describes the verses as "a great passage. It helps me when I've been away from the Word and I get anxious. Also, I look to Colossians 3:23, if I'm pressing. It helps me to realize that I'm not out there alone."

Scott Karl

You've seen the "No Fear" T-shirts. For a while they seemed to be everywhere, expressing the boldness and the macho image of the age: "I'm not afraid of anybody or anything."

In 1996, Scott Karl received a unique opportunity from the people who make the "No Fear" shirts. He had noticed that the company made shirts for other baseball players, and that sparked an idea. "I approached them and said, 'I understand if you feel it would be a conflict to put a Christian verse on a shirt, but if you would, I'd greatly appreciate it.' They accommodated me, and I had them make up some shirts that had 2 Timothy 1:7 on them. It says, 'For God did not give us a spirit of timidity, but a spirit of power, of love, and of self-discipline.'"

Left-handed pitcher Scott Karl is fairly new around the American League, having arrived in 1995; but he has already established himself as one of the good young pitchers in a league that has been striking fear in pitchers' hearts for years. After all, this is the league where scores of 12–10 and 14–9 have become as commonplace as splintered bats. It's the league where an ERA of 4.00 makes you a star. It's the league of the small strike zone, the home run, and the lead that is never safe.

There is plenty to fear when you stand 60 feet, 6 inches from Juan Gonzales, Albert Belle, Mo Vaughn, and Mark McGwire day in and day out. Yet in 1996, just his second year in the majors, not even the prospects of those kinds of threats stopped Karl from winning thirteen games for the Brewers. And it didn't stop him from getting his first major league shutout against the team that boasts one of those vaunted sluggers, Vaughn's Boston Red Sox.

Some pitchers in the American League have been able to face down the fear factor by coming to the mound with an awe-inspiring weapon of their own. John Wetteland, Roger Clemens, and Randy Johnson don't have to fear because they bring a gun to work with them—a gun that fires bullets past hitters at near-ly 100 miles per hour.

Scott Karl's weapon of choice is not nearly as frightening. He relies not on heat, but on deception and location. He depends heavily on a change-up, a slider, and an assortment of other off-speed pitches that he throws with menacing accuracy.

So, what about this young pitcher gives him the courage to go out to the mound with a "No Timidity" T-shirt under his Brewers' uniform?

It could be a number of things from his past—incidents along the way that have emboldened Karl and given him the inner strength to face down baseball's best hitters.

Possibility #1: It could be the courage he learned back in high school when he had to overcome a career-threatening injury.

Scott grew up playing two sports—soccer and baseball. "I started playing soccer when I was five years old," he says of his growing-up years in Southern California. "We lived on a long street with lots of kids, so we just started playing soccer. I was one of the tallest, fastest kids back then, and it was something I was good at."

But a soccer career would not be in Karl's long-range plans. As he explains with a laugh, "I think I'm as fast right now as I was when I was five. Everyone else got faster, and I got slower."

Slow or not, he continued to play soccer throughout high school. As a senior at Carlsbad High School, his love for soccer came dangerously close to costing him his baseball career. Toward the end of his last season of soccer, he was seriously injured.

"A kid slid into me on a cheap shot. He kicked my ankle,

but my foot never left the ground. My ankle snapped. I had to have surgery on the ankle, and they put in three screws to hold it together."

The injury not only ended Scott's high school soccer career, but it also jeopardized a baseball career that had begun in Little League and progressed through high school. So steady was his improvement that by his junior year at Carlsbad High School, he was named All-League and was scouted by the universities of the Pacific-10 Conference.

Then came the soccer injury. It took so long for his ankle to heal that by the time Scott was ready to play baseball, half of the season was over. By then, the Pac-10 schools had packed it up and gone home. They told him, "We like you, but we're not sure if you're ever going to play again. We just can't go forward with this."

Even in the face of that bad news, Karl battled back and returned to baseball that spring. In the thirty-plus innings he had left in his final high school season, Karl held opposing batters to no earned runs.

One afternoon, Carlsbad had a game against a team whose coach had attended the University of Hawaii. Karl made such an impression that the opposing coach called the staff at Hawaii and told them, "This kid was dropped by some schools, but he looks like he's going to make it. Why don't you give him a shot?"

Soon the Fighting Rainbows were on the phone, offering Karl a full scholarship to play on the islands. "We needed that," Scott recalls, "because our family didn't have a whole bunch of money." As the son of a correctional lieutenant in the California prison system, Scott knew funding a college education would place a heavy financial burden on the family.

"It turned out to be the best thing for me," he says.

Possibility #2: It could be the courage Karl learned while pitching for Hawaii—faced with a situation that would call for perseverance in the face of certain defeat.

The ability to face down baseball's best hitters may have developed as he was completing less-than-sparkling series of pitching performances. It seemed that any chance Karl had to be noticed by major league scouts was fading. Yet he would have one more opportunity.

It was the spring of 1992, and Hawaii was in the NCAA regional baseball tournament. The competing teams played a round-robin format in which the loser doesn't go home but continues in the losers' bracket. By battling its way back up through that bracket, a first-round loser could conceivably vie for the championship.

In the opening game of the tournament, Karl was on the mound against Pepperdine University, a strong baseball team. "Every single major league team was out there with scouts, watching the game," Scott recalls. It was the right place to be for a kid who had major league dreams.

However, it was not the right time for Scott. "I didn't throw very well. I was disappointed." Hawaii lost the game, meaning the Rainbows would have to claw their way back through the losers' bracket. It also meant that Karl's chances of impressing major league scouts were slim.

Hawaii swept through their bracket and stood face-to-face with Pepperdine again. But to win the regionals, they would have to beat Pepperdine twice in one day. The first game of the day was in Karl's hands. This time he prevailed, coming away with a complete game victory. But would it make a difference to his baseball hopes?

"On that last day, most of the major league scouts had already gone. But Milwaukee had stayed. They saw me throw, and that really turned them on," Scott recalls.

A few weeks later, the Brewers proved their interest. They used a sixth-round draft pick to nab Karl and make a professional baseball player out of him.

Possibility #3: It could be the courage Karl learned after a minor league setback.

In previous years, Scott had proved his tenacity and perseverance. He had overcome the high school injury. He had dealt successfully with a loss in what might have been his only chance to be scouted. But then he was faced with the worst situation a minor league player can encounter—he was demoted to a lower classification.

As his minor league career began, Karl was the quintessential upwardly mobile baseball player. He spent his Rookie League season in Helena, where he was 7–0 with a 1.46 ERA. The league leader in ERA, Karl permitted his opponents a paltry .240 batting average while showing the Milwaukee brass that he was ready to move on.

At Double A El Paso in 1993, it was more of the same. Karl led the league in innings and tied for the league in starts, complete games, and shutouts. In just about every category, he was near the top of the league. After two years in the minors, he had nowhere to go but up.

In April 1994, he had moved up another rung on the ladder—he was with the Triple A New Orleans Zephyrs when the season started. That's when he felt the sting of demotion. In late April, Karl, the youngest pitcher in the American Association, suffered a bout of shoulder tendinitis. The Brewers thought it best to ship him back to El Paso for some rehab.

Karl had a tough time thinking of the move as purely rehabilitation. To him, it was clearly a step backward. "I was really angry," he recalls. "I was mad about the whole situation. I had already done well at the Double A level. Why did I have to go back to El Paso?"

Once more, it seems, a great opportunity was threatening to pass him by. Mired in self-pity and worried about his future in baseball, Karl began to do some soul-searching. He thought back on some things he had heard while in New Orleans— things his manager, Chris Bando, had told him.

Bando, who has developed a reputation among young players for his baseball teaching abilities and for his dedication to Jesus Christ, had not been afraid to talk about his faith. Also, while with the Zephyrs, Karl had been befriended by Steve Sparks, another pitching prospect in the Brewers' organization at the time.

"Steve took me for who I was and kind of fed me in small pieces," Karl says. "He just kind of allowed me to be drawn in instead of trying to beat me over the head with Christianity. I kept asking questions, and he'd give me places to read to find answers. He loved me for who I was, and I learned more and more about Jesus."

At that time, Karl was searching for answers, but he had not yet made a commitment to follow Christ.

"I was in my hotel room one night, trying to figure out why I was so mad. *Why am I angry at everybody?* I realized right then that there was Someone who could take away all this anger for good. I had felt this yearning through the last year of college and the first couple of years of pro ball. I hadn't known what it was until the Christians on the Zephyrs showed me that it was Jesus."

Faced with an uncertain future in baseball, Scott made the decision to secure his *eternal* destiny. "I got down on my knees and asked the Lord to come into my heart and life. I said, 'Lord, my life is Yours. Please lead me and guide me every day. Please remove this anger and bitterness from my heart. Help me to be a servant to You.'"

Immediately, things improved for Karl—at least on the inside. "I really felt a change in my attitude. I was there [in El Paso] for six weeks, but instead of being angry, I thought, *Okay, I'm here for a reason. The Lord placed me here. Let's not question Him. Let's just do it and do the best we can and deal with the circumstances.*"

His new attitude paid off, as he pitched well again at El Paso. After losing his first outing, he won five straight games and allowed just 2.96 earned runs per nine innings. Soon he was back where he started the season—New Orleans.

"When I got back to New Orleans, I told Steve [Sparks] that I had become a Christian, and he was all fired up. We had Bible studies on the team. And Chris Bando continued to help me grow."

Courage had won out over adversity again. He now had a true source of courage and a reason to conquer timidity. He came away with a faith he could use wherever his baseball travels would take him.

And it was a good thing too, because the 1995 season would be a travel year for Karl as he went back and forth between New Orleans and Milwaukee. His itinerary looked like this:

Opening day of minor league season: New Orleans

Opening day of major league season: Milwaukee (the

strike had delayed the first game of the major league season to a date later than the minor league's opening day)

May 14: Back to New Orleans after three relief appearances and a 5.07 ERA with the big club

May 23: Brought up to Milwaukee

May 25: Back to New Orleans

June 27: Brought up to Milwaukee

Finally, on July 1, Scott Karl stood on the pitcher's mound at County Stadium, ready to make his first major league start. He was twenty-three years old.

"That was unbelievable," he says of that game. "I was pitching against the Yankees, but I had such peace. As nervous as I had been before the game, after I threw that first pitch, I was fine. I knew that I was filled with the Spirit, and I was being guided. Steve Sparks and I had said a quick prayer before the game, and he was cheering me on."

So were family and friends back home in Riverside, California. The game was on national TV that day. Although the Brewers lost 3–1, Karl pitched well, allowing just five hits in seven innings while recording six strikeouts.

"When it was all over, I just gave thanks to God—thanks for the peace, thanks for keeping me safe, thanks for the courage. It was a great way to start. It was a blessing."

The 1995 season proved that Karl belonged in the majors. One of eight rookie pitchers on the Brewers that year, Scott won six games, including an end-of-the-year complete game against the Red Sox for an 8–1 victory.

What's more, the following season showed that Karl was one of baseball's up-and-coming young pitchers. His thirteen victories and 207 innings pitched established him as a mainstay on the Brewers' young staff. He also ranked in the top twenty-five of all American League pitchers in ERA, just behind Mike Mussina of the Orioles. Among pitchers who found themselves looking up at Karl in the ERA race were Doc Gooden, Jack McDowell, and David Wells.

As the 1996 season unfolded and Karl began to make a name for himself, he noticed some things that contributed to his success.

"One of the biggest keys is that I've learned consistency with my abilities. I've learned to throw more strikes—lower strikes, better strikes. And I've learned to stay on an even keel emotionally—never too high, never too low. And I've learned to stay focused."

He discovered too that consistency on the mound is in part a result of consistency in his spiritual life. "I know that when I've been in the Word and fellowshipping with other Christians, I feel stronger. And when I've been away from the Word and sort of struggling, I feel that my season is a drag. Baseball focus and spiritual focus go hand in hand."

Having battled and defeated various challenges that might have ended his baseball career, Karl seemingly could relax a bit now, knowing that he had made it to the big time. But two new challenges continued to keep him looking at that Second Timothy T-shirt for reminders about his source of courage.

For one, as Karl entered the 1997 season, he was still a very eligible bachelor. And he knows what kinds of challenges that brings.

"Being single, a Christian, and a major league baseball player is one of the toughest things to do. My eyes are open to the truth. If my eyes were blinded to the truth, it would be easy. But I know what is right and what is wrong. One of my biggest temptations is having to meet people, but having to go to certain establishments to meet them. They expect to meet at social scenes that aren't the best places to go. These places seem to be surrounded by Satan. That's why it is so good to have accountability partners like Steve Sparks and Mike Matheny. We can talk about these things and keep each other accountable."

Another challenge Karl faces is something that many professional athletes have not even attempted to overcome—pride. "I learned a lot in 1996 about humility," Karl says. "I believe you have to be humble—whether you are an athlete or not. If you're good, people will know. You don't have to tell them. You don't have to act like it. Besides, you're *blessed* with talent—it's not like you get it on your own. For me to be ignorant and to say 'I did this all on my own' is terrible. I've had a lot of support—from family, from teammates, from God."

You cannot be timid if you attempt to make your way through the American League schedule with a fastball in the 80s and an off-speed pitch as your main guns. And Scott Karl has proved that he is anything but timid. His comeback courage got him to college despite screws in his ankles and doubts from some of the top West Coast coaches. And his dogged determination in the NCAA play-offs let him salvage a good game and another look from major league scouts.

Yet it wasn't until he stopped depending on himself and started trusting in the Lord Jesus Christ that he found out what true courage was all about. And now he's eager to display that courage to others—not just on a T-shirt, but in his entire life.

Q & A WITH SCOTT KARL

Q: *You grew up with just one sibling, a sister. What was the relationship like?*
Scott: She and I didn't always get along when we were growing up, but now we are very tight. Stephanie is three years younger than I am. When I went away to college in 1989 in Hawaii, we both realized how much we missed each other. She looks up to me as a baseball player and for my accomplishments. I have a lot of respect for her. She's always worked hard and has always been a caring, loving person.

Q: *What is the fellowship like on the Milwaukee Brewers?*
Scott: I'm pretty blessed to be on a team with four or five really strong Christians. At least once or twice on a road trip, sometimes even more, we have Bible studies after the games. We get together and share ideas and what we've been learning.

Q: *The Brewers have struggled in the past few years but have a good, strong nucleus. What do you think of this team?*
Scott: I'm excited about it. I think our team is headed in the right direction with as many young guys as we have. We're all learning, but in the next couple of years, we'll have enough experience. We'll be in the prime of our years, but we won't be

inexperienced. Cleveland did it like this, and I think we can too.

Q: *What kind of ministry do you enjoy?*
Scott: I like to work with Unlimited Potential, Inc. That's Tom Roy, Don Gordon, Tim Cash, and Chris Bando. Tom and I speak out quite a bit. We've also worked at some camps, telling the kids about how to play baseball and then sharing the gospel. Also, Tom is always looking out for me because I'm a single Christian. I also do what I can to help Ron Rightnower, who used to pitch with us in Milwaukee and now works with Fellowship of Christian Athletes in Toledo.

THE ROAD TO THE MAJORS

• Selected by the Milwaukee Brewers in the sixth round of the 1992 draft

Minor league stops: Helena, El Paso, New Orleans

Minor league highlight: With El Paso in 1993, led the league in innings pitched and tied for first in starts, complete games, and shutouts

Year	Team	W	L	PCT	G	SV	IP	H	R	ER	HR	TBB	SO	ERA
1995	Mil	6	7	.462	25	0	124.0	141	65	57	10	50	59	4.14
1996	Mil	13	9	.591	32	0	207.1	220	124	112	29	72	121	4.86
2 Years		**19**	**16**	**.543**	**57**	**0**	**331.1**	**361**	**189**	**169**	**39**	**122**	**180**	**4.59**

Keith Lockhart
The Late Bloomer Blossoms

VITAL STATISTICS

Born November 10, 1964, iin Whittier, California
5 feet 10, 170 pounds
Attended Oral Roberts University
Position: Infielder
Throws right, bats left
Family: Wife, Lisa, and two children, Danny and Sydney
1997 Team: Kansas City Royals

CAREER HIGHLIGHTS

- Tied for team lead in doubles with 33 in 1996
- Led Royals in hitting with a .321 average in 1995
- Received Royals' Joe Burke Award for special achievement in 1995

WARMING UP

When Keith Lockhart first joined the Kansas City Royals, he was "a behind-the-scenes kind of guy." But a year later, he had taken over the leadership of the Royals' chapel program because the previous leaders, Greg Gagne and Gary Gaetti, were gone. Each Sunday, he would organize the chapel for chaplain Mike Lusardi. "I've kind of had to step up and organize it," he says.

FAVORITE BIBLE PASSAGE

"Trust in the Lord with all your heart and lean not on your own understanding; in all your ways acknowledge him, and he will make your paths straight" (Proverbs 3:5–6). "I also like Romans 8:28, which is a verse I put on a baseball card with my testimony."

Keith Lockhart

W hen Keith Lockhart was a fifteen-year-old high school baseball player in Covina, California, he played against a skinny kid from nearby La Puente. A kid with a first name everyone pronounced oddly. The kid's name was Cecil—a Fielder who would one day be known more as a Hitter!

Sixteen years later, Keith Lockhart and Cecil Fielder met again on the baseball diamond. If Fielder had noticed Lockhart on that prep baseball field back in 1979, he probably didn't recognize him when they met again in 1995.

By the time they competed a second time, Fielder had played four years for the Toronto Blue Jays, spent a year playing for Hanshin in Japan, had pounded out more than 200 home runs, and had turned into the major league's top power hitter of the first half for the '90s.

A lot of things had changed for Keith Lockhart too. But in the seventeen years that had passed between that forgettable high school contest and the game between the Tigers and the Royals in 1995, Lockhart's career had been routed much differently than Fielder's. It had taken him to Mount San Antonio Junior College, Oral Roberts University, Billings, and minor league stints in Cedar Rapids, Chattanooga, Nashville, Tacoma, Louisville, and Las Vegas. By the time the rematch took place, Lockhart had played in more than eight hundred minor league baseball games and had logged only about seventy days of major league service. He had also celebrated his thirtieth birthday.

To say that Keith Lockhart came to the major leagues late in his baseball life is like saying Jeff Gordon is a good young race car driver. You won't find anyone to doubt those statements.

While others his age had finished their careers or had peaked and were on the downward slide, Lockhart was just getting his career cranked up. In 1995, for instance, as a thirty-year-old rookie for the Royals, Keith hit .321 for the season after getting a call-up from Las Vegas on June 5. In his first month with the team, he hit .422.

The infielder's success was so unexpected by the Royals that, after the season, Keith Lockhart was awarded the Joe Burke Award, which is given to a player on the Kansas City team who goes beyond expectations.

No one expects much from a baseball player who graduated from high school as a 5 feet 2 inch infielder and not even the best player on his team. "I didn't make all-conference or all-city or anything like that," Lockhart says. "There were some guys on my team who were much better than I was. A lot of guys on my team were really good athletes and could hit pretty well. I never hit for a lot of power. I was a steady player. I was a good hitter for the average, and I was a good defensive player."

Lockhart was the middle of three boys in his family. When he was nine, his parents separated, leaving him and his brothers confused by the new situation. "As a little kid, I didn't care what the reason was—we just knew one of our parents wasn't there. It was frustrating. It was tough. I really missed not having a dad around."

Now that he's the father of two children, Lockhart looks back on his own difficult childhood as a reminder of how important his marriage is. "Nothing could be that bad to separate parents and keep them from their kids."

Fortunately for young Keith Lockhart, he had an outlet for his frustration and turmoil—sports. All kinds of sports.

"I played in the Pop Warner football league. I was pretty small for football, though. In high school, I started playing soccer, but after my freshman year, I concentrated on baseball. I was better at that." And besides, growing up in Southern California, Lockhart was able to play baseball all year.

After graduating from high school, it seemed as if baseball would not be a wise career choice. In fact, the direction he was heading would have landed him in a firehouse long before it would put him in a baseball clubhouse.

"I didn't know what I wanted to do after high school," he recalls. "My dad was a fireman, and I always wanted to be a fireman too." In pursuit of that dream, Lockhart enrolled at Mount San Antonio Junior College in Walnut, California, where he could study fire fighting. Besides offering courses in his chosen field, the college was inexpensive. "It was like fifty bucks for tuition," he recalls.

But fire fighting and money saving weren't the only reasons Lockhart matriculated at Mt. SAC, as those who attend the college call it. He also discovered that he was wanted there because he could play baseball. To Lockhart, this was a new, exhilarating feeling.

"I was playing in a summer game [before college], and we were in the play-offs," Lockhart says. "The Mount San Antonio coach happened to be at the game. He came up to me afterward and asked if I'd like to come out for the junior college team. Just having that kind of invitation led me to Mt. SAC."

As unlikely as it seems that a walk-on at a JC could eventually land a starting position on a major league team, it was even more unlikely that Lockhart was able to make the Mount San Antonio team in the first place. The coach may have invited him, but it was by no means an exclusive invitation.

Incredibly, when Keith showed up for the first day of practice at Mt. SAC, there were 128 guys trying out for the team. That coach must have watched a lot of summer games that year!

To increase the odds even further, Lockhart was immediately eliminated from his favorite position—third base. "I started taking ground balls at third base," he recalls. "I had taken one or two ground balls, and the coach said, 'You'll never play third base for me, kid.' I looked over and there were only about six guys playing second, so I ran over to second. We were doing double-play drills, and he was impressed with what he saw."

Out of 128 would-be players, the coach made the skinny, short, firefighter-in-training one of his selections. After the shaky audition at third base, the coach, Art Tazmanian, and Keith Lockhart hit it off. "The coach took me under his wing. He taught me how to turn the double play. He liked how I hit. I just think he didn't like my size at third."

Remember, Keith was 5 feet 2 inches tall, so it was no wonder Coach Tazmanian was hesitant about putting him at third. He probably thought he'd have to use the pitcher for a relay to get the ball to first.

Besides finding a mentor, Keith Lockhart had other good things happen as he played in obscurity in Walnut. First, he began to grow. By the time he was done with his two years at Mt. SAC, he was up around 5 feet 6 inches.

But more important than his physical growth was his personal growth, which was helped along by Coach Tazmanian, who was a Christian. At the time, Lockhart, who was not a Christian, had grown interested in another college activity besides baseball—partying. Yet he knew that scene led to trouble. "A lot of the friends I hung around with—and it was a tough group— were into drugs and partying and alcohol. I felt that if I went to schools locally, I'd get wrapped up in that. I needed a fresh start."

That's when Coach Tazmanian's help came in handy. "He really promoted me and marketed me while I was at junior college," Lockhart recalls. "I was getting letters from all these different colleges, which was very surprising. Coach asked me where I wanted to go to school, and he said he'd help me get in when my two years at Mt. SAC were over."

Lockhart decided he wanted to finish his college career at the University of Houston. "A buddy of mine—a pitcher—and I were all set to go. Houston called us every day for a month."

But then something unusual happened. Out of the blue, someone from Oral Roberts University called Lockhart late one night. Apparently, Coach Tazmanian, who knew the head coach at Oral Roberts, Larry Cochell, had made a phone call to Tulsa.

The night after the phone call, Lockhart and his friend were off to ORU on a recruiting visit. And they were impressed with what they saw. "As we were in our hotel room getting ready to leave, we looked at each other and said, 'The University of Houston better be pretty good!'"

It must not have looked good enough, because Lockhart chose Oral Roberts. He didn't even know it was a Christian school when he decided to go. "The one thing I didn't like about it was that we had to wear a tie. And we had to go to chapel twice a week."

What he did like, though, was ORU's coaching staff. Coach Cochell was greatly respected, and he has since gone on to win a national championship at Oklahoma. The pitching coach was Jim Brewer, a former major-league pitcher. What's more, Oral Roberts regularly ranked in the Top 10 nationally.

One of the advantages of playing for such a program is the presence of scouts. Not that Lockhart knew anything about why they were there.

"Even when I was a junior in college, I was unaware of what the major league baseball draft was," he says. "I remember that we had a guy who was drafted from my junior college team, and I thought it meant he went right to the big leagues. He came to visit us with all his Oakland A's stuff, and I thought he was in the majors. I wasn't even aware of the minor league stuff."

Naive as he was, he could still play ball. Having grown to a height that was at least acceptable to scouts, Lockhart got the attention of Jim Brewer. "He really liked me, and he used to talk to scouts all the time about me. He used to ask, 'How'd you like to play for the Cincinnati Reds?' I thought, *That would be great.* There were Reds scouts at most of our games and practices."

So when Lockhart was twenty-one years old, and before he had enough credits to graduate from college, he was picked by the Reds in the 11th round of the 1986 major league draft. Let's hope someone had warned him that he wouldn't go straight to the big show, for if he thought he would, he had a nine-year surprise in store. He wouldn't receive his first major league paycheck until April 1994. Nobody can ever accuse Keith Lockhart of not being patient.

While Lockhart was given a boost athletically by coaches Cochell and Brewer, he received a spiritual boost by two friends, Steve Hecht and Rich Bordas. But that spiritual development was not without some obstacles.

"I had friends I went to parties with, and I had Steve and Rich that I did other stuff with—good stuff. After a while, I had more fun with Steve and Rich. They used to make Christian music tapes for me to listen to. We just hung out. They never challenged me with anything. They never asked me if I wanted to be a Christian. They just lived their lives, and I noticed that they had a foundation. They had stability."

He maintained his friendship with Steve and Rich even after he left Tulsa in the summer of 1986 to begin his baseball career—not in Cincinnati but in Billings, Montana. In the fall, Lockhart returned to Oral Roberts to continue pursuing his degree.

"I went to chapel one day, and I was sitting with the athletes in the balcony. The speaker that day had a message that challenged everybody about their personal faith in Jesus Christ. The speaker said, 'Ask the person next to you if he or she wants to receive Christ.' A guy we called 'Bombie' was standing next to me. He kind of nonchalantly asked me if I wanted to accept Christ, and I said, 'Yeah!' I think I kind of threw him off, but he led me in a prayer for salvation.

"Right away, I told Rich and Steve about it, and they began looking after me spiritually. They really encouraged me."

For Lockhart, the decision was genuine, but it left him with an odd feeling. "I thought something would happen. I said a prayer, and nothing happened. I thought I didn't do it right. I remember praying that prayer four or five times back in my room, waiting for something to happen."

What Lockhart needed to discover was that his growth as a new Christian would be gradual. "Once I started reading through the Bible and praying, things began to happen. I realized that my language was better. Sure, I had watched what I said around certain people before, but now I had a conviction not to cuss.

"I lost the desire to drink beer. I had tried to do that on my own, but it didn't work. It was a cleansing process. God started with the major things back then, and to this day He's still working on me."

Lockhart had a newfound faith to take with him on the second leg of his minor league excursion. After being named MVP of the Rookie League at Billings, he was sent to Cedar Rapids, where he was a Midwest League terror. He hit .313, pounded 23 home runs, knocked in 84 runs, and stole 20 bases. Cincinnati wasn't quite in full view, but it seemed to be just over a couple of hills.

The first hill was the big one in Chattanooga, Tennessee, where Lockhart spent his third minor league season with the Double A Lookouts. True to form, he had another outstanding season (12 home runs and 67 RBI), helping the Lookouts to the Southern League championship.

"The dream was slowly coming to be something reachable," Lockhart says of his seemingly straight trip to Cincinnati.

And to make matters even better, he had a friend at the top.

"Pete Rose had come to the Instructional League where I was playing, and he really liked me."

And why wouldn't he? They both were scrappy. They both had to overcome the disadvantage of a small stature. They were both late developers. This appeared to be a player-manager relationship that begged to work.

The 1989 season saw Lockhart heading for that final hill—Nashville—before he could move to Cincinnati to play for Pete Rose. Would it be the final minor league stop? Another good year (.267 average, 14 home runs, 58 RBI) made it look that way. And for the 1990 season, Keith Lockhart was penciled in as a part of the Reds' forty-man roster.

Yet there were problems ahead at the crest of the hill. Pete Rose had fallen from favor. His problems with gambling had cost him his seat on the Reds' bench as skipper. Lockhart's ace in the hole was gone.

In his place was Lou Piniella. Great manager. Great person. But he didn't know Keith Lockhart from any other minor league prospect. To make matters worse, there was a lockout during spring training of 1990, and there wasn't time for the rookies to show their skills. Lockhart was cut from the Reds' roster on the last day of spring training.

He was headed back to Nashville. "I thought sure I'd be back up there right away," Lockhart says. "I was doing well down there, but there were no injuries or anything [on the Reds' team]. So I stayed there for 1990 and 1991." The vision of Riverfront Stadium was slipping away. Lockhart would be twenty-seven years old by the time the next season rolled around.

"After the 1991 season, it just didn't look good. So Reds General Manager Jim Bowden came up to me after the season and said that if something doesn't happen, they would try to trade me."

That's what happened. The following spring, Lockhart was dealt to the Oakland A's, which meant only that his Triple A team for 1992 would be Tacoma instead of Nashville. But it also meant something else extremely significant. He played for Bob Boone.

Boone, a former major league catcher, was also working his way up the minor-league ladder. He was in Triple A, learning about the fine art of managing a baseball team. It would be a fortuitous relationship, for if the Pete Rose-Keith Lockhart connection never paid off, perhaps this one would.

After a year playing for Boone and the A's Triple A, affiliate, Lockhart moved to the Cardinals organization. At an age when most players would give up and go look for an insurance company to work for, Keith decided to stick with it. "When you're that close, it's hard to just give up. You see so many people who stick around, and someone gets hurt, then they get called up."

For Keith and his wife, Lisa, whom he had met at Oral Roberts and had married in 1989, another consideration was what God wanted them to do. They decided to leave the decisions in His hands. "Our prayer was that the Lord would just close the doors if He didn't want us to keep pursuing baseball. If I couldn't get a job, we'd know to give it up."

Playing for Louisville in 1993, Lockhart had an outstanding year, hitting .300, slugging 13 home runs, and knocking in 70 runs. He started on the All-Star team. He did everything a guy could do to get the call.

The problem was, the Cardinals had more infielders than they knew what to do with. "There just wasn't room for me," Lockhart says.

If the Lockharts were praying for closed doors to be their cue to quit baseball, the winter of 1993 was a clear message to stay. A dozen teams showed interest in Keith, and his agent narrowed the list down to San Diego as the best option.

Spring training with the Padres pitted Lockhart against Harold Reynolds. Reynolds was a talented second baseman who had spent several years with the Mariners and had been a two-time American League All-Star. But at thirty-four years of age, some people thought his career was coming to a close. Lockhart was twenty-nine and still looking to begin his. Both men were Christians who were trusting God to show them the way.

Lockhart won that battle, and on April 5, 1994, he entered a major league baseball game for the first time as a pinch hitter against the Atlanta Braves. Two days later, Lockhart collected his first major league hit against Greg McMichael. "The next day, I got my first start and hit my first two home runs. I really started with a bang."

Yet Lockhart's career with the Padres ended with a whimper. Forty-five days after his first big league season began, it ended when he was optioned to Las Vegas. Soon the strike ended the 1994 season, and Keith Lockhart was right back where he started. Great prospect. No team.

Still, Lockhart had been around long enough to make a few friends. One of those fortunate acquaintances was Jeff Cox, who had been Lockhart's first manager in Billings. That year had been a first for both—Cox as a minor league manager and Lockhart as a minor league player. But their backgrounds overlapped even more: Jeff Cox was a former infielder who'd put in a stint with the Oakland A's; he was from Covina, California; and most incredibly, he had attended Mount San Antonio College.

"I read that Jeff got the third base [coaching] job with Kansas City," remembers Lockhart. "I told Lisa, 'I know Kansas City is going to call because Jeff knows what I can do.' Sure enough, a couple of days later, they called."

Besides the Cox connection, there was another important contact in Kansas City—Bob Boone, who had been named manager of the club. "I finally had some people in my corner," says Lockhart. "It seemed like a great place to be." On November 7, 1994, three days before his thirtieth birthday, Lockhart signed a minor league contract with the Royals.

If you've been paying attention, you know that no matter how good things look for Keith Lockhart to lock into a solid major league position, there will surely be some obstacle. And sure enough, another one cropped up. This time, it was replacement baseball. When the players went on strike and spring training came along, the owners put together replacement teams of non-major league players. The Kansas City Royals wanted Lockhart to be a replacement player.

"I was a great candidate to do that," he says. "I was thirty years old with forty-five days of major league experience. But I really didn't feel like I should do it. After thinking about it and praying about it, I knew the only reason I would have done it was for the money. We didn't want that to be our motivator.

"I knew that if I played as a replacement, I would possibly play one more year and that would be it. I'd be labeled by the players. Our minor league coordinator, Bob Hegman, called me into his office. I knew he was a Christian. We had a pretty nasty confrontation about helping the organization. When I left, I said to myself, *I wonder what team I'll be playing for next week.* I had buried myself with the Royals, and this was my best shot."

But it wasn't just the Royals' brass who pressured him to join the replacement team; manager Bob Boone wanted him to as well. "Everything looked terrible because I wouldn't do it," Lockhart says. "We drove to Omaha. We had our van and a rental truck holding all our furniture. We were sitting in a hotel. My agent called, and he said I could always go back to Louisville. And the Cubs wanted me."

When the minor league season began, Lockhart stayed with Omaha, the Royals' Triple A team, where he shellacked American Association league pitching. While wondering if he'd ever get another crack at the majors, he hit .360 for the junior Royals.

In June, Chico Lind inexplicably left the Royals, opening a spot for Lockhart. On June 5, he was called up. Bob Boone told him, "You're hitting third and playing third." He went 4–7 in his first series and was a fixture in the Royals' infield for the rest of the season. As a thirty-one-year-old rookie, he played in ninety-four games, hit .321, and won the hearts of Kansas City fans.

It was more of the same for Lockhart in 1996 as he proved that he belonged by hitting .273 in 138 games for K.C.

"It's amazing how the Lord restored favor to me. All these people who I thought didn't like me because of the replacement thing—God turned the whole situation around. My wife and I think back to where we were in that hotel room. Our backs were against the wall, but God restored everything."

Remarkable. The skinny kid from Covina had made it. Not easily. Not without enough struggles to break most athletes' spirit. But he made it.

"I played so long in the minor leagues," he says. "After that 1995 season, we'd go to a restaurant and someone would say, 'There's Keith Lockhart.' That's the first time people ever recognized me."

The late bloomer had finally come to full bloom.

And now even Cecil Fielder knows who Keith is.

Q & A WITH KEITH LOCKHART

Q: *What do you and Lisa do to stay strong spiritually?*
Keith: We do a lot of reading. Also, we've always been involved with a church. I used to teach lessons for kids. Church fellowship is very important to us.

Q: *Because you left Oral Roberts University early, you didn't get a chance to graduate. Are you still pursuing a degree?*
Keith: I'm seventeen hours short of graduating. I'm planning to finish my degree through correspondence.

Q: *You didn't make the All-Star team in 1996, but Bob Boone said, "It would make my managerial career if I saw Keith Lockhart in the All-Star game."*

Keith: It was really nice to be thought of that way. The last week or two before the All-Star game, people were asking me about the game. I probably started thinking about it a little too much. It would have been great to go. It was nice to see other players and coaches respond with their comments. To earn their respect on the field is what counts. I didn't make the team, but I was thought of, and that really means a lot to me.

Q: *You've learned to play several positions. Was that by design so you would have more opportunities?*
Keith: When I was with the Reds, they had Chris Sabo, Ron Oester, and Jeff Treadway. They had a lot of second and third basemen. They thought I'd better be a utility player. During my first big-league camp, I played left field in my first spring training game. Eric Davis was in center and Paul O'Neill was in right. Here I am in left field, and I had never played a game at that position in my life. I prepare myself every day for two infield positions—second and third.

THE ROAD TO THE MAJORS

- Selected by the Cincinnati Reds in the eleventh round of 1986 draft
- Traded to the Oakland A's on February 4, 1992, for Robert Carlsen
- Signed by the St. Louis Cardinals on December 18, 1992
- Signed by the San Diego Padres on January 7, 1994
- Signed by the Kansas City Royals on November 7, 1994
- Traded with Michael Tucker to the Atlanta Braves on March 27, 1997, for Jermaine Dye, and Jamie Walker

Minor league stops: Billings, Cedar Rapids, Chattanooga, Nashville, Tacoma, Louisville, Las Vegas, Omaha

Minor league highlight: In 1994, Lockhart played the following positions, in order of frequency: outfield, shortstop, second base, third base, pitcher, catcher

THE LOCKHART FILE

Year	Team	G	AB	R	H	2B	3B	HR	RBI	BB	SO	SB	BA	SLG
1994	SD	27	43	4	9	0	0	2	6	4	10	1	.209	.349
1995	KC	94	274	41	88	19	3	6	33	14	21	8	.321	.478
1996	KC	138	433	49	118	33	3	7	55	30	40	11	.273	.411
3 Years		**259**	**750**	**94**	**215**	**52**	**6**	**15**	**94**	**48**	**71**	**20**	**.287**	**.432**

Mark McLemore
Looking for Honesty

VITAL STATISTICS

Born October 4, 1964, in San Diego, California
5 feet 11, 207 pounds
Position: Infielder
Throws right, bats both
Family: Wife, Capri, and three children, DeMarca, Darien, and
    Derek
1997 Team: Texas Rangers

CAREER HIGHLIGHTS

- Led Rangers in triples (5) in 1995
- Led Orioles in multi-hit games (49) and infield hits (23) in 1993
- Led AL pinch hitters in slugging percentage (.818) in 1992
- Established California Angels record for sacrifice hits for a rookie (15) in 1987

WARMING UP

Mark and Capri McLemore spend their off-seasons in Phoenix, Arizona. Mark is a season-ticket holder for his favorite basketball team, the Phoenix Suns.

FAVORITE BIBLE PASSAGE

"Finally, be strong in the Lord and in his mighty power" (Ephesians 6:10). Mark notes that the verse "reminds me every day to protect myself when I go out. Put on the breastplate of righteousness and know that God is with me and protecting me. You have to reinforce that every day."

Mark McLemore

Thirty-five years. That's how long the franchise now known as the Texas Rangers had played baseball before they earned the right to appear in their first postseason game. Since 1961, when the Washington Senators began play as an expansion team in the American League, this organization had done everything possible to earn a shot at World Series glory.

In the team's history, they had tried some of the best baseball names in the game as field managers: Ted Williams, Gil Hodges, Billy Martin, Don Zimmer, Bobby Valentine. In 1994, the Rangers came close to their goal when they ended the season in first place in the AL West. But it was a shallow victory that year; the strike stole the postseason and left the Rangers with yet another empty October.

In 1995, three new people moved to the Texas franchise to seek their fortunes as Rangers and to help end the dry spell. All three had previously spent time together in Baltimore.

On October 10, 1994, the Rangers hired Doug Melvin to be the team's general manager.

On October 14, 1994, Doug Melvin hired Johnny Oates to be manager.

On December 13, 1994, the two of them signed second baseman Mark McLemore to a contract with the Rangers.

The Baltimore connection was complete. And combined

with the addition of other top personnel, the Rangers were on their way to the upper echelons in baseball.

For McLemore, the opportunity to play for Oates and Melvin again was just what he had been looking for. He knew there was something special about them, and he was glad they wanted him.

When he signed with the Rangers, Mark McLemore was looking for one thing—honesty. He knew Melvin and Oates would give it to him because they had done so before, in Baltimore.

"When I first went to Baltimore," McLemore says, "I talked with Doug about honesty. He told me, 'My word is good— whether you like what I say or not.' That's all I could ask for. With all the things I had gone through over the years, I really hadn't been able to find anyone who would just be truthful with me."

That's quite a statement, considering that McLemore had played for twelve different baseball clubs in three different major league organizations since he had first signed with Baltimore in 1982.

So on July 5, 1991, McLemore put his career in Melvin's capable hands, anxious for the honesty he had been seeking. He got that—and a chance to prove his stuff.

And that's all McLemore ever really wanted. His baseball career began in the neighborhoods of San Diego, when, through the influence of his three brothers, McLemore discovered that he could compete with anybody around, regardless of age. "I was always better than people older than me," he says, without sounding boastful. "Sometimes I was as good as people four or five years older."

In McLemore's neighborhood, it paid to be good, because the competition was pretty stiff. Among Mark's friends as a kid were future sluggers Sam Horn and Kevin Mitchell, football legend-to-be Marcus Allen, and future NBA player Cliff Levingstone. "We had quite a few kids who were very good," McLemore says in a huge understatement.

Although McLemore lived in the land of the Padres, he was a Dodgers fan. Among his favorite players was Davey Lopes,

L.A.'s great infielder. It was a thrill for McLemore when he was with Baltimore to have Lopes as one of his coaches.

As a prep player at Morse High School in San Diego, McLemore and Horn made up a two-man show. "I would get up and get on, and Sam would knock me in," Mark says. "That would be pretty much it."

But even if the team wasn't very good, he and Sam were good enough to be drafted after their senior year. Although Mark was also sought out by some local college football coaches who wanted him to play defensive back, McLemore was sure he wasn't going to take their offers.

"I didn't want to stay in San Diego," he says. "I would like to have been drafted by the Dodgers, but I just wanted to be picked. I thought I was going to be chosen by the Astros."

Instead, the California Angels picked McLemore in the ninth round. "I was surprised to go to California. The Astros' people had been talking to me every day. But it really didn't matter. I just wanted to play."

After five minor league seasons, McLemore became a fixture at second base at the Big A in Anaheim, playing in 138 games. But the remainder of his stay in California was spotted by frequent visits to the disabled list. In September of 1989, the Angels sent McLemore to Cleveland.

Eight appearances with Cleveland in 1990 and then twenty-one games with Houston in 1991 could easily have been the swan song for McLemore. The Houston Astros had released him on June 25 after he had spent about six weeks on the disabled list. McLemore toiled for the remainder of the 1991 season in Rochester, the Orioles' farm team, where he hit .281. Still, there was no guarantee he would have a job for 1992. In fact, McLemore was declared a free agent after the season, meaning he was not bound to Baltimore. Yet the Orioles invited him to spring training, and he won a job.

At that point, McLemore was twenty-seven years old and had played in only 301 major league games, most of them in 1987 and 1988 with the Angels. But when he arrived in Baltimore, he found an advocate in Johnny Oates.

"I had heard that Johnny was a Christian, and I knew Johnny would be fair. That's all anyone could ask for."

During the 1992 season, McLemore started 52 games and played in another 49, while catching the attention of the Orioles skipper. "It was exciting being in Baltimore," Mark says. "It was an opportunity to play every day. At California, I didn't have that chance. Also, playing in Camden Yards was special. You look out there, and you've got 45,000 people there every night. No matter who you play or how you're playing, it's full. It was definitely nice."

Things got even nicer in 1993, when McLemore became an Orioles regular—starting 119 games in right field, 20 at second, three at third, and one as designated hitter. He set career highs in every offensive category except steals. His outstanding season (.284 batting average, 72 RBIs, 21 stolen bases) led to his being tied for second in team MVP voting. Only four other players in team history had reached the 70-plus RBI, 20-plus steals plateau before McLemore accomplished it.

Inserting McLemore into the lineup was just one of many good decisions Johnny Oates made that year as he was named the American League Manager of the Year by *The Sporting News*.

The following season, McLemore turned in another solid performance. In fact, 1994 saw him play in 104 of the team's 112 games. He looked to be a longtime fixture for the Birds, whose continued improvement propelled them to a second-place finish in the strike-shortened '94 season.

But major league baseball teams often do mysterious things, and on September 26, 1994, the Orioles gave the word *mystery* new meaning. After Oates had helped the Orioles become a team that could contend for a division title, Baltimore management decided he was not their man, and he was dismissed. He left behind some remarkable stats, including a 237–199 record in his last three years with the O's. And he had become the first person who had ever played for the O's, managed a Baltimore minor league team, and coached and managed at the major league level.

The good news for Oates, though, was that his friend Doug Melvin was the new Ranger general manager. A week after Melvin moved into his offices in Arlington, Oates was hired as the field boss. And a couple of months later, Mark McLemore was in the fold.

"Johnny doesn't know to this day what he has meant to my career," McLemore says.

Before 1991, it might not have meant much to McLemore that Johnny Oates was a man of God. That year, while McLemore was a member of the Astros organization, McLemore and his wife, Capri, were encouraged by Capri's cousin to consider Christianity.

"She started talking to us about Jesus Christ and about what He could do for us," McLemore says. "When she started talking to us about it, our ears were wide open. It was kind of strange. We were so ready to listen."

Not only did Mark and Capri listen, but they also heeded the advice to follow Christ. They both prayed and accepted Jesus as their Savior.

"It made a tremendous difference in my life to know Jesus," Mark says. "I was calm. I was peaceful. Things didn't worry me or bother me as much. Always before when things came up, I'd say, 'How can I handle this?' I'd worry about this and that. With Jesus, I could just give things to Him."

Even the outstanding 1996 season, which turned out to have enough highlights to make anyone's career, brought times when McLemore had to turn to his source of strength. Before the season began, there was trouble. On November 1, 1995, McLemore underwent arthroscopic surgery to repair a partial tear in the rotator cuff in his right shoulder. Two months of rehab followed, leaving him ready just in time for spring training.

At the Rangers' camp, McLemore showed that he had come all the way back, but he did have a minor setback in the middle of March. After he hurt his rib cage, someone asked him how he treated it. "I rubbed chicken soup on it," he replied. "Chicken soup works for everything—colds, headaches, strains."

For the Texas Rangers, the 1996 season was chicken soup for a first-place-starved team and its fans. And one of the main reasons for the team's success was their steady, dependable second baseman. While Juan Gonzalez, Will Clark, Mickey Tettleton, and Ivan Rodriguez grabbed the headlines, the team relied heavily on the quiet consistency of McLemore, Rusty Greer, Kevin Elster, and Daryl Hamilton.

One of the strengths of the 1996 Rangers was solid defense, and McLemore was a critical component. In fact, the Rangers came within one game of setting a major league record for consecutive games without an error. They went fifteen games without a miscue between a Kurt Stillwell error on August 3 and Elster's drop of a perfect McLemore throw for a force at second on August 20. For his part, McLemore compiled a .985 fielding average for the season. "Fielding has always been an emphasis with me, and I know it's always been important to Johnny," says McLemore.

But McLemore continued to shine when he put his glove down between innings, having his best year at the plate. He posted a career-high .290 batting average and a personal-best .379 slugging percentage. For the fourth straight year, McLemore stole more than 20 bases, and he scored 84 runs. In addition, he became an important clutch hitter for the Rangers, batting .322 with runners on base.

Even as he was having a banner year with his bat and glove, McLemore struggled with a loss that far exceeds anything an athlete experiences on the field. Early in the season, his father died. It was then that McLemore's decision to play for Johnny Oates was confirmed.

When McLemore went home to California for his father's funeral, Oates called him long distance and prayed with him. "That's something you wouldn't normally expect to hear from a baseball manager," McLemore notes. But then most players and managers don't share the strong faith that McLemore and Oates do.

Late in the season, McLemore experienced another difficult incident. On September 4, while the team was warming up at The Ballpark to play the Twins, McLemore was hit in the mouth with a bat. He was jogging to the batting cage to take batting practice when coach Bucky Dent was hitting ground balls to the infield. McLemore didn't notice Dent, and he ran right into the path of one of his swings. The Ranger second baseman had four of his lower teeth bent back, he suffered a lacerated lip, and his jaw was bruised. Fortunately, nothing was broken or permanently damaged, and McLemore was soon back in the lineup.

Three weeks later, he was in the middle of the biggest game in Rangers' history. On September 26, the Rangers were playing the Angels, and the American League Western Division title was theirs for the taking—and that's just what McLemore did. He stole second and scored the Rangers' fifth run of the game, and then later scored the winning run as the Rangers beat the Angels to capture their first title. In all, McLemore scored half of the Rangers' runs that night.

Yet he and the Rangers knew that they had accomplished only part of their mission. When he was asked in September to name his personal major league highlight, McLemore said simply, "It's coming up this fall."

Things did not turn out for the Rangers as they had hoped, though. After knocking off the Yankees in Game 1 of the first round of the American League play-offs, Texas was unable to win again. The Yanks took the series 3–1. The World Series would have to wait for another year. But all in all, it had been a fabulous year for McLemore and the Rangers.

"Doug and Johnny have made the difference in Texas," McLemore says. "Of course the players have to go out and do the job, but Johnny sets the tone. If players can trust their manager, it makes a big difference."

Trust and honesty. Isn't that just what baseball needs?

Q & A WITH MARK MCLEMORE

Q: *Who has the biggest impact on you spiritually?*
Mark: My wife. She knows when I'm feeling a little down or if I'm getting away from the Lord. She'll just say to me, "We need to pray."

Q: *What has it meant to you to be a father?*
Mark: It's made me think about everything I do—how I say things, how I react to things. I have the responsibility to raise three kids in Christ, and it's a big challenge.

Q: *How do you think Major League Baseball is doing in getting the fans back?*
Mark: I think they're doing an OK job, but I think they could be doing a lot better. One of the biggest things is the labor agreement. Once that's done, that will show the way. If that's done, you'll have baseball for the next five or six years nonstop. We do care about the fans.

Q: *Are fans treating the players differently now than they did before the strike?*
Mark: Yes. We have people in our society who still feel negatively toward the players. I don't take it personally.

Q: *What skills do you think are most important for young kids who want to be good infielders?*
Mark: They need to develop good hand-eye coordination and good footwork. And they need to know that they can get better with hard work.

THE ROAD TO THE MAJORS

- Selected by the California Angels in the ninth round of the 1982 draft
- Traded to the Cleveland Indians on September 6, 1989
- Released by Cleveland on December 13, 1990
- Signed by the Houston Astros on March 6, 1991
- Released by Houston on June 25, 1991
- Signed by the Baltimore Orioles on July 5, 1991
- Signed as a free agent by the Texas Rangers on December 13, 1994

Minor league stops: Salem, Peoria, Redwood, Midland, Edmonton, Palm Springs, Colorado Springs, Tucson, Jackson, Rochester

Minor league highlight: While playing with Edmonton of the Pacific Coast League in 1989, Mark was named the best defensive second baseman in the league

THE MCLEMORE FILE

Year	Team	G	AB	R	H	2B	3B	HR	RBI	BB	SO	SB	BA	SLG
1986	Cal	5	4	0	0	0	0	0	0	1	2	0	.000	.000
1987	Cal	138	433	61	102	13	3	3	41	48	72	25	.236	.300
1988	Cal	77	233	38	56	11	2	2	16	25	28	13	.240	.330
1989	Cal	32	103	12	25	3	1	0	14	7	19	6	.243	.291
1990	Cal	20	48	4	7	2	0	0	2	4	9	1	.146	.188
	Cle	8	12	2	2	0	0	0	0	0	6	0	.167	.167
1991	Hou	21	61	6	9	1	0	0	2	6	13	0	.148	.164
1992	Bal	101	228	40	56	7	2	0	27	21	26	11	.246	.294
1993	Bal	148	581	81	165	27	5	4	72	64	92	21	.284	.368
1994	Bal	104	343	44	88	11	1	3	29	51	50	20	.257	.321
1995	Tex	129	467	73	122	20	5	5	41	59	71	21	.261	.358
1996	Tex	147	517	84	150	23	4	5	46	87	69	27	.290	.379
11 Years		**930**	**3030**	**445**	**782**	**118**	**23**	**22**	**290**	**373**	**454**	**145**	**.258**	**.334**

Greg McMichael
The Kid with No Future

VITAL STATISTICS

Born December 1, 1966, in Knoxville, Tennessee
6 feet 3, 215 pounds
Attended the University of Tennessee
Position: Relief pitcher
Throws right, bats right
Family: Wife, Jennifer, and two children, Erin and Slade
1997 Team: New York Mets

CAREER HIGHLIGHTS

- Pitched in 73 games for Atlanta with a 3.22 ERA in 1996
- Appeared in three World Series games (2.70 ERA) in 1995
- Led Braves in saves (21) and tied for first in appearances (51) in 1994
- Recorded saves in first 15 save opportunities in rookie year, 1993

WARMING UP

Do relief pitchers get anxious before entering a game? Listen to Greg McMichael: "I don't ever *not* get nervous. The hardest part for me is when I'm sitting in the bull pen, watching the game and waiting for my moment when I might be called on. Once I get up and start warming up, I think the nerves go away because I'm able to do some activity."

FAVORITE BIBLE PASSAGE

"God did not give us a spirit of timidity, but a spirit of power, love, and of self-discipline" (2 Timothy 1:7).

Greg McMichael

S tarters John Smoltz, Tom Glavine, and Greg Maddux got more glory. And closer Mark Wohlers occupied the bull pen position of choice. But on a pitching staff that has garnered the most attention in the '90s, Atlanta Braves pitcher Greg McMichael was as steady and dependable as any of them. As the setup man for Wohlers, McMichael quietly compiled one of the best ERAs in the league during his four years with the Braves.

Although McMichael wears a World Series ring and enjoys the rewards that came with being a member of baseball's most successful team in the past decade, he understands how close he came to having none of it. In fact, the obstacles he had to overcome to reach the major leagues make his story one of the more remarkable ones you'll ever hear.

One of the most significant hardships came when Greg was fourteen years old and doctors in Knoxville, Tennessee, delivered the news every young athlete dreads hearing: "Son, we hate to tell you this, but you'll never play baseball again."

It was his knees. An unusual cartilage disease had set in, and it looked as if any dreams the youngster had of playing baseball were over.

"It was pretty devastating," McMichael recalls. "I was playing every sport, so when the doctor said I couldn't play again, I didn't know what to feel. For an eighth-grader who thinks sports is his career choice, that's a big blow."

Greg and his brother, Jeff, had spent their formative years playing sports. While Greg concentrated on the diamond activities, his older brother pursued football. "I remember growing up watching him run all over the field."

Eventually, Jeff earned a scholarship to the University of Tennessee, where he played linebacker. Although the younger McMichael had dabbled in the gridiron game, he confesses that "I don't think I had the heart for it."

For the McMichael brothers, though, the worst news of their young lives was not the knee disease that appeared to sideline Greg's hopes on the field. The toughest part was the breakup of their parents' marriage three years earlier.

Young McMichael had been hit by a double whammy: No happy home, and now, no sports. It was more than he could handle. Soon, he was out looking for trouble.

"All I knew was that I wouldn't be able to do the things I wanted to do," he says. "That's when I got involved with the wrong crowd. I was a freshman hanging out with seniors. I got into some bad habits and was drinking and smoking dope."

The family was in shambles. The athletic career was deader than the humid air on a hot Tennessee night. And Greg McMichael was on his way to being a regular drug user. It's a long way from the halls of Webb High School to Atlanta Stadium taking this path, but soon an unlikely turn of events would begin to show him the way.

Although the family had attended a Baptist church before Greg's parents had parted ways, none of the McMichaels were Christians at the time of the breakup. Yet as Allen McMichael was working his way through the divorce, some friends convinced him to attend church, and eventually, he put his faith in Jesus Christ.

Yet there was still no indication that Allen's newfound faith would mean a reconciliation with his wife.

"It wasn't until several years later that my mom came to know Christ," Greg recalls. "She went through some serious spiritual warfare first."

As she struggled, Sylvia McMichael went to some friends

for help. One of those friends knew just what she needed. So she took Sylvia to the home of the women's pastor, who led her to faith in Christ. Greg's parents were still apart, yet they now had the kind of foundation that could lead them back together.

"When my mom became a Christian," Greg says, "that's when God started impressing on her heart that she needed to get back together with Dad. Yet it wasn't until about a year or two later that she actually pursued it."

But when she did, it was just what her son needed. "As I was at the farthest point from the Lord, my parents' lives were changing," Greg says. During his freshman year of high school, Allen and Sylvia McMichael picked up the remnants of their marriage and tied them back together.

His parents' remarriage had a profound effect on their son. "I saw for the first time who God is and what He can do," Greg says. "It's a great example of how God takes chaos and creates order. Our family was going in different directions. God brought us back together and into a tightly knit group. I knew that if He could do that for my parents, I wanted to follow Christ too."

But it didn't happen overnight.

At the time, Greg McMichael was not willing to give up his partying lifestyle. "It took me about two years. I knew what I was doing was wrong, but it was the only fun I was having. I was going out a couple of nights a week looking for fun.

"Then I started struggling. I had some spiritual warfare in my life. They call the Holy Spirit the hound of heaven, and that's what it really felt like. I'd lie awake at night for hours with this battle going on. I couldn't sleep."

Finally, at the beginning of his junior year, Greg sat down with his parents and prayed to receive Christ as Savior.

"The next day, I went to school with new eyes. It was difficult facing my friends, but it wasn't something I weighed before I made my commitment. I knew it was a really important task for me to tell my friends what had happened.

"My best friend, Shawn Lowe, always drove me to school. I told him about it that morning, and he said that he had done that [accepted Christ] years before. Shawn ended up rededicating his life to the Lord a few days later. Also, I remember walking around the track sharing my story with another friend. Some of the guys who I thought were my friends were just my drinking buddies, and they fell away. And some didn't believe me. They just had to wait and see."

Despite the skepticism, McMichael forged ahead in his new faith. "I started a Bible study. We had about fifteen to twenty kids, and we'd meet once a week. Here I was, a baby Christian, trying to rally all the Christian kids at my school. It really made a difference in my life."

Not only did McMichael have a newfound faith to motivate him, he also had renewed hope where baseball was concerned. With the help of three surgeries, his knees improved enough for him to try to play again.

"My knees steadily got better, and I was able to endure the aches and pains," he recalls. "The winter after I became a Christian, I really dedicated myself to baseball. I couldn't play football. I couldn't play basketball. So I became more disciplined toward baseball. I became more goal-oriented. Now God had instilled in me discipline, endurance, and perseverance."

Soon McMichael was catching the attention of college scouts, especially from the University of Tennessee. Just like his brother, Greg earned an athletic scholarship to play for the Volunteers. At first, there was still not much in Greg's game to suggest that he would one day pitch in the World Series. During his freshman and sophomore seasons, McMichael struggled with a 3–7 record and a 6.82 earned run average. Yet things improved so much by his junior year that the Cleveland Indians drafted him.

If this was the highway to baseball heaven, though, it was not clearly marked. Along the way, McMichael was sidetracked by two more detours that nearly left him back where he had been as a young teen—without a future in the game.

After two successful seasons of Class A and Double A ball, Greg hit a major roadblock as he tried to make the leap to Triple A. Although the Indians had moved him up to Colorado Springs, their Triple A affiliate, for the second part of the 1990 season, those bothersome knee problems resurfaced.

McMichael underwent surgery again, and he began to

make plans to get back on the mound. "First, the Indians told me just to take it easy and get myself back into shape, that there was no rush. Then all of a sudden—*boom!* They tell me, 'We don't think you can play anymore. We're concerned about your health. We think you should retire and think about your future.'" Fearing the worst, the Indians released McMichael.

He had clawed his way to the verge of entering the major league ranks. He had overcome the serious knee problems of his teenage years, and his faith had led him out of the quicksand of substance abuse. Yet he was hearing the same shattering news as before: You'll never play this game again. At age twenty-four, it seemed he was a washed-up former minor leaguer.

"That was a time when I had to reflect and evaluate where I was," he says. "I was flying home after that, and I was praying, 'God, where do You want me to go from here? Are You trying to tell me something? What's Your desire for my life?'"

The answer came after McMichael arrived home in Tennessee. "When I got there, I think God really impressed on my heart not to quit," he says. "He instilled in me a desire to play."

Fortunately, McMichael had a connection that could help him get back in the game. And it would take some help—after all, it is not easy for a Double A player with bad knees and a release slip to get another opportunity. But McMichael's contact—the scout who had drafted him with the Indians, Roy Clark—could indeed give him a boost. Clark had changed tribes, and was now a scout for the Atlanta Braves. He remembered being impressed with Greg earlier.

A tryout was set up, and McMichael pitched in front of Braves officials. He pitched well enough to earn a chance with Atlanta, but there was one catch: He would have to start all over again. After working his way up to the Triple A level with Cleveland, he was now relegated to a level that McMichael calls "the lowest point you can go." Two days at the Braves extended spring camp earned McMichael a call-up to Single A Durham. "I went to Durham and started back up the ladder."

It was 1991, Greg's fourth year in professional baseball, and he was no closer to the big time than he had been in 1988.

Coming off knee surgery as he was, he did not pitch with the same effectiveness he had displayed during his climb through the Indians' system. "It takes about a year to recover fully from knee surgery," he explains.

But while the knee was getting back into shape, he developed still another problem. Tendinitis in his shoulder, combined with the knee difficulty, made every outing a chore. "It was a crucial time for me," McMichael says. "I was coming out of the bull pen and my ERA was around 5.00. I was pitching terribly and my arm was hurting. I couldn't pitch the way I wanted to."

Then he hit rock bottom. The first half of the season was drawing to a close, and Durham was playing in Kinston, where McMichael had pitched when he was with the Indians. Greg was the starting pitcher for the game when Kinston secured the first-half championship.

"A guy hit a grand slam off me to clinch the first half," he recalls. "I was at the lowest point in my career. Here I was pitching terribly and getting clinched on by the team I was with before. I'd get up in the morning and my knees were hurting. I decided I was going to quit. I went to the ballpark the next day, and I was going to tell the manager that I had quit."

Yet a couple of things happened to stop McMichael from cutting short a career that would eventually lead him to the pinnacle of his sport. First, when he got to the park that day, he ran into Roy Clark, the scout who had signed him originally with the Indians and who had recommended him to the Braves. When Clark asked Greg how he was doing, he got an unexpected reply.

"I'm doing terrible," Greg responded. "I'm going to quit."

The scout knew exactly what to say. "You know," he told the frustrated right-hander, "if you quit now, you may look back and say, 'What if?' But if you stick it out, you'll know you gave it your best. Let the chips fall."

At about the same time, Greg received a letter from his friend David Driver. The two had met earlier when McMichael accompanied the sports outreach organization Athletes In Action on one of its tours. Driver, AIA's sports information director, requested that McMichael speak to his Sunday school class the next time the Durham team traveled to Driver's town.

"I knew if I quit, I couldn't do it," Greg says.

Those two unrelated messages—one about his career and one about his ministry as a Christian athlete—changed McMichael's mind. Instead of hanging up his glove, he returned to the field and began ringing up the hitters in the Carolina League.

"The whole year turned around," he recalls. "My knee felt better. My tendinitis went away. And I developed a change-up that year. That was the pivotal point in my career."

After that turning point, he got on the fast track to the majors. He began the 1992 season at Double A Greenville, where he pitched in fifteen games. In his first twenty-six innings for Greenville, he allowed just two earned runs. Soon he was promoted to Triple A Richmond—one step away from the big leagues. At Richmond, McMichael recorded an unremarkable 5–4 as a starting pitcher.

Would that be enough to earn him a spot in Atlanta? McMichael didn't think so. "I didn't really put an exclamation point on my year," he says.

To do that, he journeyed to Puerto Rico for some winter baseball. For the next three months, he opened some eyes. He led the league in innings pitched, strikeouts, and ERA, and he made the All-Star team. It was enough for the Braves, who invited McMichael to spring training as a nonroster player. No guarantees, but at least they would give him a good look.

What they saw was a pitcher who knew how to get people out. The team was looking for a closer—someone who could take the mound late in the game and preserve a lead. Although McMichael had been a starter the previous year, he seemed to fit into the closer role perfectly for the Braves.

He pitched so well that one of his teammates, Sid Bream, approached Greg with about a week left in spring training and told him, "There's a 90 percent chance you're going to make this team." This was a team that already had a monster starting lineup—not to mention people like Mark Davis (44 saves in 1989), flame-throwing youngster Mark Wohlers, and veteran Steve Bedrosian in camp vying for spots on the roster.

Fearing a letdown, McMichael told Bream, "Nah, there's probably a 10 percent chance I'll make the team."

As self-fulfilling prophecies go, that one would turn out to be highly inaccurate, but McMichael did proceed to make things tough on himself. "I started putting pressure on myself to do more. I really struggled. So, after two days of that, I got down on my knees and gave it all back to the Lord. And I began to pitch the way I had before."

As spring training wound down, the Braves were in Atlanta to play the Boston Red Sox. McMichael's wife, Jennifer, was there, along with his parents. After the game, Braves manager Bobby Cox called Greg, Jay Howell, and Steve Bedrosian into his office.

"We've decided to go with you guys," Cox said. "We've released Davis, and we've sent Wohlers down."

After two tries, Greg McMichael had reached the top rung of the ladder. He was a major league pitcher.

"I went outside, and Jennifer was waiting for me. I hugged her. My parents were all excited. It was really emotional. We had gone through a lot that spring."

Looking back on his minor league experience gives McMichael a fresh appreciation for what he had accomplished, and he is sure most fans don't understand what most players go through to reach the top.

"The minor leagues is a difficult situation," he says. "You're in a smaller town, and you're traveling across the country in buses with a group of guys. You're living in apartments with three or four guys, and you're earning about $800 a month. In Single A ball, you get about $10 a day for meal money when you're on the road. All the while, you're battling people for a job. You've always got guys trying to take your position. At the same time, you're trying to stay healthy. It's a difficult task to make it through the minor leagues."

Once established in the major leagues, Greg was determined to prove his ability. In his first year with the Braves, he went from being an unknown commodity to being the team's top closer while finishing as runner-up in the voting for Rookie of the Year. He was so good to start the year that he converted his first 15 save opportunities and ended the season with 19 saves. He appeared in an incredible 74 games that year. Again in 1994, McMichael served as a closer, this time racking up 21 saves in 51 games pitched.

Yet the arrival of Mark Wohlers would soon mean a change in roles for Greg. It's the kind of change that turns many pitchers into malcontents. The glory role in the bull pen belongs to the closer, who can strut in from the bull pen with his invincible pitches, squelch rallies and run-scoring threats night after night, and receive accolades from players, fans, and reporters alike. The setup role, though, is a little like being a stock man in a grocery store. It's work that has to be done, but no one really pays it much attention.

Nevertheless, when McMichael was asked to switch to setup man, he handled it with the grace that is a trademark of his career. "Whatever I've been asked to do," he says, "I've wanted to do it to the best of my ability. I knew that even when I was a closer for the Braves, I wasn't the closer they wanted. I knew I was just an interim. There are more guys who are kind of like me than there are guys like Mark Wohlers. He's a classic. He's the guy you'd want there, and that's understandable.

"I enjoy my position [as setup man] because I get to pitch a little bit more and in more situations. There's less pressure from the media standpoint. There's less glory, and all that stuff, but that's fine with me."

Glory came in huge portions to the entire Atlanta ball club in 1995 when they defeated the Cleveland Indians to win the World Series. For his part, McMichael again contributed greatly to a pitching staff that had all the pieces in place. He made 62 appearances in 1995, posting a 5–2 record and a 3.07 ERA.

No matter how successful McMichael and his team are, he doesn't appear to be any different from the guy he was while struggling in the minors. "I'd like to think being in the World Series hasn't changed me," he says. "Sure, it's the goal of every player to win the Series, but I don't think I'm any happier now than I was before. I'd like to think I was as happy making $800 a month in Class A ball as I am now."

The key to Greg McMichael's life, it seems, rests not so

much with his role as a baseball player, but with his relationship with Jesus Christ. "I know I wouldn't be in the majors if I hadn't come to Christ when I was in high school. And if my parents hadn't been obedient to God and remarried, I wouldn't be here. Through everything I endured to make it to Atlanta, if it wasn't for the things God has taught me and instilled in me about acceptance and performance, I wouldn't have made it.

"God taught me ten years ago that my performance does not dictate how I should feel about myself," he continues. "God says I am totally loved and accepted and forgiven. He loved me the same ten years ago as He loves me now that I'm a world champion. His love doesn't change. When I discovered that, I was freed up to be the best athlete I could be. I no longer had to look to the fans or my coach or the newspaper or the awards to get self-worth. When I started to understand that about my Christian walk, that's when I started to blossom as a pitcher."

He's been at the absolute bottom in baseball with little chance of even playing again. He's been at the top of the game, celebrating on the field as world champion. He's had success in the postseason, and he's endured the scorn of fans after a disappointing performance in the 1996 play-offs.

But for Greg McMichael, life is so much more than baseball. Real satisfaction for him comes in his personal relationship with Christ. When the knees finally do betray him for the last time, his relationship with Christ is something he'll be able to stand on forever.

Q & A WITH GREG MCMICHAEL

Q: *Is there anything about being in the major leagues that you don't like?*
Greg: Your privacy is taken away. I can't go to the store without people saying, "Aren't you Greg McMichael?" I wear my glasses and people don't recognize me as much. Being asked for autographs is not really a problem, but you feel invaded a little bit.

Q: *What do you do about the pressure you must live under as a major league player?*

Greg: There's a lot of pressure. You can read in the paper about everything you did—plus what the owners think, what the fans think, what the coaches think, and what the writers think. You can get caught up in that and let that be how you feel about yourself. So putting my trust in the Lord, I knew that I didn't have to be concerned with all that. Sid Bream told me once, "Let's not even read the papers. It's not worth it. Let's put our trust in what God says about us and not the papers—good or bad." My trust in the Lord keeps me on a level plane.

Q: *Were you a baseball fan as a kid?*
Greg: I went to one Reds' game when I was really little, but I don't remember anything except going to the food stand. Other than that, I didn't watch my first major league baseball game until I was a junior in high school. I lived in a football town, and we never watched baseball. I guess I was always out playing it.

Q: *What kinds of ministry opportunities do you enjoy?*
Greg: I see my focus as youth and high school groups. That's when I became a Christian, and I've always felt that's where God would have me work. I do a lot of speaking in the off-season. I do some camps with Unlimited Potential [a ministry that uses baseball as a tool for evangelism and discipleship]. I usually do two of those during the season and two during the off-season. I really limit my appearances during the off-season to about two a month. The season is such a grind, so in the off-season I try to give my time to my family.

Q: *What was your reaction to being traded to the Mets in November 1996?*
Greg: I knew a trade was one possible scenario with my change in position [he became eligible for arbitration after the 1996 season]. So it's not a complete shock. But it's hard when you've established your home and you enjoy being there year round. I've been thinking of my wife and kids.

THE ROAD TO THE MAJORS

- Selected by the Cleveland Indians, seventh round of the 1988 draft
- Released by the Indians on April 4, 1991
- Signed by the Atlanta Braves as a free agent on April 16, 1991
- Traded to the New York Mets on November 25, 1996

Minor league stops: Burlington, Kinston, Canton, Colorado Springs, Durham, Greenville, Richmond

Minor league highlight: While pitching with Canton in the Eastern League in 1989, McMichael pitched 36 consecutive scoreless innings.

THE MCMICHAEL FILE

Year	Team	W	L	PCT	G	SV	IP	H	R	ER	HR	TBB	SO	ERA
1993	Atl	2	3	.400	74	19	91.2	68	22	21	3	29	89	2.06
1994	Atl	4	6	.400	51	21	58.2	66	29	25	1	19	47	3.84
1995	Atl	7	2	.778	67	2	80.2	64	27	25	8	32	74	2.79
1996	Atl	5	3	.625	73	2	86.2	84	37	31	4	27	78	3.22
4 Years		**18**	**14**	**.563**	**265**	**44**	**317.2**	**282**	**115**	**102**	**16**	**107**	**288**	**2.89**

Mike Muñoz
A Real Firefighter

VITAL STATISTICS

Born July 12, 1965, in Baldwin Park, California
6 feet 2, 192 pounds
College: Cal Poly Pomona
Position: Relief pitcher
Throws left, bats left
Family: Wife, Lee Ann, and one child, Kailey Ann
1997 team: Colorado Rockies

CAREER HIGHLIGHTS

- Pitched in all four of Colorado's play-off games versus Atlanta in 1995
- Pitched in 32 straight games without giving up a home run in 1994
- Allowed left-handers only 14 hits in 73 at bats (.192) in 1992
- Pitched in 65 games for Detroit in 1992

WARMING UP

When Mike Muñoz signed his 1996 contract with the Colorado Rockies, he did something not many players are willing to do. He took a $20,000 pay cut to stay with the team. He had been with the Rockies since 1993 and was eager to stay put. "Playing with the Rockies is a career highlight," he says.

FAVORITE BIBLE PASSAGE

"If you confess with your mouth, 'Jesus is Lord,' and believe in your heart that God raised him from the dead, you will be saved" (Romans 10:9).

Mike Muñoz

What little boy doesn't dream at one time or another of swooping into a dangerous situation dressed in uniform and bringing his equipment with him, ready to put out a fire that is threatening to grow bigger and bigger?

While that description clearly describes every little boy's dream of becoming a firefighter, it also depicts the dream many sandlot baseball players have of becoming a successful major league relief pitcher.

For Mike Muñoz, growing up in Southern California meant having both dreams. As he worked his way through the youth leagues of Baldwin Park, Muñoz was torn between the dream of becoming a major leaguer and becoming a firefighter.

"To tell you the truth," Muñoz says, "my biggest dream was to be a firefighter. It was something I really wanted to do."

One might assume that Muñoz wanted to battle conflagrations because his father was a fireman, but that wasn't the case. In fact, what career influence his dad did have on Mike had more to do with throwing baseballs than with spraying water.

"My dad was my biggest influence in baseball," Mike says. "He had some college experience and had a slight chance of playing pro ball. So he had a really good idea about baseball. My dad was my coach through Little League. He saw my potential and he didn't want me to waste it."

Jess Muñoz saw something in his son that a lot of other people might not have noticed when Mike was in high school. Mike Muñoz was good enough to garner All-City honors for Bishop Amat High School in Los Angeles, but he was slender and had a mediocre fastball. No one offered him the kind of scholarship he wanted or a spot in the major league draft. "I was scouted a little bit, but I was too small," Mike says.

The potential his dad had encouraged him to develop was there, but he didn't have anybody convinced he would some-day be earning his livelihood as a flame-throwing lefty. There-fore, when it came time to go to college, Muñoz first pursued an education in flame-*quenching*. He attended a junior college near his hometown so he could study fire science.

Soon, though, the love of baseball took over the love of fire fighting. "After the first year," Mike says, "that got a little old, and I dropped the fire science thing. I think baseball just became more important, and I wanted to do everything to make it."

One of the best things he did to reach his potential was to change schools, leaving Backdraft 101 behind and heading to California Polytechnic University at Pomona. Cal Poly Pomona had shown an interest in Muñoz when he was in high school, but not enough to attract him. Although the school did not offer scholarships for baseball players, Coach Scalinus, who was a well-respected teacher of the game, drew Muñoz to Cal Poly for his second year of college.

By now, Muñoz had begun to mature physically, and the Broncos were the beneficiaries. In his sophomore year, Muñoz established himself as the kind of pitcher major league scouts were scouring the country looking for. He went 16–6 for the year and was named an NCAA Division II first-team All-American.

Because of the rules of Major League Baseball, though, Muñoz was not drafted after his breakthrough year. If a player does not go into the draft after high school, he must remain an amateur until his junior year is finished. So Muñoz stayed at Cal Poly and had another impressive year. As a starter, he stayed in every game until at least the seventh inning. Plus, he won his last ten decisions as he led the Broncos to a second-place finish in the Division II World Series.

It was time for the next big step. In the June 1986 free agent draft, the Los Angeles Dodgers picked Muñoz in the third round, and Muñoz was off to the minor leagues.

In his first year of pro ball, Muñoz went to Great Falls, Montana, to play for the Dodgers' Pioneer League rookie team. Still a starting pitcher, Muñoz fashioned a 4–4 record with a 3.12 ERA to earn his way to the next rung of the ladder. Single A Bakersfield was his next stop.

For Muñoz, that season-long stay with the California team would transform his life as a pitcher. "I was a starting pitcher during the first half of the season," Muñoz recalls. "But I was having trouble getting past the fourth or fifth inning. So the manager sent me to the bull pen to find myself. All of a sudden, in the first or second day at that position, they stuck me in save situations, and they told me that they had found my place."

Muñoz had decided against professional fire fighting several years earlier, but now he was back in the danger zone. He was asked to sit in the firehouse (bull pen, actually) and wait for the bell to ring (well, the telephone from the manager). He was a fireman after all.

In 52 appearances for Bakersfield in 1987 (just 12 as a starter), Muñoz was 8–7 with a 3.74 ERA. And he had a brand-new statistic to his credit: saves (nine).

So how does a 22-year-old pitcher adjust to the dramatic switch from starter to reliever? After hoping that someday he would walk to the mound at Dodger Stadium as a starting pitcher, how does a pitcher cope with the idea that his major league life will be spent in a bull pen, waiting every day for the chance to come in and smother the sparks left by opposing teams' bats?

For Muñoz, it seemed almost like a blessing.

In the first place, Muñoz had created something of a problem for himself as a starter, and it had nothing to do with the way he pitched. It had more to do with the way he prepared to pitch. "The days I pitched, I was a basket case," he recalls. "I had these little rituals I did, and if I couldn't do the rituals, I knew things weren't going to go well that day."

When the Dodgers asked Muñoz to become a relief pitcher, then, the first relief was his. He was free from the rituals. "When

I switched to relieving, I knew I had a chance to pitch every day. If the phone rings, it does, and if it doesn't, it doesn't. I decided, *If I worry like I did when I was a starter, I'm really going to be a mess.*"

Free of the need for pregame rituals and the jitters they brought, Muñoz excelled as a reliever. And he enjoyed the fact that the Dodger organization placed him in a key relief role. "I wasn't just a mop-up guy. I had a key role. I felt important on the team. I just took off with it."

Good things were on the horizon for Muñoz as he began the 1988 season in San Antonio. First, he had a remarkable season coming out of the Missions' bull pen. Appearing in 56 games, all in relief, Muñoz crafted an outstanding 1.00 ERA, striking out 71 batters in 71 innings pitched. He compiled a 7–2 won-loss mark during that season.

But even better than that, he met Lee Ann, who would later become his wife. Although Mike and Lee Ann made their first acquaintance in 1988, it wasn't until the next year that they began dating. By then, Muñoz had climbed up another rung of the ladder, to Triple A Albuquerque. Once Mike and Lee Ann became an item, she would venture to Albuquerque and stay with an aunt and uncle while visiting Mike. In 1990, after Muñoz had gotten his feet wet as a major league pitcher with the Dodgers, they were married.

Mike's first major league appearance had come on September 6, 1989, after a successful year at Albuquerque. As the Dukes' top left-handed relief pitcher that summer, Mike had appeared in 60 games, striking out more than a batter per inning pitched. In addition, he allowed just two home runs in 72 innings of work.

Yet in a cruel irony, something went wrong for Muñoz on that early September day when he finally got his initial big league opportunity. The Dodgers were in Cincinnati to meet the rival Reds. When Tommy Lasorda when to his bull pen to find someone to shut down the Reds, he selected Muñoz. The first batter he would face was Jeff Robinson.

Muñoz went into his stretch and fired a fastball toward home plate. Before the ball could arrive at its destination,

Robinson took a robust, Riverfront Stadium swing and knocked it into next week. In one pitch, Muñoz had given up half as many home runs as he had all summer in Albuquerque. "What else am I going to pitch in my first time in the league?" he says of his first, fat fastball. "And he was ready for it."

It was a bad start for the new kid in Tinseltown. And it wasn't long until the Dodgers decided that Muñoz was not in their future. He was traded to the Detroit Tigers in late September 1990.

Concerning his less-than-successful stint with the Dodgers, Muñoz thinks he's figured out the problem. "I had eighty games in the major leagues. I can remember being more scared than anything—just being this young guy called up. They had hopes for me being the next left-handed reliever for them. They had continually looked for someone since Steve Howe left. So that's what I was doing in the majors, trying to be the Dodgers' left-handed closer. I put way too much pressure on myself—instead of going up and enjoying it and having fun. I was just twenty-three. I had every right to be scared."

With the L.A. experience to build on, Muñoz went to work for the Tigers, attempting to become part of a team that was in the early stages of rebuilding. The 1991 season was spent mostly at Toledo, Detroit's Triple A team, with a six-appearance major league entree during June and July.

Going into the 1992 season, Muñoz's career didn't look much more promising. In spring training, he was given little chance to make the team. But there were some important things that needed to take place in his life during the summer of '92; and as it would turn out, he would have to be in Detroit for them to happen.

An outstanding spring training convinced Sparky Anderson that Muñoz should travel north with the team. Ol' Spark had no idea, but his decision to keep Muñoz on the team would bear all kinds of spiritual rewards for the tall lefty. And it was a boon to the team as well.

On the baseball side of the ledger, Muñoz enjoyed his first full season of major league action, staying with the big club from opening day to the final out of the season. Also, Muñoz was the most called-upon pitcher on the squad in 1992, making sixty-five appearances. Facing mostly left-handed hitters, Muñoz allowed only fourteen base hits all year as opposing hitters batted just .192 against him.

But it was on the spiritual side of the ledger that made 1992 a permanent highlight for Muñoz.

During his previous years in pro baseball, Muñoz had been aware that there was a spiritual battle going on in his heart. "I was searching," he says of those times. "I was going to Bible studies, but I was still living the way I wanted to live. I was going out and drinking and things like that. From what I know now, I wasn't a Christian. I didn't have a personal relationship with the Lord.

"I was raised to know the story. I knew Jesus died on the cross for me, but as far as accepting Him personally, I thought it was done for me. It was hard for me to grasp the idea that I had to accept Him into my life. It was hard to understand that no one could do it for me."

While Muñoz was in Detroit during his best year in the majors, he got to know two people who would finally help him understand the gospel and the commitment he needed to make. Jeff Totten, the chaplain for the Tigers, and Frank Tanana, a pitcher for Detroit who had more than 200 career wins, came alongside Muñoz to help him.

"Frank took me under his wing," Muñoz says. "He didn't let me stray too far. He didn't try to jam the Bible down my throat, but he was a godly man. I watched him live. Here's a veteran guy who had eighteen or nineteen years in the majors, and here I was a rookie. [Muñoz had not accumulated enough innings while with L.A. to lose his rookie status.] And we were going to lunch all the time together. At first, I was saying, 'Wow! I'm hanging out with Frank Tanana.' But then I began to think, *He's just a man just like I am*. When you start to think about him in that way, you totally forget what he's done on the field. What he's doing off the field is so much more important.

"Also, Jeff Totten and his Bible studies were helpful. And Ed and Gwen Diaz, who live in Lakeland, Florida, where we trained in the spring, were helpful to my wife."

Through the assistance of these mentors, Mike and Lee

Ann Muñoz finally realized they had to put their faith in Jesus Christ for salvation—and that's just what they did.

It wasn't long after becoming a Christian that Muñoz discovered the hard truth that trusting Christ does not mean problems disappear. It just means that when problems arise, you have Someone to provide strength and guidance.

Spring training of 1993 did not go as well for Mike as the previous one had. After just eight appearances on the mound for Detroit, Muñoz was told he was headed back to the minors. The problem for Detroit was that Mike told the Tigers he wasn't going. In baseball parlance, that essentially means he had asked to become a free agent. Soon the Colorado Rockies were on the phone, and on May 14, he signed with the new club in the mountains.

This did not mean, however, that he could bypass the minor leagues altogether. Energized by his affiliation with a new club and hopeful for a new start, he went to Colorado Springs. There, he figured, he could work his way back to the major leagues. Playing for the Sky Sox, Muñoz appeared in forty games, fashioned a 1.67 ERA, and showed Rockies skipper Don Baylor that he was ready for another crack at the big show.

On August 22, 1993, he was back in the land of charter flights and big-time meal money. On August 23, he notched his first win for the Rockies. He had found a new baseball home.

During his first four years with the Rocks, Muñoz experienced a variety of successes and disappointments on the field, yet he cherishes an unusual experience for a relief pitcher as one of his highlights. In 1995, pitching against the Pittsburgh Pirates, he got his first major league hit off Jim Gott. It was a double, and it knocked in a run for the Rockies.

Other top memories for the lefty include pitching for the Rockies in the 1995 play-offs and being a part of the team when Colorado opened Coors Field in 1995.

Yet what really encouraged Muñoz as he carved out a career in Colorado were the friendships he established on the team with fellow Christians Darren Holmes and Walt Weiss.

"We always get together," Muñoz says. "We like to get into the Word on the road. Those guys are really important to me.

Even if we're just getting together to watch TV, we have something in common, and that's the Lord. We're always doing something clean. Even when we're sitting in front of the TV, we can be talking about Him. There are times when we get into the Bible—we'll start at 11:00 at night and suddenly we look at the clock and it's 4:00 in the morning. We think, *What are we doing? We just get into the Word!*"

During the 1996 season, there were times when it appeared that the Bible study group could be broken up. Muñoz struggled often during the season—at one point he wondered if he might face a return to the minor leagues for the first time since 1993. Yet his attitude remained upbeat.

"It's tough to deal with that kind of stuff," he said early in the 1996 season, referring to his ballooning ERA and the possibility of returning to Colorado Springs. "But I've been through it before. It's not anything to look forward to, but wherever I go, that'll be the best thing for me."

Muñoz was able to turn his season around, however, and finished with a 2–2 record and an improved ERA. Part of the reason for the turnaround was the confidence Rockies' manager Baylor put in his lefty. "Even when I wasn't pitching well, he was putting me in games, giving me a chance to pitch my way out of it," Muñoz recalls.

It had been more than a decade since Mike Muñoz had studied fire fighting. Yet there he was, still waiting for the signal to sound—summoning him to take the hill and extinguish an opponent's rally. For a relief pitcher, that's all a guy can ask for: A chance to put out the fire.

Q & A WITH MIKE MUÑOZ

Q: *How did your dad influence you to play baseball? And how does that affect the way you think kids should be taught?*
Mike: My dad never pushed me or made it unattractive. It was not an "everything you do" kind of thing. He didn't say you have to live or die for sports. But there were times when I got lazy, and he knew when to step in and push a little bit. I know

how fathers can get by being too pushy, and I don't want to get that way with my children.

Q: *Who are some of your spiritual mentors?*
Mike: We have so many people who are important to us. We see Frank and Cathy Tanana once in a while. Jeff Totten is really good about calling me on the phone. Sometimes after a tough game, he'll call up and encourage me. Also, since we live in the Dallas area, John Weber, the chaplain for the Rangers, is important to our family. We have Bible studies as a family.

Q: *Who helps your wife with spiritual concerns?*
Mike: Bobby and Gari Meacham have been so good. Bobby is a former major leaguer and a current minor league coach. Gari has been supportive of my wife. She does a lot of studies with the wives in Denver, and she provides materials for them to read.

Q: *What has been the biggest difference for you in becoming a major leaguer after not attracting much attention in high school?*
Mike: I weighed 150 pounds when I was a senior in high school, and I weigh 192 now. My velocity then was nowhere near what it is now. I've added 10 miles per hour on my fastball since high school.

THE ROAD TO THE MAJORS

- Selected by the Los Angeles Dodgers in the third round of the 1986 draft
- Traded to the Detroit Tigers for Mike Wilkins on September 30, 1990
- Signed as a free agent by the Colorado Rockies on May 14, 1993

Minor League Stops: Great Falls, Bakersfield, San Antonio, Albuquerque, Toledo, Colorado Springs

Minor League Highlight: Posted a 1.00 ERA and a 7–2 record for San Antonio in 1988

Year	Team	W	L	PCT	G	SV	IP	H	R	ER	HR	TBB	SO	ERA
1989	LA	0	0	- - -	3	0	2.2	5	5	5	1	2	3	16.88
1990	LA	0	1	.000	8	0	5.2	6	2	2	0	3	2	3.18
1991	Det	0	0	- - -	6	0	9.1	14	10	10	0	5	3	9.64
1992	Det	1	2	.333	65	2	48.0	44	16	16	3	25	23	3.00
1993	Det	0	1	.000	8	0	3.0	4	2	2	1	6	1	6.00
	Col	2	1	.667	21	0	18.0	21	12	9	1	9	16	4.50
1994	Col	4	2	.667	57	1	45.2	37	22	19	3	31	32	3.74
1995	Col	2	4	.333	64	2	43.2	54	38	36	9	27	37	7.42
1996	Col	2	2	.500	54	0	44.2	55	33	33	4	16	45	6.65
8 Years		**11**	**13**	**.458**	**286**	**5**	**220.2**	**240**	**140**	**132**	**22**	**124**	**162**	**5.38**

Dave Nilsson
An Aussie in Milwaukee

VITAL STATISTICS

Born December 14, 1969, in Brisbane, Australia
6 feet 3, 231 pounds
Position: Outfielder/Infielder
Throws right, bats left
Family: Married to Amanda
1997 team: Milwaukee Brewers

- Finished 10th in AL in batting average with the bases loaded in 1995
- Knocked in five runs in one game versus Oakland on July 17, 1995
- Named Milwaukee Brewers Most Valuable Player in 1994
- Was part of the first Australian battery in big league history when he caught Graeme Lloyd on April 14, 1993

WARMING UP

At first glance, Dave Nilsson appears to be a laid-back person. He's quiet and calm. Yet he is also driven. "Down inside," he says, "I want things to happen a lot quicker than they sometimes would happen." As a relatively new Christian, though, he has found his faith to be a great source of patience. "It's very easy to get caught up in this game and let it consume you, but when you keep your eyes focused on the Lord, that just doesn't happen. It's just so reassuring to know Him, and He keeps you so level. There's not so many ups and downs as this game normally brings."

FAVORITE BIBLE PASSAGE

"One hasn't really stuck out to me yet. It would be good if I could find one. It's funny, because a lot of people ask me about that. I used to feel bad that I didn't have a favorite, but it'll hit me when it hits me."

Dave Nilsson

Dave Nilsson doesn't see much difference between the cultures of the two countries he splits his time between—the United States and Australia. In fact, the countries are so much alike that Nilsson spends summers in both places. When he leaves the States after the baseball season ends, Australia is just beginning to warm up for its solstice.

Even when Nilsson arrived in the U.S. in 1987 as a seventeen-year-old free-agent signee of the Milwaukee Brewers, he had no trouble adjusting. "There's not much of a difference, really," says the Brisbane-born Brewer. "It was just the same as another kid from another state. It's just a little bit farther from home and a little bit more expensive to call."

But what about baseball, the game that is just now beginning to gain widespread popularity in the land of cricket and rugby? Even that, Nilsson says, is no different. "The game's pretty much the same. The only difference is in the level of play."

Surely Nilsson has discovered *some* difference between the U.S. and his native land. Well, yes, there is one tiny difference—mosquitoes. Both countries have them, but only in Australia can they do what they did to Nilsson in 1995. In March of that year, Nilsson contracted Ross River Fever, a virus that is carried by Australian mosquitoes. When it hit, Nilsson was afflicted with chronic fatigue and swelling in the joints.

After the baseball strike was settled in April and the players had agreed to begin the season a month later than usual, Nilsson was still unable to play. Ross River Fever had drained him of his energy.

The year before, Nilsson had established himself as one of the best young hitters in the American League. With his size and steady improvement at the plate, he was considered a burgeoning power hitter in the Brewers' lineup.

In 1994, he had 109 hits, 43 of which went for extra bases. His .451 slugging average served notice that he was a dangerous hitter. It was his first full season in the majors, yet Nilsson led the Brewers in RBIs, hits, doubles, and games played. Four times during the year he collected four hits in one contest. The future, it seemed, was limitless.

Until the mosquitoes got him.

Suddenly, this 6-foot-3, 231-pound slugger was powerless. "I was just so lethargic," he recalls. "I never really had much energy."

To try to play his way back into shape for the 1995 season, Nilsson retraced his steps through the minor league system, playing three games in Beloit, five games in El Paso, and three games in New Orleans while on a rehabilitation assignment. On June 24, he was back in Milwaukee, where he put up some good numbers the rest of the way, matching his 1994 home run total with 12 dingers and hitting .278.

Yet that season showed signs of a power shortage for Nilsson in two areas. First, of course, was the lack of strength he felt throughout the season because of the illness. The second was a deficiency of a spiritual kind. That season, he felt an emptiness inside that needed to be filled by something besides baseball.

"I had been through nine years of professional baseball, and now that I was in the big leagues I began to notice something about myself," he says. "When I was recovering from the fever, I had a lot of time to myself. I realized how much baseball, even though I enjoyed it, was not really that big a part of my life.

"Growing up in Australia, sport was a big priority in our family. And down there, a lot of people think that if you can achieve something—if you can be at the top—you're going to have peace and happiness and everything that comes with it. After finally getting to the big leagues, I started to get an emptiness inside. I started to wonder what was really important."

For someone who was wondering about life and how to find true meaning, there was no better team for Dave Nilsson to be on than the Milwaukee Brewers. The backbone of the team, both spiritually and athletically, were guys like Kevin Seitzer, Bill Wegman, and Cal Eldred. The Thumpers, they called themselves—taking what someone thought was a derogatory term, "Bible Thumpers," and turning it into a name of honor. Those three and others often spent hours in Bible study, and they were always aware of the importance of their testimony as Christians.

For Nilsson, the spiritual influence in the Brewers organization had begun back in 1990 when he had roomed with Eldred on a team managed by Chris Bando, who is known for his ability to share the gospel and disciple Christians. In 1995, as Nilsson continued his spiritual search during his time of physical weakness, he watched his teammates closely.

"It was not as much them going after me or me going after them," he says. "They just kind of lived their lives, and I knew they were Christians. I never had the faintest idea what that meant, but you can definitely see the life of a Christian. There was a lot of peace and a lot of happiness through times of turmoil.

"In the game of baseball, you see guys making a lot of money, and those you think should be the happiest are really the most miserable people when you get to know them. That's something the public doesn't understand."

As he observed Seitzer and the other believers, though, he saw that they were not like that. When Nilsson talked to some of his Christian teammates about their faith, they gladly shared it with him. "They explained to me about Christ, and on July 23, 1995, I decided to accept Him."

Just a month or two before Nilsson prayed to receive Jesus Christ, his girlfriend, Amanda, had done the same thing. A few months later, they were married. For Dave, their new faith made the wedding ceremony an extraspecial occasion.

"It was a true blessing to have God in the middle of our relationship when we got married," he says. "I've been to a lot of weddings that, quite honestly, didn't mean a lot. To us, the words really meant something because we were including God in our vows. Now we're together in God, which is very special."

As Dave and Amanda spent their off-season in Australia after the 1995 season, he had still not recovered from the fever. He continued to feel groggy and listless, and this was seven months after contracting the virus. As he sought help, he discovered a man named Errol Amerasekera, a medical practitioner who specialized in treating Ross River Fever sufferers.

Amerasekera discovered that some of the listlessness was related to allergies Nilsson didn't know he had. Once the allergens—dairy and wheat products—were flushed out of Nilsson's system, he began to regain strength.

Nilsson thought so much of Amerasekera and his efforts that he took him along to spring training in 1996. Whatever Errol prescribed for the big guy from down under certainly worked. Nilsson played in 123 games for the Brewers in 1996 and hit .331, the sixth-best batting average in the American League. His slugging percentage of .525 dispelled any doubts about his strength.

On one enchanted evening in Seattle in July—in fact, one year to the day after he had committed his life to Jesus Christ—Nilsson outslugged Jay Buhner on Buhner Buzz Cut Night III. For this Kingdome promotion, anyone who arrived with a Jay Buhner-like shaved head got in free. A total of 22,378 fans—including 3,321 buzz-cuts, 3,293 of whom were men—were on hand that night to see their favorite hairless hitter in action.

Buhner lived up to his part of the festive evening: in the fifth inning, he buzzed a Scott Karl pitch into the seats to tie the game at 3–3. But then the spotlight turned on the only right fielder on the turf that night who needed a comb. Nilsson led off the seventh with a solo shot off Blas Minor. Two innings later, he blasted Blas for a two-run shot, and the Brewers went away with a 7–3 victory. It was Nilsson's third multi-homer game of the season.

With 17 home runs and 84 RBIs, Nilsson edged closer to being the power hitter the Brewers projected him to be years ago when they signed him as a weekend club team player in Australia.

Which brings us to the question that begs an answer. How did Dave Nilsson get to Milwaukee? Why was he among only five major leaguers in the history of the game who hailed from a place noted more for its wombats than its ball bats?

Surprisingly, Nilsson came by his baseball instincts the same way many Americans do—his dad was a ballplayer. But his dad was more than that—he was also a cricket player.

"We were a sporting family," Nilsson says. "Our lives revolved around sports. We played a lot of cricket and a lot of football, which is actually a rugby league."

Nilsson's dad, who ran a printing factory when he wasn't out on the pitch batting a cricket ball or on the diamond hitting a baseball, introduced his four sons to the American game. "It wasn't a real popular sport then," Dave admits. "But there was always a league where you could get into games on the weekend."

While in high school in Brisbane, Nilsson played one year of baseball, but he didn't stay with it because "it wasn't taken too seriously." Instead, he stuck to playing club baseball for several local teams.

In 1986, a senior team of Australian baseball players visited the United States on an exhibition tour, and they asked Nilsson and a couple of other younger players to join them. Nilsson was sixteen years old. "We came for two weeks and played a lot of college teams. Some scouts saw me when I was over here."

When Nilsson returned to his homeland, he continued to play for the weekend clubs. At the time, he says, "I think there were two or three scouts in Australia. A part-time scout for the Brewers, Kevin Greatex, just happened to see me."

Impressed with what he saw, Greatex signed Nilsson as a free agent. Because he was from another country, Dave did not have to wait for the spring draft. So on January 28, 1987, just six weeks after his seventeenth birthday, Nilsson signed up to become a member of the Milwaukee Brewers organization.

Not that he knew anything about the Brewers. "I followed American baseball as much as I could, but there wasn't much about it on TV or anything. I had heard of the big guys, like Pete Rose. But I couldn't tell you one person on the Brewers."

Within a few weeks of his signing, he was off to spring training in Chandler, Arizona, to meet a whole camp full of new friends.

What would seem to be a daunting new situation for someone so young did not cause Nilsson much of a problem. As already mentioned, he didn't find the culture appreciably different, and he feels that his upbringing prepared him for being thrust into the adult world. "I was the youngest child in our family," he says. "I was left to grow up on my own because of that. My parents had been through it all five other times, so I was left to do a lot of things on my own."

What Nilsson did find challenging was surviving the economics of minor league baseball. After the extended spring training camp, he was sent to Helena, Montana, in the Rookie-class Pioneer League. There, he and his fellow underpaid major-league-wanna-bes were faced with subsistence-level living. And he found that for the next three years, the lifestyle would not be much different as he went from Helena to Class A Beloit to Class A Stockton.

"Every minor league player goes through periods when he wants to quit and give it up," says Nilsson. "The lifestyle those first three years was difficult. We had very little money. The living standard wasn't much. There would be three or four of us who would put our money together to get a place. It would have no furniture. We used to love to go on the road and stay in hotels, because at least we'd have a bed and a TV and all that stuff."

By the fourth year of his minor league sojourn, Nilsson must have grown accustomed to the living conditions and the pitching, because he had a good year in Stockton in 1990, hitting .290 with 22 doubles. Those numbers were good enough to convince the Brewers to move him past the minor league holding tank that is Class A and give him a shot at Double A.

At El Paso in 1991, Nilsson was hitting an incredible .418

for the Diablos when he was moved up to Denver, then the Brewers' Triple A affiliate. After ninety-four games with Denver, spread over two seasons, Nilsson was ready for the big club.

On May 18, 1992, he arrived at Tiger Stadium in Detroit for his first taste of major league action. In that game, Nilsson belted a double off Tiger hurler Kevin Ritz for his first big league hit.

Injuries would make his first two seasons in the majors a checkered success; but by the time 1994 rolled around, Nilsson had earned his shot at being a regular part of the Brewers. He stuck with the club throughout that strike-shortened season.

It's not been a particularly easy road for Dave Nilsson as he has carved out his major league career far from home. Injuries and that bizarre illness—plus that most American phenomenon, the baseball strike—have taken a chunk of playing time out of his record.

And his first few years with the Brewers were played at a time in the team's history when they weren't in contention for a divisional crown. Yet Nilsson doesn't fret about these uncontrollable circumstances. Instead, he lets his faith dictate his feelings about such things.

"You go out to win every game. But the hard thing to explain is that God is in control. He knows what's going to happen before it happens. But that doesn't stop you from giving a strong effort. At the end of the day, He's in control. Everything is in His timing. I try to keep my focus on trusting God."

No matter if you're a baseball player from America or a cricket player from Australia, that's an attitude that can't be beat. Now, if they could just do something about those mosquitoes.

Q & A WITH DAVE NILSSON

Q: *During the 1996 season, the Brewers lost Kevin Seitzer to the Indians. What was the team's reaction to that situation?*
Dave: Obviously, when you take him away from the team, it changes things, but I think everyone was happy for him. He final-

ly has his chance. We were just pleased for him and his family.

Q: *What goals do you have for yourself individually?*
Dave: I'm not one to set goals. During the course of the season, I might have a week's goal or a month's goal, but I think my goal is to be available to the team every day. I've always been kind of injury prone. I want to be as consistent as I can every day. That's where having Christ gives me the advantage.

Q: *You began as a catcher but have changed positions. What do you prefer to play?*
Dave: I was catching and then I was in the outfield and then DH. I just kind of leave that up to the team. Whatever is best for the team. I want the team to win, and whatever is best for it, that's what I want to do.

Q: *What kind of ministry opportunities do you and Amanda like to get involved in?*
Dave: I manage a baseball team in Australia. With the higher profile I'm starting to get down there, we look at that as a chance to minister. I plan to do a lot of clinics and things like that. We can reach a lot of people with baseball. The main thing we are trying to do is live our lives as best we can to show Christ in what we do.

THE ROAD TO THE MAJORS

• Signed as a non-drafted free agent on January 28, 1987

Minor league stops: Helena, Beloit, Stockton, El Paso, Denver

Minor league highlight: While splitting the 1991 season between El Paso and Denver, Nilsson had the best batting average of a full-season player in the minors (.366).

THE NILSSON FILE

Year	Team	G	AB	R	H	2B	3B	HR	RBI	BB	SO	SB	BA	SLG
1992	Mil	51	164	15	38	8	0	4	25	17	18	2	.232	.354
1993	Mil	100	296	35	76	10	2	7	40	37	36	3	.257	.375
1994	Mil	109	397	51	109	28	3	12	69	34	61	1	.275	.451
1995	Mil	81	263	41	73	12	1	12	53	24	41	2	.278	.468
1996	Mil	123	453	81	150	33	2	17	84	57	68	2	.331	.525
5 Years		**464**	**1573**	**223**	**446**	**91**	**8**	**52**	**271**	**169**	**224**	**10**	**.284**	**.451**

Terry Pendleton
Most Valuable Person

VITAL STATISTICS

Born July 16, 1960, in Los Angeles, California
5 feet 9, 195 pounds
Attended Fresno State University
Position: Infielder
Throws right, bats both
Family: Wife, Cathy, and two children, Stephanie and Terry
1997 Team: Cincinnati Reds

CAREER HIGHLIGHTS

- Played in five World Series (1985, 1993–96)
- Hit a home run in his first at bat as a Marlin on April 25, 1995
- Voted to the All-Star team in 1992
- Named NL Most Valuable Player in 1991
- Hit two grand slam home runs in the 1985 World Series

WARMING UP

Being a leader is tough, and Terry Pendleton knows one reason why. "It's a fight every day because people who are unbelievers are always looking for you to slip up. They're paying more attention to you. People who want to believe, who want Christ, pay close attention to you."

FAVORITE BIBLE PASSAGE

"I can do everything through him who gives me strength" (Philippians 4:13).

Terry Pendleton

t's October 28, 1995, and the Braves are on the verge of capturing their first World Series title since moving from Milwaukee in 1966. In fact, it would be the Braves' first championship since 1957, the year Hank Aaron won the National League Most Valuable Player Award and Warren Spahn won the Cy Young Award.

In 1995, as the Braves await their chance to make the final out against the Cleveland Indians and scamper onto the field in celebration, they too had a Cy Young Award winner—a guy named Greg Maddux.

One person was missing, though, from the mad rush to the infield after the final Indian had been retired and the Braves rushed wildly into a sea of delirious excitement. Missing was their MVP—or at least the most recent Atlanta Brave to win the National League Most Valuable Player trophy. He was at home in Duluth, Georgia, tantalizingly close to Atlanta, but he may as well have been a million miles away.

Terry Pendleton watched that landmark game on television instead of from third base. And when it came down to the final out and the Braves spilled out onto the field, he couldn't watch anymore. An ache the size of Fulton County Stadium filled his heart because he realized that he very well could have been there—moshing in that championship dance.

"I was very happy for the guys," he says, "but I was jealous somewhat. I wanted it."

And why not? It was Terry Pendleton, as much as anyone, who had ushered in a new era of baseball success in Atlanta in 1991.

In 1990, Pendleton had a thoroughly miserable year for the St. Louis Cardinals, a team Terry had been affiliated with since 1982 when they had drafted him after he hit .397 for Fresno State University. That 1990 season was marked first by a damaged hamstring, and then by the arrival of a new third baseman.

A young catcher named Todd Zeile was impressing the Cardinals coaching staff so much that they pulled him out from behind the plate and put him at third during Pendleton's injury. Pendleton never got his job back. In September of that season, Terry made just one start for the Cardinals, making it clear to him that his days in St. Louis were numbered.

Fortunately for Pendleton and the Atlanta Braves, he was a free agent after that season. On December 3, 1990, Pendleton signed a contract with the Atlanta Braves. It was a bold move for the veteran infielder. In 1990, the Braves had finished in last place for the fourth time in the previous five years. They had not won more than 72 of the 162 games on the schedule since 1984. Between 1985 and 1990, they had finished an average of 27 games out of first place. And in 1989, the Braves' record was 65 and 97. This was hardly the kind of team someone would join and expect to contend for a spot in the postseason—let alone play in the World Series.

Incredibly, the long period of Atlanta Braves' ineptitude ended in 1991. And who would lead the charge for them as they climbed from one of baseball's worst teams to one of the game's best? It was Terry Pendleton who carried the banner up championship hill. It was Terry Pendleton who would be a key leader in planting the National League pennant at the top of that hill.

Pendleton's acquisition by the Braves was so important in their resurgence that team general manager Stan Kasten called it "the greatest free-agent signing of all time." A look at TP's performance throughout the 1991 season would lend credence to that grand proclamation.

Although Pendleton hadn't hit over .300 since his first year in the majors in 1984 (.327 in 67 games), and despite the fact that the previous three seasons he had hit .230, .264, and .253, he won the National League hitting title in 1991 with a .319 average. He also led the league in hits with 187. That marked the first time a Braves hitter had sat atop the hitting race since Ralph Garr sang that duet in 1974. Pendleton's .319 average was the best ever for a Braves' third baseman.

In addition to being the first Atlanta player to win the Most Valuable Player award since Dale Murphy in 1983, he was also feted by *The Sporting News* as the National League's Comeback Player of the Year. As if that weren't enough, he led the league in total bases (303) and multi-hit games (52).

Terry Pendleton brought a winning attitude to a team that had had enough of losing. While in the Gateway City, TP had been a part of two teams that had gone to the World Series (1985 and 1987), so he had the wisdom of experience on his side. "He's been the cornerstone of change," Braves' executive John Schuerholz said during the 1991 season.

On his arrival in Atlanta, he instantly became a leader in the Braves' clubhouse—willing to come alongside struggling players and help them back toward success.

Unfortunately for the Braves, another upstart team sneaked into the spotlight at the end of 1991 and denied them a championship. The Minnesota Twins beat Atlanta twice in Fulton County Stadium to capture the sixth and seventh games of the Series and earn the title World Champions. Although Atlanta fell short, Pendleton contributed greatly to the Braves' attack, hitting .367 with two home runs in the Fall Classic.

Despite their disappointment, Pendleton and the Braves were back for another shot at the title in 1992. And again, TP was a key part of the Atlanta attack, knocking in 105 runs, banging out 199 hits, and putting together his second straight .300-plus season. For his efforts, he was voted to the National League All-Star team—the first Brave to be so honored since 1986.

Again the Braves made it to the World Series, and again they were denied the title. This time the powerful Toronto Blue Jays, behind the same pitching nemesis who had done them in during the 1991 Series, Jack Morris, defeated Atlanta four games to two.

Surely 1993 would be different.

This time, however, things didn't look good early. In early May, Terry Pendleton was hitting a measly .148 and the team was playing poorly. But after the All-Star break, TP and his teammates—including new acquisition Fred McGriff—went on a tear, winning 54 games and losing just 19. Pendleton hit nine home runs during a 25-game stretch, and he ended up hitting .272 with 17 home runs and 82 RBIs for the season.

After that hard-fought comeback, the Braves' season would be determined by one game. Incredibly, San Francisco and Atlanta had both won 103 games, and the final game would mean the difference between going on or going home. Playing separate teams, the Braves won, the Giants lost, and Atlanta snagged the division championship again.

In the play-offs, though, the Braves ran into an overachieving Philadelphia Phillies team and lost the National League Championship Series, four games to two. During the series, Pendleton hit safely in all six games, batted .346, and hit his first NLCS home run. He also set records for most career NLCS at bats (129) and games played (32).

Would that surprising loss to the Phillies signal the end of Terry Pendleton's World Series dreams? It sure appeared so.

In 1994, of course, there was no World Series. During the strike, the Braves gave Pendleton his release. Just as the Cardinals' move of Zeile to third had spelled the end of Terry's St. Louis career, so did the Braves' transition of Chipper Jones from short to third make Pendleton expendable again.

Again he was going to a team with a losing tradition, but not even the acquisition of Pendleton could turn the Florida Marlins around in 1995.

And that brings us back to October 28, 1995, with Pendleton at his Duluth home, flipping channels with his brother—unable to watch as his Braves buddies celebrated. It looked as if his World Series dream was as dead as a marlin out of water.

But the story doesn't end there. In a move that shows that front office people in sports do have heart, the Atlanta Braves rescued Pendleton from the Marlins in August of 1996 and gave him another shot at winning a World Series ring when they traded minor leaguer Roosevelt Brown to the Marlins in exchange for him.

"It was a great feeling," Pendleton says about that midsummer dream deal. "My wife, Cathy, and I prayed an awful lot about that. We wanted to be back in Atlanta. Atlanta is home for us. To have God answer that prayer just one day before my wife and kids were going to fly from Miami back home to Atlanta for school, that was great! Believe me, no matter what happened with the world championship, I gained the whole world."

And he's not just talking about baseball, for his whole world revolves around his family and his faith. He and his wife have been married since October 27, 1984. They had dated off and on for nine years before that, having known each other since their days at Channel Island High School in Southern California.

Terry has a tremendous amount of respect for what his wife has gone through in their long baseball odyssey. "My wife has been great," he says. "Through the great times in life, through the bad times in life, through the ups and downs in baseball, she has helped me to know that baseball is not the most important thing. Worshipping Christ and knowing that your family is there for you are the most important things in life."

As with all baseball families, Cathy and the Pendletons' two children, Stephanie and Terry, have had to learn to adjust to an unusual lifestyle.

"People don't understand this game of baseball. First of all, the game of life is tough enough on a wife and kids—just the everyday schedule you have is rough. The game of baseball—or football or basketball—adds triple-time to you. The travel takes players away from home so much. Your kids have things to do, but you're never there for them. Your wife needs you to just be there. To give her that hug. Just to know you're there. But you're not.

"The phone call doesn't do it. The kids don't want to speak to you on the phone. Because you're not there, it's out of sight, out of mind. So it gets tough. But for wives in general, it's tough on an everyday basis. I've traded places with my wife so she could go out while I took care of the kids. Believe me, you can have that job. I don't want it. I have to give wives a lot of credit for what they do."

Despite the drawbacks that come naturally from being a major league player, Pendleton has discovered that his family doesn't view him any differently because of his job. "My kids are great. I can go 0 for 4 and strike out four times, but when I come home, I'm still Dad—regardless of what happens on that field. That's the most beautiful thing in the world."

And for him, the thrill is compounded after a long road trip and he is reacquainted with his home team. "I think back to when my kids were born, and I felt like that was the most awesome feeling in the world. Well, being away from home as much as I am, it feels that way every time I come home. My kids hear the car pull up and they run to the door. I come through the door and they greet me. It's almost like having another child again. It's an awesome feeling."

A picture begins to develop of the kind of person Terry Pendleton is, and it is not hard to see why the Atlanta Braves wanted him back for the 1996 stretch run. A quality player with a big heart—that's just what a team needs as it faces the pressure-packed closing months.

So what is the secret behind this man? Why does he have such a positive attitude? What makes him the kind of man people gravitate toward?

Terry Pendleton would tell you that much of the goodness he exhibits can be traced back to a time most baseball fans look on with a mixture of anger and disgust. While the foundations of baseball were shaking and threatening to collapse, Pendleton was busy reinforcing his own foundations.

"Outside the game of baseball or even inside the game, I'd have to say that my biggest thrill was—and most people frown on this—1994 when we went on strike. When we went out, everybody was talking bad about baseball and the owners and the players and how greedy everybody was, but I had some other business to take care of. The Lord said, 'I'm going to set you aside and I'm going to do something with this heart of yours. You've gotten away from Me, and I'm going to bring you back to Me—back to the way you should be.'"

Soon he got a phone call from Tim Cash, who works with Christian baseball players to help them grow spiritually. "We sat down and talked and talked and talked. I decided that I had to rededicate my life to Christ. I had learned that baseball had pushed me away from Him, from my family, from my kids, and I was more interested in the game of baseball than taking care of my family and focusing on Christ and worshipping Him. That strike was the greatest thing that ever happened to me and my family."

Of course, the strike time off was also when the Braves let Pendleton go and he signed with the Marlins. While playing in Miami in 1995, Pendleton had an excellent season. He provided the kind of leadership the team was looking for, and his offensive game returned to its pre-1994 form. In fact, in his first at bat wearing the Marlin teal, TP blasted a Ramon Martinez pitch for a home run. It marked only the second time in club history that someone had hit a round-trip shot the first time up.

Pendleton went on to set club records for third basemen in games played (129), putouts (104), assists (250), total chances (372), and fielding percentage (.952). At the plate, he batted .290 with 14 home runs and 77 RBI. He was just the kind of leader-player the Marlins needed if they wanted to mold a winner.

The story of Pendleton's relationship with one of the Marlins' top players clearly shows the kind of impact he makes on lives. The player is Gary Sheffield, an outfielder who, despite his incredible talent, has often been seen as a troubled young man.

"Gary's had a lot of trouble in life," Pendleton admits. "But it's not necessarily always his trouble. He stepped in for a relative in a situation and took a lot of the blame for things others have done. Gary and I had lockers next to each other on the Marlins. It was done intentionally. It wasn't my choice—it was the organization's choice, because they thought I could be a positive influence on him."

And the organization was right—TP's influence was significant. So significant, in fact, that in the spring of 1996, TP and

Tim Cash met with Gary, who decided to accept Christ into his life.

"I didn't realize how much of an impact I had made on Gary until I left the Marlins and came back to the Braves. Gary was quoted in a newspaper story as saying that the biggest thing he was going to miss in the new season was me."

Sheffield told Pendleton later that "when things weren't good for me, you always knew what to say."

As Terry Pendleton tells this story, he has to pause because it brings him to tears. It's another indication of the huge, tender heart that has made TP such a respected man in baseball.

Finally, Pendleton is able to continue telling about Gary Sheffield. "It really touched me to hear a person say something like that about me. A lot of people look up to Gary Sheffield. To have him say something like that about me was a great honor."

As we have seen, honors are nothing new to Pendleton. The kind you put on your shelf *or* the kind you put in your heart. He's got them all—well, almost all.

When the Atlanta Braves fished this Marlin out of Miami, the general consensus was that they had brought him back for two reasons: he would help the team down the stretch and the Braves were giving their former main man an opportunity that had eluded him in 1995.

As usual, the Braves were headed for postseason competition, and many felt that they would go into the Hot Stove season with their second straight world championship safely tucked under their belts. And Terry Pendleton would have his first ring.

"I'm happy to be going home," Pendleton said after the trade. Happy also to be going from fourth place to first place in one day.

Yet the storybook ending was never written. It was, after all, the New York Yankees who did the victory dance on the infield at Yankee Stadium. And this time, Terry Pendleton could not flip the channel to something else. He could only sit in the visitors' dugout and watch someone else celebrate the world championship that was finally supposed to be his.

Five times Terry Pendleton had played in the World Series. Five times he had watched the other team grab the ring.

Yet in this story, the protagonist doesn't have to get the big prize to live happily ever after. This man understands life, and he's not about to let something he can't control steal his happiness.

"There are a lot of great players in this game who have never experienced one World Series," he says. "The Lord has given me the opportunity to be in five in of them. You talk about Mark Wohlers being your closer and Greg McMichael being your setup man, which the Braves had in 1996. I think I was the setup man for an awful lot of years. And I don't mind being that.

"The Lord has given me the opportunity to play with some guys and minister to some guys. This game of baseball can be very humbling, as the game of life can be very humbling. But He's really put it on my heart to appreciate what He has allowed me and my family to do with and in the game of baseball and what He's going to allow us to do outside the game. I'm just real pleased to have the opportunities He has given us."

Terry Pendleton is the kind of man all good sports fans hope would get one more chance to bring home the big prize. He seems to be the antithesis of the common perception of today's sports stars, who are often arrogant and self-centered.

Pendleton's friend Tim Cash calls him a "transparent, honest, broken man. He's not an egotist by any means. He's just a real, tender man."

And everyone who has teamed up with Terry Pendleton—whether in a clubhouse or in his home or as his friend—knows that he is more than just a most valuable player in baseball. He's a most valuable person in life—even if he never gets to jump on top of a World Series celebration pile.

Q & A WITH TERRY PENDLETON

Q: *What is your biggest thrill in baseball?*
Terry: My greatest thrill in baseball probably wouldn't be anything *I've* done. It would be in 1992 when Sid Bream rushed home in that play-off game with the winning run to send us into the World Series.

Q: *Who was a big influence on you spiritually as a young player?*
Terry: Rod Booker, who I played with in Double A ball, Triple A ball, and in the big leagues with the St. Louis Cardinals. I met Rod Booker getting on the bus at 5:00 A.M. We were leaving spring training in St. Pete, Florida, to go play Double A ball in Little Rock, Arkansas. I had never met Rod before then. This shows you how the Lord works. Rod came to our ball club because I fractured my wrist and could not play. Rod gets on the bus, walks down the aisle, and he speaks. When he spoke, I knew there was something about him. I knew he was different from other guys on the bus. Rod ended up moving into an apartment next door to me in Little Rock, and I got to spend a lot more time with him. I found out what this man had that I didn't have. He had inner peace, and he knew the Lord big-time. He was my cornerstone through the minor leagues, because he kept me in check. I had to basically be accountable for everything I did. Rod held me accountable and I held him accountable.

Q: *You mentioned Sid Bream. Was he a good friend when you both played on the Braves?*
Terry: I had met Sid Bream when he was with the Dodgers and I was with the Cardinals. I got a chance to play winter ball with him in 1984, but I never really got to know Sid until we spent some years together in Atlanta. Knowing Sid is knowing the way you should walk with the Lord. I have the utmost respect for Sid. I was once asked on live television to compare Sid Bream and myself. I said, "In all honesty, there is no comparison. If I was half the man Sid Bream is, I would do very well by the Lord."

Q: *What is the driving force in your life?*
Terry: It used to be baseball. Now it's praising God and walking and worshipping Him the way He would want me to. The biggest thing for me is that I used to just react to things too fast. Now I think about how the Lord would want me to react. That has made me stronger and has helped my family an awful lot.

It's helped me to minister to other people—or just say a few kinds words here and there to others.

THE ROAD TO THE MAJORS

- Selected by the St. Louis Cardinals in the seventh round of the 1982 draft
- Signed as a free agent by the Atlanta Braves on December 3, 1990
- Signed as a free agent by the Florida Marlins on April 7, 1995
- Traded to the Atlanta Braves for Roosevelt Brown on August 13, 1996

Minor league stops:　　Johnson City, St. Petersburg, Arkansas, Louisville

Minor league highlights: Led American Association third basemen in fielding percentage (.964) and putouts (88) in 1984

THE PENDLETON FILE

Year	Team	G	AB	R	H	2B	3B	HR	RBI	BB	SO	SB	BA	SLG
1984	StL	67	262	37	85	16	3	1	33	16	32	20	.324	.420
1985	StL	149	559	56	134	16	3	5	69	37	75	17	.240	.306
1986	StL	159	578	56	138	26	5	1	59	34	59	24	.239	.306
1987	StL	159	583	82	167	29	4	12	96	70	74	19	.286	.412
1988	StL	110	391	44	99	20	2	6	53	21	51	3	.253	.361
1989	StL	162	613	83	162	28	5	13	74	44	81	9	.264	.390
1990	StL	121	447	46	103	20	2	6	58	30	58	7	.230	.324
1991	Atl	153	586	94	187	34	8	22	86	43	70	10	.319	.517
1992	Atl	160	640	98	199	39	1	21	105	37	67	5	.311	.473
1993	Atl	161	633	81	172	33	1	17	84	36	97	5	.272	.408
1994	Atl	77	309	25	78	18	3	7	30	12	57	2	.252	.398
1995	Fla	133	513	70	149	32	1	14	78	38	84	1	.290	.439
1996	Fla	111	406	30	102	20	1	7	58	26	75	0	.251	.357
	Atl	42	162	21	33	6	0	4	17	15	36	2	.204	.315
13 Years		**1764**	**6682**	**823**	**1808**	**337**	**39**	**136**	**900**	**459**	**916**	**124**	**.271**	**.394**

Andy Pettitte
Baseball's New Houston Rocket

VITAL STATISTICS

Born June 15, 1972, in Baton Rouge, Louisiana
6 feet 5, 235 pounds
Attended San Jacinto Junior College
Position: Pitcher
Throws left, bats left
Family: Wife, Laura, and one child, Joshua Blake
1997 team: New York Yankees

CAREER HIGHLIGHTS

- Won 21 games for the Yankees in 1996
- Led the majors with 11 pickoffs in 1996
- Member of the world championship team in 1996
- Led American League rookie pitchers in victories in 1995

WARMING UP

During the off-season following the Yankees' World Series championship, Andy Pettitte was in great demand in the Houston area—especially in churches. He could have been in a different church every weekend, wowing the congregations with his baseball stories. Instead, he decided that the best place for him spiritually was to be in church, listening to his pastor and helping with the church young people. "I need to grow closer to the Lord," he said. "If I had taken those opportunities to speak, I would never have been getting the preaching I need. I felt like that is what the Lord was telling me to do."

FAVORITE BIBLE PASSAGE

"Mostly, my wife and I like to read the Bible."

Andy Pettitte

Not too many years ago, a young, strong-armed pitcher graduated from a Houston-area high school with dreams of a major league baseball career coursing through his mind. In high school, this young man had been named to the All-State baseball team, and his team had played in the state championship game.

When he was drafted by one of the New York teams in the major leagues after high school, he chose not to sign. Instead, this pitcher went directly from high school to San Jacinto Junior College to continue his baseball pursuit.

Later in his career, he would pitch in the American League All-Star Game and the World Series. And eventually, his name would be connected with the name of Toronto Blue Jays pitcher Pat Hentgen.

Who was this young man?

Two major league pitchers could answer to that description—two pitchers who were born ten years apart in two different states but whose careers have taken parallel paths in many ways.

When New York Yankees pitcher Andy Pettitte was growing up in Deer Park, Texas, a suburb of Houston, he had two pitching heroes. One was Nolan Ryan, the power pitcher who spent much of his career pitching in the Houston Astrodome.

The other pitcher was Roger Clemens.

"I liked to watch Roger pitch," Pettitte says. "I didn't fashion my game after him because I was left-handed, but I enjoyed the way he pitched."

It is the careers of those two pitchers—Roger Clemens and Andy Pettitte—that seem in many ways to be mirror reflections of each other.

- Clemens was born in Dayton, Ohio, in 1962; Pettitte in Baton Rouge, Louisiana, in 1972.
- Clemens's family moved to Houston, where Roger attended Spring Woods High School; Pettitte's family moved to Houston, where Andy attended Deer Park High School.
- Clemens earned All-State honors as a baseball player, and he led his team to the state championship; Pettitte was the Greater Houston Area Player of the Year in 1990, and he led Deer Park to the state finals with a victory in the semifinals. Deer Park lost in the state championship game.
- In 1981, the New York Mets drafted Clemens with the 12th pick of the draft, but he did not sign; in 1990, the New York Yankees chose Pettitte in the 22nd round, but he did not sign.
- After high school, both Clemens and Pettitte spent one year at San Jacinto Junior College as preparation for their next move in baseball.

Of course, their paths took different routes from then on, but similarities continued even in the majors. Clemens pitched in his first All-Star Game and in the World Series and was a Cy Young Award candidate in 1986; Pettitte accomplished these feats in 1996.

How does Pat Hentgen enter the picture? In Pettitte's case, he is the pitcher who went head-to-head against Pettitte for the 1996 Cy Young Award. And the Roger Clemens connection began in the spring of 1997, when Clemens became Hentgen's teammate with the Toronto Blue Jays.

In Clemens's distinguished career, he has earned the nickname "Rocket," and no one would dare bestow that moniker on any other player. Yet there is a sense in which Pettitte is baseball's new Houston "Rocket." His meteoric rise to fame in his first two years in the majors shot him into baseball's top levels, and his live left arm should keep him there for years to come.

As Andy Pettitte thinks back on his road to the majors, he is not afraid to give credit to the people who have helped him move from Little League ball in Houston to the big show at Yankee Stadium. The first person to set him in the right direction was his dad, Tommy.

"My dad always loved sports," Pettitte says of his father, who played mostly football when he was growing up. "He always coached me. He was always a big influence on me."

When Pettitte reached his sophomore year of high school, he concentrated all of his sports attention on baseball, leaving football, a game he liked, behind. "I wasn't very big. I didn't think I would be big enough to play football," says the 6 foot 5 inches 235-pound Pettitte. It was soon after he gave up the gridiron that Pettitte began to fill out. "After my sophomore year, I shot up about five or six inches."

Then it was time for a second mentor to step in and take the budding pitching star to another level. "I had good coaches at Deer Park High School," Pettitte says. "I had a real good relationship with our assistant coach. He was able to help me out a good bit with my pitching."

By the time he was a junior, his size, his newfound knowledge, and his instinctive pitching skills had begun to attract some attention. "I had always dreamed of playing pro baseball, but I never really thought about it until my junior year of high school. That's when the scouts started to talk to me. First, college coaches came and asked me to come to their schools. We were a large high school, so people knew about us."

Pettitte's senior year put a huge punctuation mark on a high school baseball career that just got better and better. His ERA was less than 1.00 that year, and he was named the top high school player in the entire Houston area. And although his team fell to Duncanville in the state championship with another pitcher on the mound, Pettitte's pitching in the tournament continued to impress the scouts—the major league variety.

Before the major league draft of 1990, however, Pettitte signed a letter of intent to attend the University of Texas (it's not surprising that this is the school Roger Clemens attended after his year at San Jacinto). "I didn't really know what I was going to do," Andy says. "But when I got drafted, I realized I didn't want to go to school for three years, which I would have had to do if I had gone to Texas. I wasn't really big on studying." (A player who is drafted and then goes to a four-year school must stay there three years before he can sign.)

So he went to San Jacinto Junior College. "I wanted to go there for a year, and I was hoping that after one year I could go to the pros. I needed to get stronger and throw harder."

At San Jacinto, a third mentor took the fledgling lefty under his tutelage. As head coach Wayne Graham observed his young hurler, he made an observation that seems more than appropriate coming from a coach at San Jacinto: "He's a left-handed Roger Clemens," Graham said. "If anybody will pitch in the big leagues, it will be Andy Pettitte."

Graham should know. He coached both of them at the Texas school.

As far as Pettitte is concerned, Graham's teaching ability was just as accurate as his ability to predict major league success. "I came out of high school throwing 85, maybe 86 miles per hour. Coach Graham had me throwing 92 mph. That was a lot of fastball speed to gain in one year."

The New York Yankees noticed. Because Pettitte had an agreement with the Yanks that no one else could sign him for the first year, he was bound to them. When scout Joe Robison put a contract in front of Pettitte on May 25, 1991, Andy was ready to sign. The extra year of growth had paid off.

At the time Pettitte signed with the Yankees, he was still eighteen years old. Although he had the confidence of his J.C. coach and the assurance that the Yankees wanted him, the biggest confidence builder in his life at that time was his faith. As he headed for his first professional camp, he was another in a growing number of young baseball players who had put their faith in Jesus Christ.

Pettitte's journey of faith had begun seven years earlier. Although his family was religious during the first twelve years of Andy's life, he was not taught the need for a personal relationship with Jesus Christ. That new concept was impressed on his family in 1984 when Andy's sister began attending a Baptist church in Deer Park.

"She started saying that we needed to go to this church, so we did," he recalls. One Sunday the pastor gave an invitation to people who wanted to learn more about Christ to come forward after the service. "I went down front and the people showed me how to be saved."

Andy and his sister weren't the only Pettittes to find salvation at this church. The whole family came and was saved. Later, a friend invited Andy to visit another church down the street from the one they had started attending. When Andy went, he liked what he saw. Well, at least he liked what he saw when he looked at the pastor's daughter. Her name was Laura. They began dating and did so throughout high school.

When Pettitte signed with the Yankees in 1991, then, he left Deer Park with a growing faith in Jesus Christ, a growing love for Laura, and a growing desire to play major league baseball.

The Yankees knew exactly what they wanted Pettitte to do in preparation for that third thing to happen. "They told me coming in that they would want me to throw about 500 minor league innings." Although Pettitte would feel at times that the pace was too slow for his tastes, their guidance seemed to work out just right. By the time Pettitte entered the majors in 1995, he had accumulated 572 innings and had proved that he was ready.

In a minor league career that began with Tampa in 1991 and ended with a brief stint with Columbus in 1995, Pettitte never had a losing record, posting a 42-20 mark in those four seasons with six Yankee farm teams. His 2.56 ERA proved his consistency.

Looking back on his minor league career, two things stand out for Pettitte. First is the source of his success. "It's because the Lord was with me that I was able to do well in the minors. I was putting Him first in my life." That philosophy, like his growing pitching repertoire, has stayed with him throughout his career.

The second thing that stands out to Pettitte about his minor league experience was the difficulty of it all. "I think back about how hard it was. I was married for two years in the minors, and it was tough on my wife. We didn't have much money, and I had to be gone so much. It's a tough road. It is so much different when you get to the majors."

Ah, the majors. For the Pettittes, it was doubly different. Not only were they now thrust into the usual limelight of major league fame, but Andy was also playing in a city known for chewing people up and spitting them out. And he was playing for an owner who doesn't tolerate anything but success. Being a rookie in New York and playing for George Steinbrenner can be hazardous to a young man's health.

"It was a tough transition," Pettitte says. "You're trying to figure out if you belong or not. A lot of people don't make it, and you're wondering if the Yankees are going to stay with you. If you have a couple of bad games in New York, they're ready to send you back down to the minor leagues. It's just a lot of pressure being in New York."

For proof of that, look at the file on former Yankees infielder Bobby Meacham. He was a can't-miss prospect who seemed destined for a grand career with the Yankees. He was dubbed "the Yankee shortstop for the next ten years." Yet between 1983 and 1987, Meacham rode the dreaded New York-to-Columbus (Yanks' Triple A farm team) shuttle nine times—sometimes coming up for one game and then being trucked back to Ohio. Meacham never fulfilled the potential that had been predicted.

Fortunately for Pettitte, he had to make that shuttle trip only once, and even then he knew why it was happening. "They told me I was being sent down just to get a couple of starts in so I could be ready to go into the rotation. It wasn't a big deal for me."

Although Pettitte would eventually experience the same kind of success he had enjoyed at every level of baseball, his first outing as a major leaguer didn't make anyone predict greatness. "The first game I pitched was against Kansas City, and it was freezing cold. I got the first guy out, and I thought, *This is easy*. Then all of a sudden, they scored two runs on me in one inning. I gave up four hits, and I knew it wouldn't be as easy as I thought."

But that trip to the mound was an aberration. He discovered that he really could compete at this level—and even thrive. Pitching in Yankee Stadium, a place that could be a nightmare for young players, Pettitte became a fan favorite. "I love pitching in Yankee Stadium," he says. "When I take the mound at Yankee Stadium, I feel like my stuff is going to be better than ever."

In 1995, Pettitte started 25 games for the Yankees and finished with a 12–9 record and a 4.17 ERA. Besides his ability to get batters out, he also established himself as an expert at getting runners out, too. Pettitte's lightning-quick move to first helped him nab 12 runners who had strayed too far from their base. "I've always had a great pickoff move. I've tried to make my move exactly like I was going to home plate, except step to first."

It was 1996, though, that was his real breakthrough year. From the opening series of the season on, Pettitte was the Yankees' ace. He even won the right to pitch in the Yankee home opener, making him the youngest New York pitcher to do so since 1910 when Hippo Vaughn did the job at age twenty-two.

By fashioning a record of 21-8 during the 1996 season, Pettitte became the first Yankee pitcher in eleven years to win 20 games. The last was Ron Guidry, another Yankee pitcher with Louisiana roots.

By picking up his 15th win in the 99th game of the season, he reached that plateau quicker than any other pitcher in Yankee history. And in one of the most important statistics for a starting pitcher, Pettitte was 13-3 pitching after a Yankee loss. To be the ace of a staff, a pitcher has to be able to stop the team from suffering a losing streak, and he did just that.

Case in point. In early September, the Yankees took off for the West Coast for a long road trip. The Baltimore Orioles had awakened from a season-long slump and were beginning to threaten the lead the Yankees had built up in the East. Twice during the excursion west, Pettitte went to the mound after losses and won for the Yankees—once after a four-game skid.

Yankee manager Joe Torre said at the time, "He's equal to the task every time we lose a game. Not that I look forward to us losing games, but he comes through for us. It is incredible for his limited experience. He's got a resolve about him."

Pettitte's 1996 success is even more incredible when you consider that he pitched much of the time with a sore arm. "That was a tough season for me," he says. "Sure, it ended in a dream, but it was tough. For three months of the season, my arm was hurting so bad I could hardly straighten it after games. I was having a lot of trouble with my arm; but I was winning, so the Yankees wanted me to keep going out there and pitching.

"I don't know what the problem was. My elbow was tender. But eventually, the pain just went away. The doctors never knew what was wrong or why it stopped hurting. By September, I was feeling better."

As the season wound down and the Yankees headed into the play-offs, many baseball experts had Pettitte pegged as a surefire pick to win the Cy Young Award. He had led his team to a divisional crown, he had won twenty-one games, he had picked off eleven runners, and he had helped his team avoid protracted losing streaks.

Yet winning that award was not as important in October to Pettitte as winning something else—the World Series.

Coming into the Series, the Atlanta Braves and the New York Yankees were on two completely different tracks. The Braves had been forced to roar back from a 3–1 deficit against the St. Louis Cardinals, and they had done so in impressive fashion. They had blasted the Cardinals in Games 5 through 7 of the National League Championship Series and appeared to have the energy of a runaway monster truck as they pulled into Yankee Stadium.

The Yankees, on the other hand, cruised through their tussle with Baltimore and were calmly waiting to see who would come out on top in the National League. By the time the Braves had dispensed with the Cards and were ready to begin the World Series, it had been seven days since the Yankees had played a real game.

Game 1 of the series pitted the Yankees' ace, Andy Pettitte, against the Braves' big-time winner, John Smoltz. It was probable American League Cy Young winner vs. shoo-in National League Cy Young winner.

It was no contest. The Braves hammered Pettitte all over Yankee Stadium 12–1, leaving the Yankees looking like pinstriped road kill. "It's beyond me what happened out there," Pettitte said after the game, an outing in which he was pulled in the third inning after giving up seven runs and six hits.

But Andy Pettitte was not done. And neither were the Yankees. Despite being down two games to none after losing the second game to the Braves 4–0 behind the revitalized pitching of Greg Maddux, the Yankees did not die.

By the time Pettitte climbed onto the mound again, the Series was knotted at two games each. Pitching in the last game ever played at Atlanta's Fulton County Stadium, Pettitte again faced John Smoltz.

Instead of a laugher as Game 1 turned out to be, this one turned into a classic. In the fourth inning, the Yankees finagled a run out of Smoltz when Charlie Hayes, who had reached base on an error, scored on a Cecil Fielder double.

In 8⅓ innings against Pettitte, the Braves couldn't come up with anything. In the bottom of the ninth, after Pettitte retired the first batter, Joe Torre came out and gave him the rest of the night off. He knew it was time for his incredible closer, John Wetteland.

For a competitor like Pettitte, it's tough to leave the finishing up to someone else, but if it had to be anyone, his good friend and Bible-study partner Wetteland was just the guy.

Pettitte repaired to the dugout to see if his buddy could preserve the tenuous lead and assure the Yankees of a 3–2 Series lead as the teams headed back to the Bronx. Sitting on the bench, Andy draped a towel over his head and slumped over, his face toward the floor. Noticing this, the TV announcers declared, "Pettitte can't bear to watch."

While that might have been true for many die-hard Yankee fans, that was not the case with Pettitte. He wasn't in denial. He was in prayer.

"I told the reporters after the game, 'I was praying.' They

like to downplay it when you say something like that, but I was just praying. I pray for John every time he goes out there, and I was just praying for him again."

Wetteland made quick work of the Braves, and the Yankees had the Series advantage. When they won Game 6 back at their stadium 3–2, the celebration began. Andy Pettitte, in only his second year in the majors, had accomplished what Roger Clemens had never done—he had captured a Major League Baseball World Series ring.

The Series championship decided, there was one more matter to be settled: Would Pettitte pick up that coveted Cy Young Award—the one everyone thought he should get?

On November 13, the announcement was made. The votes, which had been cast before the postseason began, had been counted. The American League Cy Young Award winner was . . . Pat Hentgen. The Blue Jays' pitcher received 110 points and the award; Pettitte picked up 104 points and a lot of sympathy.

"I was disappointed," Pettitte says. "I had been telling everyone that I really didn't think I was going to win it when the season ended. Then I continued to pitch while the season was over for Pat. So all you heard was people talking about me and how I was going to win the Cy Young Award. I started thinking, *Hey, if everyone says I'm going to win it, then obviously I'm going to win it.* That's why it was a blow for me not to win. Yet deep down inside, when the season ended, I thought Pat deserved it."

For a pitcher as young as Pettitte to come that close in his second year is quite an accomplishment. And because he is young, he may have other opportunities to capture the award.

Whether he does or doesn't, Andy Pettitte has already served notice that it's not odd at all to compare him to his boyhood hero—the original Rocket, Roger Clemens.

After all, the similarities are astounding.

Q & A WITH ANDY PETTITTE

Q: *What do you do to stay strong spiritually?*
Andy: During the season, we try to have fellowship on the team. We stay involved in the chapel program. There were a few of us

in the chapel program, but I wish there were more. During 1996, we had John Wetteland and Joe Girardi and a few others.

Also, my wife and I are involved in a church. When we get home in the off-season, our lives revolve around our church. We both work in the youth department with high school kids during the off-season. It's pretty easy to stay strong then.

Q: *What do you plan to do with your son to help him make it in this society?*
Andy: Stuff goes on now on TV and other places that is different from stuff we had when we were growing up. We try to keep him surrounded by good people and not bad people. We try to keep him at church and hope it will rub off on him.

Q: *Describe Andy Pettitte to someone who doesn't know him at all.*
Andy: I would say I try to be real humble, and I love my family. I would rather be by myself or with my family than in the public and recognized.

Q: *When you speak about your faith to reporters, they often react in unusual ways. Why is that?*
Andy: They don't know what I'm talking about. They ask, "How can you handle the pressure?" and I say, "I put my pressures on the Lord, and let Him take care of them." They don't have a clue what I'm talking about.

THE ROAD TO THE MAJORS

- Selected by the New York Yankees in 22nd round of the June 1990 draft
- Signed as a free agent with the Yankees on May 25, 1991

Minor league stops: Oneonta, Greensboro, Prince William, Albany, Columbus

Minor league highlight: Named Yankee organization Pitcher of the Year in 1994 after posting 7–2 records with both Albany and Columbus

THE PETTITTE FILE

Year	Team	W	L	PCT	G	SV	IP	H	R	ER	HR	TBB	SO	ERA
1995	NYA	12	9	.571	31	0	175.0	183	86	81	15	63	114	4.1
1996	NYA	21	8	.724	35	0	221.0	229	105	95	229	72	162	3.8
2 Years		**33**	**17**	**.660**	**66**	**0**	**396.0**	**412**	**191**	**176**	**244**	**135**	**276**	**4.0**

Tim Salmon
Disney's Top Angel

Born August 24, 1968, in Long Beach, California
6 feet 3, 220 pounds
Attended Grand Canyon College
Position: Outfielder
Throws right, bats right
Family: Wife, Marci, and one child, Callie
1997 Team: Anaheim Angels

CAREER HIGHLIGHTS

- Named to *The Sporting News* All-Star team in 1995
- Tied AL record for most hits in three straight games (13) in 1994
- Hit home runs in four straight games May 11–15, 1994
- Named American League Rookie of the Year in 1993

WARMING UP

Tim Salmon has a rule of thumb about negative press. He will not read it. Or positive press either, for that matter. "I'm kind of naive to what reporters say about me because I stay away from the media. I don't read the paper. It's a good way to go. Every player, whether he's a Christian or not, should abide by that."

FAVORITE BIBLE PASSAGE

Proverbs 3:5–6. "That was the first verse I committed to memory. I thought, *this is a no-brainer. This is what it's all about. This is living by faith. I can't understand everything that's going on around me, but I believe there's a God, and I'm going to trust in Him.*"

Tim Salmon

The California Angels have never won a world championship, but they are going to Disneyland. Actually, they are not just going to Disneyland, they are now part of it. Not only that, they are not even the California Angels anymore—they are the Anaheim Angels.

Decked out in redesigned uniforms that reflect more of the Disney theme than their traditional outfits, these Angels in the outfield and infield are now the baseball cousins of pro hockey's Mighty Ducks. Both teams are owned by the Walt Disney Company and are part sport, part logo—and all entertainment.

Standing tall as a key figure among the new Angels is a player who, if he were given to such shenanigans, could get some great publicity out of his name. If Disney can have Mickey *Mouse* and Donald *Duck*, then isn't it only appropriate that one of their stars is Tim *Salmon?*

But don't look for Tim Salmon to be modeling for the lead story in an animated cartoon anytime soon. It wouldn't fit his style.

Tim Salmon will give the Anaheim Angels his usual 100 percent effort on the field. He'll drive in his traditional complement of nearly 100 runs. He'll pound 30 or so home runs. He'll have a slugging average over .500. And he'll be proud to wear the colors the team's new owners have chosen. But he probably won't agree to let his likeness be turned into a Saturday morning cartoon character.

Don't get the wrong idea. Salmon is no stuffed shirt. He is bright, friendly, and easygoing. And it doesn't hurt that he's big, strong, and handsome. But it's not publicity, untold wealth, and worldwide fame that Tim Salmon is after.

"There's a lot of opportunity for me with Disney owning the club. I could take this thing as far as it can go with marketing and ride off into the sunset," Salmon says, speaking as a former employee of Gene Autry ought to speak. "But the people who know me realize that's not me. I told my agent, 'That's not what I'm here to do. I'm here to play baseball—and my family is a big part of that. I'm not going to allow extracurricular things to take away from that.'"

Salmon seems determined to remain the same person he's always been—despite his fame as one of baseball's best outfielders.

That's one reason he looks forward to returning home to Arizona in the off-season—so he can hook up again with a group of friends who meet for a weekly Bible study. "Just normal people," he calls them. People who will answer a question that nags at Salmon: "Has the game changed me? I want to know, 'How do they see me?' They keep me accountable."

Another reason Salmon enjoys getting away from Disneyland and settling into his off-season home is that his good friend Shawn Boskie, a former Angel, is close by. "Probably one of the biggest influences I have is Shawn. He's one of my best friends. We live close to each other during the winter, so we're really plugged in. We get together and enjoy the fellowship—whether we're talking about faith or not. Here's somebody who believes the same things I do and has the same values. We always keep each other accountable."

But the biggest reason Salmon is jealous of his time—and not so eager to let it go to people who could turn him into a poster boy for what is right about baseball—is a woman named Marci and a little girl named Callie.

"Our philosophy is to be a family during the off-season," says Salmon. "I really try to just pull everything in."

The only tension Salmon feels in this regard relates to his faith. While he will not be lured by big bucks and big names, Salmon does feel the urge to get out and tell others about his faith in Jesus Christ.

"I acknowledge that I have a platform, and I do take the opportunity to speak. I do five or six speaking engagements during the off-season. I'd love to speak to as many groups as I can, but so many people, when they find out that I'm a Christian and a ballplayer, want me to speak. I just can't do them all. My family has to be my priority."

Family has always been important to Salmon—even though the family he grew up in was not as stable and happy as the one Tim and Marci are trying to create. The Salmon family of Tim's boyhood had to deal with divorce. Tim and his brother, Mike, were young when their mom and dad split, and like all children of divorce, they endured some difficult times.

"I kind of bounced around between my mom and dad," Salmon recalls. "I lived in California and Texas with my mom and in Phoenix with my dad. I went to seven different schools." As a result, Salmon wonders, "Maybe I didn't learn as much as I could have if I had stayed in one school."

But despite the hardships, Salmon can see two positive results that came from his nomadic lifestyle as a kid. First, his mom understood the importance of sports in the lives of two boys who didn't have a full-time dad at home and whose mom had to be at work much of the time.

"When we were living with our mother," Salmon says, "we were playing sports all the time, out in the street. She got us involved in Little League and Little Tikes football and soccer. She was a single mom, and she was gone a lot, so instead of having us be home while she was at work, she figured, 'Why not have them out playing?' It was good for us. My brother and I could always sharpen our skills and be together while we did it. Sports was the backbone of our lives growing up. There was always a season going on wherever we went, and that helped us fit in."

And all that sports playing paid off, as both Tim and Mike Salmon have enjoyed careers in pro sports (Mike has played in the NFL).

The second positive aspect of his migratory upbringing was learning how to adjust to new situations and establish new relationships. "I was always in a new environment and I had to make new friends," he says. "I played sports, so I was always having to establish myself every year or every time we moved to a new team. I always came in as the unknown. It was probably more difficult than I remember, but I'm thankful for it. To become a major league player, I've had to establish myself at every level. I developed that pattern as a young kid. I always had to do more than the rest because I was new and didn't have a familiar name."

Tim Salmon began establishing his name while he was a student at Greenway High School in Phoenix. As a senior, he posted a .381 batting average and .905 slugging average and was named to the All-State baseball team. That year, he was also named the Phoenix-area Player of the Year.

In addition, Salmon played in a Babe Ruth League and for an American Legion team. It was while competing in those leagues that Salmon experienced his high-school-era highlights. "One year, I played on a Babe Ruth All-Star team that got to go to the regionals in Utah. The next year, I played on a Legion team that was undefeated. We went to Santa Clara for the regionals. I had more fun on the summer teams than on the high school teams."

It was around that time that Salmon was asked to make a change in his game—one that assisted him in his pursuit of the major leagues. "I started out as a pitcher and a catcher. On one team, another guy and I were the best pitchers on the team— and the best catchers. When one of us was pitching, the other was catching. We were the battery."

A wise high school coach, though, broke up that battery during Salmon's junior year. "Ted Blake was the coach. He moved me to the outfield because he said there were more opportunities to move up in baseball as an outfielder. I started playing outfield that year, and I've been playing it ever since."

Despite Salmon's astronomical stats while at Greenway High, it wasn't as if he were ready to leap straight to pro baseball. He was drafted by the Atlanta Braves in the 17th round—

and they made him an offer he *could* refuse. Their deal would have given Salmon $15,000 and a shot at a future in the game, but Salmon simply was not ready for that step.

"I was really raw," he says. "I was not ready to make that jump. I was not mature."

To make sure he was doing the right thing, Tim called Coach Blake and asked his opinion. Blake suggested that he not turn pro.

Also, Salmon got some advice from an unusual source. "The scout who was there to sign me said, 'I like you, and I think you're going to be a good player, but my recommendation is for you to go to college.'"

Turning down the Braves, he concentrated his efforts on picking a college. Curiously, not many schools recruited Salmon. He did get some interest from local junior colleges, but his preference was a four-year school. The University of Arizona seemed at one time to be interested in him, but they eventually dropped out of the race.

While Salmon was seeking some kind of indication as to what he should do, Coach Blake had a conversation with the coach at nearby Grand Canyon College (now University). "My high school coach and the Grand Canyon coach, Gil Stafford, were good friends, and they always did clinics together in the winter."

At first, it seemed to Salmon that Grand Canyon wasn't all that interested in him. "I didn't really hear much from them," he recalls. He would soon discover, though, that the lack of contact was not because they weren't interested but because they were already familiar with him. They knew so much about him that it took just one recruiting trip for the coaches at Grand Canyon to make up their minds.

"One day the coaches came and saw me take batting practice. When I was done, they said, 'We'll offer you a full ride.' That was really my only offer to a four-year school, and I took it."

What he didn't realize was that his stay at Grand Canyon would represent a watershed time in his life. Of course, Tim expected that to be the case with baseball, thinking he would ride a great college career right into the pros once he was again eligible for the draft. But he didn't expect that his time at Grand Canyon would change his life spiritually as well.

Grand Canyon, a National Association of Intercollegiate Athletics (NAIA) school at the time, had a growing reputation as a sports school. The basketball team would take the national championship under the guidance of Paul Westphal, and the baseball team was strong nationally as well. But what really changed Salmon's life was the fact that Grand Canyon was a Christian school.

"I didn't know a whole lot about Grand Canyon," Salmon explains. "I thought, *It's a four-year college and they have a pretty good baseball team, but we have to go to chapel twice a week.* I decided that wasn't so bad. I wasn't expecting what I found there."

What Salmon found was a fellow baseball player who had a passion for something besides seeking a national championship. His name was Acey Martin, and he was a senior catcher on the team.

"He was a very devout, sound Christian," Salmon says. "You expect that at a Christian school everybody would be a Christian. But they weren't. I wasn't. Acey was pretty outspoken. He took me under his wing—a senior taking care of a freshman. He would always strike up conversations about the Lord."

At the same time, Salmon's exposure to spiritual things was broadened by the chapel services and an Old Testament class he was required to take.

"It was the time in my life when thoughts of God and Jesus were starting to spark in my mind. It was a point when everything was just coming into place. The Lord put everything together at the right time."

Before going to Grand Canyon, Salmon says, he was "a typical jock who loved to party and dated a lot of girls and did the typical things high school kids in my situation would do. When I went to Grand Canyon, playing baseball and the time it took weaned me away from my high school friends."

Away from those influences and touched by what he heard from Acey Martin, professors, and chapel speakers, Salmon decided to trust Jesus as his Savior. "Acey led me to the Lord," Salmon says.

After that happened, many of his former activities lost their pull. "God was showing me that those things were not right if you want to do what God thinks is righteous. God was showing me that I was caught up in a lifestyle that wasn't the best way to please the Lord.

"It was really a maturation of my faith. I won't say I figured everything out my freshman year. But at that point, I decided that I didn't want to go out and party with the guys. Maybe it's best, I decided, that I don't put myself in situations where I'm available to do that."

Tim Salmon had gone to Grand Canyon to find a pathway to the majors. But he found something far more important—faith in Jesus Christ.

But there was more. He also found Marci Hustead.

"She was a very solid Christian woman who came from a strong Christian family," Salmon says. He and Marci began to date a month after he became a Christian. "The Bible says we should surround ourselves with other believers. Well, I had a believer in Acey with me in baseball, I had other Christian friends on campus, and now I was dating a Christian woman. My eyes were opened to the fact that this was a totally different way of dating. She was a great influence on me."

On the baseball field, the new Tim Salmon was the same old baseball player—hitting everything with stitches out of sight. In his three years at the Phoenix school, he compiled these numbers:

1987	.421 batting average	15 home runs	61 RBIs
1988	.382 batting average	17 home runs	63 RBIs
1989	.356 batting average	19 home runs	68 RBIs

Salmon set records at Grand Canyon for runs scored (225), home runs (51), and runs batted in (192).

During his second year with the Antelopes, Salmon led the team to a second-place finish in the NAIA World Series. In addition to his friendship with Acey Martin, Salmon became friends with a fiery player named Chad Curtis. A few years later, Curtis and Salmon would be reunited in the outfield at Anaheim Stadium as Angel teammates.

When Salmon became eligible for the draft this time around, there would be no guesswork. The Angels selected him in the third round of the June 1989 draft. That summer, Salmon paid his Rookie League dues at Bend, Oregon, without giving the Angels any indication of what he would do for them later. He hit just .245 with five home runs, although he did lead the team in triples with five.

That fall, Salmon joined up with Marci for a journey of a lifetime. On November 3, the courtship that had begun three years earlier culminated in their marriage. They didn't know what was ahead of them—whether they would ever see a major league paycheck or not—but they were now in it together.

Salmon would make steady progress toward Anaheim. In 1990, he split the season between Single A Palm Springs and Double A Midland (Texas). The next year, while spending the whole season at Midland, Salmon began to generate the power for which he would later be known, pounding twenty-three home runs for the Angels. Those numbers earned him a trip to Edmonton in the Pacific Coast League, just one step away from the Big A—Anaheim Stadium.

It would be a season most players only can dream about. Salmon demolished PCL pitching by hitting .347 with 29 home runs and 105 RBIs. In addition, he led the league in fielding percentage for outfielders.

Baseball America and *The Sporting News* both named Salmon the Minor League Player of the Year. The PCL named him their Most Valuable Player. And the California Angels, on August 20, 1992, named him a member of their major league team. He's been there ever since.

In the great baseball scheme of things, many great minor league players have swept onto the major league scene only to self-destruct into bit players or washouts. Salmon's first partial season with the Angels could have led some to believe that he would fall into that category. After being called up in August, Salmon hit only .117 with two home runs and six runs batted in.

Yet no one was even thinking about giving up on the big right-handed slugger. From spring training on in 1993, the Angels knew they had a special player.

After struggling through April with just a .254 average, Salmon turned on the guns and got better as the season progressed. He righted himself in May, hitting .294 and raising his home run total to nine. By the time he was done with American League pitching, Salmon had put together one of the best rookie years in California's thirty-three-year history.

Salmon had the third highest batting average for a rookie (.283), the second highest run production (93), the fourth highest hit total (146), and the most home runs (31), doubles (35), extra-base hits (67), and walks (82). It was enough to make Angel fans forget Wally Joyner.

In fact, Salmon's year left him with one prize that no one else can ever claim. He was the first newcomer in Angels' history to be named American League Rookie of the Year.

And it all happened despite some distractions that could have derailed the Salmon express. He endured bouts with kidney stones. He suffered through back spasms. He was hit by a broken bat on June 8 while waiting in the on-deck circle. And on September 15, after hitting a grand slam home run off Seattle's Tim Leary, Salmon broke the ring finger on his left hand while diving for a shot off the bat of Larry Sheets. The injury ended Salmon's season.

What some might call the biggest distraction of all for Salmon during his record-setting rookie year was actually his biggest highlight. And it didn't happen on the field, which Marci was glad about. On June 18, Callie Salmon was born.

The Salmons saw their new responsibility as a gift from God that they wanted to give back to Him. "We pray for Callie every day," Salmon said shortly after she was born. "We pray that she'll come to know the Lord in a way that's even greater than I know Him. She's on loan to us, so the responsibility is to train her in a way that would glorify the Lord."

Life had certainly changed for Tim and Marci Salmon in just a few years' time. They were parents. They were an established major league family. And they would soon be very rich.

After the remarkable rookie year, the Angels inked Salmon to a contract that would pay him several million dollars, and Tim knew the dangers incumbent on him with this newfound wealth.

After signing the deal, Salmon said, "My wife and I talk about how it was only two or three years ago that we were scrapping by in the minor leagues, trusting the Lord for that next meal, and all of a sudden—wow!"

The man who does not want to be changed knew where to turn to keep from letting the big money go to his head. "I feel a tremendous sense of responsibility. I think about stewardship and doing what the Lord would have me do with it, and it's a scary thing. I really have to step up my faith, listen to His Word and guidance so I can use His money well. It is His money, after all."

On the field, Salmon has continued to excel for the Angels. In 1995, for instance, the season that almost resulted in a division title for the Angels, Salmon hit .330 with 34 home runs and 105 runs batted in.

Among the many outstanding feats Salmon has already accomplished in his young career, the one that stands out in his mind was a series of games in early 1994. In May, Salmon went on a hitting tear that he still calls his major league highlight. About a week before, Salmon had been hitting .225. Angels' hitting instructor Rod Carew took Tim aside and told him to be more aggressive.

See if this sounds aggressive. In a three-game span, Salmon went 13-for-15, bringing his batting average up to .336. During the spree, he tied the American League record for hits in three straight games. In those three contests, Salmon homered three times, tripled once, doubled twice, and banged out seven singles. "I was just unconscious," he says of his .867 three-game power play. "It was an unbelievable run."

During Salmon's third year of his contract, 1996, the Angels suffered through a season they would rather forget. Picked by many to win their division after a strong 1995 showing, the Angels never got on track. Unexpectedly poor pitching and untimely injuries spelled doom for the Halos. For Salmon, it was a test of faith.

"My whole foundation of faith is what got me through that year," Salmon says. "The more I experience in life, the more I realize that it seems impossible to survive without God. How can you go through life without any peace, without any foundation—a spiritual foundation in Jesus Christ? I find it hard to understand how you can go through life without a blueprint."

Salmon's blueprint is James 1:2–4. Quoting the verse by heart, Salmon says, "'Consider it pure joy, my brothers, whenever you face trials of many kinds, because you know that the testing of your faith develops perseverance. Perseverance must finish its work so that you may be mature and complete, not lacking anything.' I've held on to that verse because of baseball. Because of all the anxiety and all the tests. It reminds me of the call to persevere."

Tim Salmon has to persevere in ways most people don't ever worry about. He has to persevere in a sometimes immoral world of professional sports to stay true to his faith and his commitment to his wife. He does that by following James 1 and Proverbs 3:5–6.

He has to persevere to avoid letting his numerous awards and accolades go to his head. He does that with Christian accountability partners, with a strong relationship with Marci, and a self-imposed vow not to read what reporters write about him.

He has to persevere against the time-robbers that can reduce his priority list—God, family, the game—to rubble. He does that by dedicating his time to his family and to fellowship with Christians.

Tim Salmon is not perfect, and he's the first to admit it. But he is an Angel, and as the Angels become more and more a part of the Disney entertainment conglomerate, Salmon may be even more in demand.

Can this Angel keep his feet on the ground? There's no doubt about it.

Q & A WITH TIM SALMON

Q: *When you were a kid, did you fashion your game after anyone in particular?*
Tim: Not really, but when I was in high school, we used to watch the Cubs games every day during the summer. That year it was Andre Dawson, Ryne Sandberg—guys like that. We would watch the game and then go out to our games or to the batting cage and try to hit like Andre Dawson or Ryne Sandberg. I was always imitating somebody in my mind—whether I looked like him or not.

Q: *The Angels had several Christians on the team in 1996. What was that like?*
Tim: Our manager, Marcel Lacheman, was a Christian. He was in our chapels. It was great encouragement to see him back Christianity on our team. He wasn't outspoken, but his presence was an encouragement. We had a great group of Christians on our team.

Q: *What do you see as your responsibility to your teammates, other than being the best player you can be?*
Tim: To set a good example for my teammates with my work ethic. The respect I show people, the way I treat them. Being unselfish. I'm being put in a situation where people are watching me, so I need to be on top of my life.

Q: *Who were your baseball heroes while you were growing up?*
Tim: Living in the Los Angeles area, the Dodgers were my favorites—Steve Garvey, Ron Cey, and their teammates. In football, I was a Dallas Cowboys fan. I liked Roger Staubach and Drew Pearson and anybody who played for them in the mid-'70s.

THE ROAD TO THE MAJORS

• Selected by the Atlanta Braves, 18th round of the 1986 draft

• Selected by the California Angels, third round of the 1989 draft

Minor league stops: Bend, Palm Springs, Midland, Edmonton

Minor league highlight: Top minor league prospect in baseball in 1992; named Minor League Player of the Year

THE SALMON FILE

Year	Team	G	AB	R	H	2B	3B	HR	RBI	BB	SO	SB	BA	SLG
1992	Cal	23	79	8	14	1	0	2	6	11	23	1	.177	.266
1993	Cal	142	515	93	146	35	1	31	95	82	135	5	.283	.536
1994	Cal	100	373	67	107	18	2	23	70	54	102	1	.287	.531
1995	Cal	143	537	111	177	34	3	34	105	91	111	5	.330	.594
1996	Cal	156	581	90	166	27	4	30	98	93	125	4	.286	.501
5 Years		**564**	**2085**	**369**	**610**	**115**	**10**	**120**	**374**	**331**	**496**	**16**	**.293**	**.530**

Kevin Seitzer
Opportunity of a Lifetime

VITAL STATISTICS

Born March 26, 1962, in Springfield, Illinois
5 feet 11, 193 pounds
Position: Infielder
Throws right, bats right
Family :Wife, Lisa, and two children, Brandon and Cameron
1997 Team: Cleveland Indians

- Selected to All-Star game twice (1987, 1995)
- Led AL third basemen with .969 fielding percentage in 1992
- Led majors by going 5-for-5 with the bases loaded in 1989
- Finished second to Mark McGwire in Rookie of the Year vote in 1987

WARMING UP

Although Kevin Seitzer's career batting average is nearly .300, he does have trouble with a couple of pitchers. He claims that the two toughest he has had to face are strikeout artists Roger Clemens and Randy Johnson. With Clemens, Seitzer hates to see his "nasty slider" and his "little two-seamer forkball." He says that with Clemens, "98 percent of the time you're going to see his best stuff."

FAVORITE BIBLE PASSAGE

"Consider it pure joy, my brothers, whenever you face trials of many kinds, because you know that the testing of your faith develops perseverance" (James 1:2–3).

Kevin Seitzer

Kevin Seitzer stood gamely before the cameras, responding to questions about one of the saddest days in the recent history of the Cleveland Indians. The favored residents of Jacobs Field had just lost a 1996 American League play-off series to the Baltimore Orioles, which rudely canceled Cleveland's plans for a repeat trip to the World Series. Seitzer, who had been an Indian for only a few weeks but who had quickly become an integral part of the team, was being asked how it felt.

"I thought we were going to win," he said, shaking his head and speaking numbly into the microphone. "I really thought we were going to win."

It was the forlorn response of a baseball player who had worked hard to earn the respect of baseball's decision makers. It was the plaintive cry of one who had toiled for losing teams far too long, forced to prove over and over that he was among baseball's elite hitters. And now, just weeks after he had been given one of the few truly good breaks in his career, he had to explain his feelings of disappointment. What may have been the opportunity of a lifetime had quickly come and gone.

When the Milwaukee Brewers traded Kevin Seitzer to the Cleveland Indians late in the 1996 season, baseball seemed finally to be giving him the advantage he so richly deserved.

"The trade was a surprise to me," Seitzer says. "There was

a lot of talk and a lot of rumors, but that's happened to me before in my career. It seems like things just never panned out. But it seems like this was a case where the Lord just blessed me big time."

What the Lord wants Kevin Seitzer to do is a concept that never strays far from his mind. Steadily growing in his faith since accepting Christ after a Pro Athletes Outreach conference in the late '80s, Seitzer has continually based his decisions about where to play baseball on prayer and faith that God will lead him.

Seitzer had attended that PAO conference in 1988 at the request of his friend from minor league days, Mike Kingery. At the time, Seitzer had just begun to let America know that he was a baseball star. He was discovering, though, that stardom did not ensure happiness. In fact, he was more miserable after having his second straight .300-plus season with the Kansas City Royals than he could ever recall.

"After my second season, my personal problems continued," he says. "I was an alcoholic. My wife, Lisa, was ready to divorce me. Our marriage was over, and my whole life was falling apart. The only thing going well for me was baseball."

Neither Lisa nor Kevin knew that the conference was a Christian event. Kevin said he and Lisa were both shocked when they walked into the conference center and discovered that it was. Yet that wasn't going to deter them. After all, Lisa had told Kevin earlier, "This is our last chance. If this doesn't save our marriage, it's over."

But first it had to save their lives. For Kevin, that statement is not an exaggeration. He admits now that he was so low he had considered suicide.

Seitzer says he knew after hearing the first conference speaker that he needed to turn his life over to Jesus Christ, but it was a tough commitment to make. "I was a proud person," he says. "It would be a big step to turn my life over to the Lord." It didn't take long, however, for him to realize he needed God's help; so that day, he asked Christ to be Lord of his life.

The next day, Lisa, who had been a lukewarm believer for a long time, rededicated her life to the Lord.

Through the years, their marriage has grown strong, as has the Seitzers' faith. In fact, they are sure each step along their baseball journey has been guided by God. So when Kevin finally landed a job on a contending team in late 1996, he knew who had planned it all.

But that wasn't the first time the Cleveland Indians had come calling for Seitzer. In early 1992, the Seitzers didn't know where Kevin would be spending the baseball season. There were even doubts that he would be spending it on a baseball field. The Kansas City Royals had released Seitzer and his .294 career batting average. At age thirty, it appeared that it may be time to find a new occupation. But they weren't ready to give up that easily.

The Seitzers worked the phones, trying to find a team that thought he could help them. New York Yankees? No. Chicago Cubs? No. L.A. Dodgers? No. San Diego Padres? No.

After several rejections, things looked grim. "I thought my career was over," Seitzer says.

Not a chance. The Milwaukee Brewers called the next day and said they were interested in Seitzer's services.

Since the Seitzers had been praying about the decision, they took this call as God's direction. Kevin instructed his agent to take the Brewers' offer, even though no one knew what kind of monetary package they were offering.

"Whatever they offer, take it," Seitzer told his agent. "I don't care if it's the minimum—take it."

Before he could sign on the dotted line with Milwaukee, though, the Cleveland Indians called and offered Seitzer triple the money he would get for playing in County Stadium. Seitzer got together with Lisa for a family conference.

When he explained the situation, Lisa said, "If you think Milwaukee is the place you ought to be, then let's go to Milwaukee."

And that's what they did. Signing for the major league minimum salary, Seitzer agreed to be a Brewer. "It was where the Lord wanted me to be. You talk about being totally at peace! I was ecstatic."

Seitzer's 1992 season with the Brewers seemed successful

statistically. He hit .270, knocked in 77 runs, and demonstrated his usual dependability in the field. Yet when it came time to sign for 1993, the best offer came from the Oakland A's.

Seitzer's stay by the Bay was short-lived. After playing in just 73 games for the Athletics in which he hit .255, Seitzer was released on July 18. Again, it looked like the end of a fine career—left incomplete without postseason play. Eleven days later, though, the Brewers reappeared and offered him a contract for the rest of the season.

Before he suited up for the Brewers, Seitzer made a decision that would affect the rest of his career, as his continually improving batting averages attest. He decided that he had been trying too hard, attempting to prove to everyone how good he was. "I finally just allowed myself to do the things I'm capable of doing," he says.

In Milwaukee, Seitzer hit .290 the rest of the season, getting almost twice as many hits as he had in Oakland in just over half the number of games. He had a new outlook and a brightened baseball future.

Many of today's players would have felt insulted if they were treated the way Seitzer had been. Despite putting up numbers that would garner some players multimillion-dollar contracts, Seitzer often faced being released, neglected, and largely unappreciated. Yet the talented batsman doesn't see it that way.

"I don't feel I've been treated unfairly. Some people might look at it like I've been ripped off. In my mind, I feel like I've been taken care of very well. I feel fortunate. I don't feel like I've been slighted in the least."

Just look at his numbers in 1994 and 1995 and see if perhaps Seitzer deserves to be mentioned among baseball's best. In his first full season back in Milwaukee, Seitzer hit .314 despite missing much of the season because of injuries.

In 1995, Seitzer made the American League All-Star team for the second time, largely on the strength of his .323 batting average before the break. He settled for a .314 average with 69 RBIs to go with his .533 batting average with the bases loaded for the season.

After the 1995 season, Seitzer's options were open once

more. As a free agent, he could have tested the market as did his teammates B.J. Surhoff (Baltimore), Darryl Hamilton (Texas), and Rob Dibble (Cubs). "We had a chance to do a number of different things, and after a lot of long, hard prayer, plus listening to God's prompting and looking for His leading, we opted to stay. That's the way we were being led, and that's what we did."

Seitzer knew he was going back to a club that was not going to be in contention. Despite having a number of good, young players such as David Nilsson, Scott Karl, and Cal Eldred, the Brewers were obviously not ready to challenge for a divisional title. At age thirty-four, Seitzer also knew that his opportunities to play for a contender were running out.

"It was hard to swallow," Seitzer says about that aspect of the decision. "They were in a rebuilding year, and they're young. I'm not really good at taking my lumps."

Early in the 1996 season, it looked like he would just have to take anything manager Phil Garner might throw his way. In fact, the Brewers' skipper had planned to not use Seitzer much during the season. He was breaking in a whole cadre of young talent, and Seitzer was the old man out. In fact, Seitzer was not at all happy with the way things were shaping up in the spring. When Garner told him that his starts would be sporadic at best, Seitzer was upset.

"I was really mad," he says. "But I went home and thought about it. I was wrong."

He decided that he would be a lousy example to the young players on the team if he pouted and griped. Good thing he didn't bust up the watercooler or turn the bat rack into toothpicks, because he never really had to sit on the bench. An injury to the Brewers' young first baseman David Nilsson put Seitzer in the lineup to start the year.

After the first six games, Seitzer was hitting .458, and he was a regular again. When forced to prove his worth once more, Seitzer handled things the best way he knows how—by hitting the baseball with authority.

Seitzer's feelings about the way things would go with the 1996 Brewers were right on target. The young players were not able to make a run at the American League Central Division title, but his presence was valuable as much off the field as it was on.

"The one thing God taught me during 1996 was that nothing—difficulties and trials and hard times—takes place that's not filtered through God's hands first. I've learned to count on that and trust in that. Just because you're going through hard times doesn't mean you're being punished or disciplined. You've got to look at it as something God knows. He understands. It's going to cause you to mature and strengthen you in your faith. Sometimes He's just trying to find out, 'How much do you really trust Me?'"

Some would say that Seitzer's trust paid off late on August 31, 1996, when the Cleveland Indians finally closed the deal they had been trying to make for a long time. Just minutes before the end of the deadline for obtaining players and having them still be eligible for postseason play, the Tribe sent outfielder Jeromy Burnitz to Milwaukee for Seitzer.

Kevin stepped into the second spot in the Cleveland batting order, sometimes playing first base and sometimes being the designated hitter.

Besides enjoying the new atmosphere of playing at popular Jacobs Field and competing on a team that was one of baseball's best, Seitzer also felt a sense of relief from some of the responsibilities that he carried at Milwaukee. "I was off the hook as the player representative, as the team chapel leader, and as the clubhouse spokesman. I could just play baseball."

His impact on the Indians was felt immediately. In the 22 games he played between the trade and the end of the season, Seitzer hit .386, had a 12-game hitting streak, and compiled a .542 slugging average. Best of all, in the game in which the Indians clinched their division, Seitzer belted a grand slam home run.

Mike Hargrove was happy with his new DH-first baseman for reasons that go beyond his good stick. Hargrove noted that Seitzer never made excuses, was always positive, and loved to talk about baseball. He called him a "breath of fresh air."

As Seitzer waited to face the Orioles, he could easily have complained. His left knee was severely injured. "It's blown pretty good," Seitzer said at the time. "But I've given it to the Lord. He knows how bad I want to be there. I've told Him that they're going to have to drag me off the field to get me out of there, but I would sure like to have that pain go away."

Pennant fever was something new for Lisa Seitzer as well. Like Kevin, she'd never had to worry about the stress and hubbub of late-season contention for first place. Perhaps that's why when Kevin one night said something to Lisa about the Indians' magic number (the combination of wins by the first-place team and losses by the second-place team that are needed to ensure that a team will finish first), she responded, "Magic number? What's that?"

The magic ended for the Indians on that October night when Seitzer was left explaining to reporters his new feeling of what might have been.

Time, and the conditions of Seitzer's knees, will tell if he will get another chance at postseason success, but the thought stays with him. "Making a couple of All-Star teams was good, but I don't like individual stuff," he says. "I want to say I won a championship—a team thing, a team goal, a team trophy."

Yet Seitzer doesn't seem to be the kind of man who will hang around at all costs to get that championship ring. He's got other priorities. "Being a dad is a highlight for me. It's really difficult when I'm away. It's a tremendous burden on my wife to have to do everything herself. I feel bad about that because my two sons need me at home. They get to an age when they try to rule the roost. I've had some long-distance discussions with them. I've threatened to get on the plane and come home to take care of things."

When Seitzer *is* home, he enjoys playing ball with his sons. "We play baseball. We play basketball. Or they'll make me be the hockey goalie and take shots on me. They just like to play with Dad."

It's not surprising, then, that Seitzer wants people to remember him not so much for what he does in baseball, but what he does at home. "I want to be a man of conviction—a man who has no compromise as far as his faith goes. I'm not as concerned about being remembered as a great baseball player as much as being remembered as a great Christian, husband, and father."

For Seitzer, that's the true opportunity of a lifetime.

Q & A WITH KEVIN SEITZER

Q: *What does Major League Baseball have to do to get the fans back?*

Kevin: A basic agreement will really launch things in the right direction toward winning their hearts back. Everybody's going to have to make some concessions for the fans, because they're the ones who have been stomped on in this whole thing.

Q: *What do you plan to do when your career is over?*

Kevin: Mike McFarlane and I have purchased an indoor baseball facility in Kansas City. We're going to teach baseball there. We have seven batting cages, four instructional tunnels, and three coin-operated pitching machines. I'm hoping that will be a stepping-stone into a ministry. We're going to be spending a lot of one-on-one time with kids. And we'll include other players, such as Joe Carter.

I don't foresee staying in baseball as a coach, but the Lord is in control. I'll go wherever He wants me to go.

Q: *What is the off-season like for you?*

Kevin: We get involved in small-group Bible studies at our church. Besides attending church, I do some speaking, but I try to keep that to a minimum. The season is so hard on a family. We really take that time to be together and to catch up. The household just goes to pot the seven and one-half months I'm away. The list of my to-do chores is very long when I get home.

Q: *What has been a spiritual highlight for you?*

Kevin: I was scheduled to speak at a father-son banquet. I had laryngitis the day before, but I knew I had to go. I took my eight-year-old son Brandon with me because he hadn't heard me speak before. By the grace of God, when I walked up on stage, I got my voice back enough to speak for thirty minutes. But best of all, my son made a decision that night to accept Christ as his Savior.

THE ROAD TO THE MAJORS

• Selected by the Kansas City Royals in the 11th round of the 1983 draft
• Signed by the Milwaukee Brewers as a free agent in 1991
• Signed by the Oakland A's as a free agent on February 1, 1993
• Released by Oakland on July 18, 1993
• Re-signed by Milwaukee on July 29, 1993
• Traded to the Cleveland Indians on August 31, 1996

Minor league stops: Butte, Charlottesville, Fort Myers, Memphis, Omaha

Minor league highlight: Led South Atlantic League third basemen with 409 total chances in 1984

THE SEITZER FILE

Year	Team	G	AB	R	H	2B	3B	HR	RBI	BB	SO	SB	BA	SLG
1986	KC	28	96	16	31	4	1	2	11	19	14	0	.323	.448
1987	KC	161	641	105	207	33	8	15	83	80	85	12	.323	.470
1988	KC	149	559	90	170	32	5	5	60	72	64	10	.304	.406
1989	KC	160	597	78	168	17	2	4	48	102	76	17	.281	.337
1990	KC	158	622	91	171	31	5	6	38	67	66	7	.275	.370
1991	KC	85	234	28	62	11	3	1	25	29	21	4	.265	.350
1992	Mil	148	540	74	146	35	1	5	71	57	44	13	.270	.367
	Oak	73	255	24	65	10	2	4	27	27	33	4	.255	.357
1993	Mil	47	162	21	47	6	0	7	30	17	15	3	.290	.457
1994	Mil	80	309	44	97	24	2	5	49	30	38	2	.314	.453
1995	Mil	132	492	56	153	33	3	5	69	64	57	2	.311	.421
1996	Mil	132	490	74	155	25	3	12	62	73	68	6	.316	.453
	Cle	22	83	11	32	10	0	1	16	14	11	0	.386	.542
11 Years		1375	5080	712	1504	271	35	72	589	651	592	80	.296	.406

John Smoltz
Best in the Business

VITAL STATISTICS

Born May 15, 1967, in Warren, Michigan
6 feet 3, 185 pounds
Position: Pitcher
Throws right, bats right
Family: Wife, Dyan, and two children, John Andrew Jr. and
    Rachel
1997 Team: Atlanta Braves

CAREER HIGHLIGHTS

- Named to four All-Star teams (1989, 1992, 1993, 1996)
- Received the Cy Young Award as best NL pitcher in 1996
- Led NL pitchers in strikeouts with 215 in 1992
- Won the game that clinched the NL West championship in 1991

WARMING UP

John Smoltz does not read the newspaper—at least not the sports page. His wife, Dyan, does keep a scrapbook of articles for the kids, but John will not read them. What's more, he does not listen to the sports pundits on the radio. "I used to listen to sports talk radio for fun, but then I would hear something I didn't want to hear and it affected me later on. Now I don't listen to any of it."

FAVORITE BIBLE PASSAGE

"I am the vine; you are the branches. If a man remains in me and I in him, he will bear much fruit; apart from me you can do nothing" (John 15:5).

John Smoltz

When baseball fans think of the 1996 baseball season, most cannot help but think about John Smoltz, winner of the National League Cy Young Award and the most overpowering pitcher in baseball.

As they think about the remarkable achievements Smoltz compiled during his eighth full year in the majors, they also should consider what the year *might* have been for the lanky right-hander from Lansing, Michigan.

The year 1996 could have been another big year for John Smoltz on the accordion. Perhaps he could have cut a brand-new polka CD or been a big hit on the accordion circuit, playing smoke-filled rooms across the Midwest.

Or 1996 could have been a summer of anonymity and lost causes as a pitcher for the team with the worst record in baseball—the Detroit Tigers. With John Smoltz on the mound going 24–6 for the Tigers, they still would have finished 15 games out of first place.

Then again, 1996 could have been another roller-coaster year for Smoltz with the Braves—like the one he had in 1991, when he was 2–11 before the All-Star break and 12–2 after it.

But none of those "what ifs" happened for Smoltz in 1996, and for good reason. It was a new John Smoltz who took the mound in April of that year—a pitcher with a fresh outlook on life, a revitalized right arm, and an improved approach to the game.

Before looking into that remarkable season and exploring what really was, what about those "might have beens"? What's the story behind those?

First, the accordion possibilities. Smoltz was born into a musically inclined family that lived near Detroit. Both his dad, John Sr., who is now the owner of an electronics shop, and Mary, his stay-at-home mom, were accordion teachers. John Jr. simply followed in their footsteps. "I was started on the accordion when I was four years old, and I played until I was seven," he says.

And he was very good. His parents entered him in accordion contests—even traveling as far away as Chicago to compete—and he often won. It was good to learn about road trips to Chicago at a young age, because he'd be taking quite a few of them later.

Despite what appeared to be a prodigious talent on the squeeze-box, John Jr. lost interest as he got older. "At seven years old, I told my parents that I didn't want to play it anymore. I wanted to play sports. I'm thankful they allowed me to do that." So are several million Braves fans.

Smoltz is lavish with his praise for his family, for besides allowing him to follow his sports interests, his family gave him a solid foundation in moral living. "I grew up in a strong family," he says. "I really believe they are the biggest reason I'm where I'm at and the person I am. We did a lot of things together. Also, from day one I was brought up to know that there are some things that are right and others that are wrong. It was a God-fearing atmosphere. It gave me a jump-start to knowing what's right."

Once Smoltz got unhooked from the accordion and hooked on baseball, he was sure that's where his future lay. "Ever since I was seven, I said I was going to be a major league baseball player." Later, Mary Smoltz took John aside and told him that it was fine to have a dream, but it was wise to have something else to fall back on if the dream doesn't come true.

"A gas station attendant looks like fun," he told her. All she could say was that he probably shouldn't tell his dad about that.

Smoltz didn't have just vague dreams of playing baseball; he wanted to play for the Detroit Tigers. "I grew up idolizing all the guys there," he says. "My grandfather worked at the stadium for twenty-one years."

Plus, he got a taste of championship fever in 1984 when his favorite team won the World Series.

As a senior at Lansing Waverly High School, Smoltz demonstrated his growing chances at fulfilling his major league dream by making the All-State baseball team. In addition to his high school success, Smoltz also played on the U.S.A. Junior Olympic team, winning gold, and in the National Sports Festival, winning silver.

Those successes captured the attention of the Tigers, and in September of 1985, Detroit signed Smoltz to a free-agent contract. He was on his way to fulfilling his dream. "I thought, *Wow, this is it! Now I'm going to play for the team I've always wanted to play for.* Not many kids get a chance to do that."

In 1986, Smoltz began his career by playing for Lakeland in the Florida State League. Right away, he let the Tigers know they hadn't made a mistake; he won his first three games and allowed just one run in his first eighteen innings of work. The rest of the season didn't go quite as well, and he finished the season with a 7–8 record and a 3.56 ERA. Still, *Baseball America* magazine rated him the sixth-best prospect in the league.

Glen Falls, New York, was the next stop on his dream quest to the majors. Playing Double A baseball, he again impressed people with his live arm and pitching maturity. Along with the Yankees' Al Leiter, Smoltz was considered the best pitching prospect in the Eastern League. This recognition came despite his 4–10 record and 5.68 ERA.

The record didn't matter, though, because everyone knew that John Smoltz was the pitcher of the future for the Tigers. Yet in 1987, the Tigers were more interested in the present. They were in a dogfight for first place in the American League East, and they needed another pitcher to go with their staff of Jack Morris, Frank Tanana, Walt Terrell, and Dan Petry. So on August 12, the Tigers handed Smoltz over to the Atlanta Braves, a team that seemed to be going nowhere, for Doyle Alexander.

Alexander went on to win ten straight games for the Tigers and help usher them into the play-offs as they sneaked past Toronto on the last day of the season. The Tigers proceeded to lose to the Minnesota Twins in the play-offs, and Alexander was never an important factor with them again.

At first, Smoltz was stunned that he'd been shipped out of Detroit. "I was twenty years old when the trade happened, and it was devastating for me. I didn't think *trade* meant *good.*"

Yet he would soon discover that it was the best move for him.

The Braves moved him immediately from Glen Falls to their Triple A team at Richmond. Less than a year after the trade, Smoltz was a member of the Atlanta Braves pitching staff, and he was only twenty-one years old.

"Atlanta gave me an opportunity to pitch at a young age with nothing to lose. They wanted me to gain experience. Also, they had a tremendous amount of good coaching and help I didn't receive in the Detroit farm system. One person who really turned my career around was Leo Mazzone [his pitching coach at Richmond]. I went to the majors and took my lumps and went through the tough times. I don't really think my development would have sped up in the Detroit organization."

With his accordion days a distant memory and his dream of playing for the Tigers gone, but not reluctantly so, it would remain to be seen what direction his baseball career would take.

But first a small romantic interlude.

One of the first—and perhaps best—results of Smoltz's move to the Braves organization was his meeting Dyan Strubel, a young woman from Atlanta. While playing for the Richmond Braves in 1988, Smoltz took a message for a roommate who had gone to school with Dyan at Georgia.

That summer, Smoltz was called up to Atlanta and got an opportunity to meet Dyan. They became friends, then began dating, and then got married in 1990.

In the meantime, Smoltz was beginning to carve out his pitching career for a team that was anchored at the bottom of the National League West. In 1988, his first year in Atlanta, the Braves were 54–106. The following season, they improved a bit, going 63–97. In 1990, they virtually repeated that record, compiling a 65–97 mark.

John Smoltz had been in the league for three years and his team had finished last, last, and last in the West. "No matter how much money you make and no matter what perks you receive, you hate losing. Losing is no fun."

Yet all was not disastrous. In 1989, Smoltz put together an 11–6 record before the All-Star break and was rewarded by being named the youngest All-Star pitcher in Braves history at age twenty-two. Only Hank Aaron and Eddie Mathews appeared as Braves in an All-Star game at a younger age.

Unfortunately, he was saddled with the loss as the National League All-Stars dropped the midsummer classic to the American League 5–3. And even worse, that loss foreshadowed things to come, for he would go 1–5 the rest of the season.

Despite the All-Star game loss, Smoltz looks back on that event as a career highlight. "For everybody who has watched or played baseball and hoped one day he could be good enough to play at the major league level, the All-Star game is a goal. It was a dream come true. It was my first full season in the big leagues. I thought for a little while that I was the chosen one because I got called up and won my first major league start—and proceeded the next year to make the All-Star team."

The up-and-down season that transpired for Smoltz in 1989 was, unfortunately, not a one-time situation. For some reason, it became a pattern. In 1990, he was 3–6 before turning things around to finish 14–11.

In 1991, Smoltz went 2–11 in the first half and 12–2 in the second. And even in 1992, when he finished 15–12, it took an 11–2 run from May to August to keep his record above .500. Batters are often noted for being streak hitters, but Smoltz had mastered the art of being a streak pitcher.

For the young Atlanta pitcher, though, there was a great measure of success in those two years as the Braves were suddenly transformed from worst to first. "In 1991 and 1992, we caught everybody by surprise. We made it to the World Series."

After the 1991 season, Smoltz knew something had to be done about his roller-coaster pattern. "That year was very difficult for me as far as my focus, thinking, and perspective," Smoltz says.

Looking for help, he turned to sports psychologist Jack Llewellyn, who helped John deal with his adversity and maintain his concentration. This helped, but it was, he says, "a temporary Band-Aid" for his career.

"I'm not discrediting it or saying it didn't help me, because it did," he says. "But it snowballed in the media. They made it look like I sat down and the psychologist gave me a book about the little choo-choo that could, and the rest is history. But it was just temporary."

In fact, John continued to struggle. Cursed perhaps by grand potential, he couldn't seem to produce the numbers that others—and he himself—wanted.

Even as the team continued its upward climb, finally winning it all in 1995, Smoltz couldn't quite get over the hump. He was a fine pitcher, to be sure, but he was only eight games over the .500 mark in his career after eight seasons.

It would take a combination of factors to help him become, for 1996 at least, the best pitcher in baseball. Without this convergence of circumstances and inner changes, the 1996 season for Smoltz may have been similar to his previous seasons—a mixture of success and failure.

Yet that was the year everything finally came together for him. You can look back over baseball history and not find many pitchers who have had the remarkable success Smoltz enjoyed in his enchanted Cy Young season.

Consider these amazing statistics: Career bests in wins (24), ERA (2.94), innings pitched (253.2), strikeouts (276), and walks (55). It had been twenty-four years since a Cy Young winner had won as many games. It had been ten years since a Cy Young winner had struck out as many hitters. In the postseason, he won four more games, giving him nine postseason wins in his career.

So what turned things around for John Smoltz? It was a combination of physical, mental, and spiritual changes.

First, the physical aspect. In 1994, Smoltz began to experience pain in his pitching arm. In August, he missed a start against the Colorado Rockies because he developed fluid in his elbow. He also had a bone spur in the elbow, a condition that he had pitched with since 1991. At the time, he was 6–10 with a 4.14 ERA and had won just one of his previous five starts.

Three days before the baseball strike began, Smoltz was sent home from Denver. He was planning to pitch with the spur if the season resumed and then have it removed during the off-season. When it was decided that the season would not continue, Smoltz had the surgery on September 8. Dr. Joe Chandler, the Braves' orthopedic surgeon, removed a large bone spur and some chips from the back of John's elbow.

The 1995 season started late and spring training was shortened because of the strike, which did not allow Smoltz the time he needed to get his arm completely ready. Yet he was greatly encouraged by the way he felt.

Despite the late start, the improvement was evident as Smoltz put together a 12–7 season and never allowed more than four earned runs in an inning. He was five games over .500 for the first time in his career, and he was pitching without pain for the first time in years.

"I've never felt better," Smoltz said in July 1995. "I never knew my arm could feel like this. Now that I've had my surgery, my career is ahead of me."

Pitching coach Leo Mazzone echoed the euphoria: "He's pitching as well as he ever has."

Besides overcoming the physical problems that had plagued him for several years, Smoltz also had to defeat the mental letdowns that affected his mound performance. To do that, he had to make both mental and spiritual decisions. John describes what went on in his mind and his heart as he struggled with the inner conflicts that did as much damage to his pitching as bone spurs did to his arm.

"As an athlete, you tend to think that you are in control. You have a work ethic, you have goals, and you have an ability that God has given you. But the way I thought and the way I approached baseball consumed me. I thought baseball was something God gave me the ability to play and the rest was up to me—it was up to me and my ability to take over every problem."

Smoltz talks about an incident at the end of the 1991 season that demonstrates how his thinking process at the time caused more harm than good.

"In 1991, it was time to negotiate my contract. During that tough off-season of negotiating a contract I had the wrong perspective, the wrong focus. I was focused on me and my ability.

"Baseball became the sole thing in my life. I was taking it home to my wife, who couldn't care less whether I won or lost. To my newborn son, who couldn't care less if I won or lost. To my dog, who definitely couldn't care less if I won or lost. Baseball ended up messing with my mind and confusing me about what was important. I truly believe that's why I started out 2–11 in 1991."

That year and 1992, of course, were the years when the Braves were beginning to enjoy their newfound success. For Smoltz, though, there was more going on than the celebrations seemed to show.

"The World Series and the All-Star games sure seemed great at the time," he recalls. "It seemed like nothing could get better. But no matter what I put my emphasis on and no matter what I put my time and focus on, there was something wrong. I wasn't able to handle the problems that came with it. I wasn't able to handle the media that so much consumed me and ate me up and spit me out."

John Smoltz was trying to handle life alone. He had a beautiful wife who could help him. He had a Savior who could help him. But he wanted to do it all himself. "I felt that I could take it all in. I felt that I could handle it. Quite honestly, I felt like I was letting God down—like He gave me the ability, and I was blowing it."

This time when Smoltz needed help, he didn't turn to a sports psychologist. He turned to some friends who could give him a permanent solution—friends like Tim Cash, a former minor league player who disciples players in the Atlanta area, and Mike McCoy, a former NFL player who does the same. They helped Smoltz see that the answers are found in a trusting relationship with Jesus Christ and a dependence on the teachings of God's Word.

"Jesus Christ definitely is my personal Savior," Smoltz says.

His journey to faith, he says, started with confusion about what Christianity meant and ended with his commitment to Christ.

"I thought doing good works and being nice was going to get me to heaven. When I was a kid, I always tried to do what was right. I found out through the help of so many great players and through Tim and Mike that that's not what it's all about.

"A relationship with Christ takes more than going to church and knowing that there's a Bible and saying, 'Okay, I know what's right—sooner or later I'll make some changes in my life.' I've seen people turn their lives around. I've seen born-again Christians talk about how they are so excited and how they've changed. But some people think, *I'll wait until I'm thirty or thirty-five, until baseball's over and all those problems are behind me, and then I'll turn my life around.*

"But then someone said to me, 'You may never see that day. You don't control the next breath and the next move and what goes on in your life.'"

That's when he made his decision to follow Christ. And beyond learning about salvation, he also learned about the help Christ can provide.

"One thing I know is that since my relationship's become vertical, since I've improved my relationship with God, I know He's going to deal with my problems. I've been freed up to know that I no longer have to carry the world's problems.

"I no longer have to listen to the radio and say, 'That guy said something false about me. I'm going to have to prove him wrong.' I can now can sit in the locker room and listen to these reporters talk about these things that used to consume me and make it difficult to perform to the best of my abilities. In a sense, my walk has changed."

In addition to finding strength from his faith, Smoltz has learned in recent years that the Bible is the source for knowing how to live. "The Bible is where the answers are. It will never change. That where I find guidance and direction."

John Smoltz no longer dwells on baseball for his happiness. He no longer seeks to take all of his problems on by himself. "You see baseball and you see the statistics and some of the things that I've done—but my heart knows that there's more in life than baseball or winning fourteen games in a row. I no longer rely on people or the game or what life can give me. Now I rely on the Lord."

The 1996 season proved to John Smoltz that life doesn't have to be full of unfulfilled potential and frustration. He reached the top of his game—and the top of his life. "He's at peace with himself now," Dyan Smoltz says of her husband. Which makes life a lot easier for everybody concerned.

Q & A WITH JOHN SMOLTZ

Q: *What was your initial reaction in 1987 when the Tigers traded you to the Braves?*
John: It was a shocking, eye-opening time for me. It was frustrating. I didn't feel like I was wanted by an organization, but I was wanted by another one. All in all, it ended up being the best thing. It gave me a chance to pitch at a younger age quicker than I ever would have with the Tigers. And it brought me to an organization that I think is one of the best in baseball.

Q: *Your profession has the downside of a loss of privacy. How does that affect you?*
John: Basically, privacy doesn't exist anymore. Some people might think that money can take care of every problem, but it's not true. There are things I don't like that are just accepted as part of the job, and one is that you basically have no private life to speak of. It's not the individual who is an inconvenience; it's the twenty individuals behind him. Once one person breaks the ice and asks for an autograph, the other twenty follow. But I try to accommodate people.

Q: *Who is the toughest hitter you face in the National League?*
John: The obvious one would be Tony Gwynn. I respect him so much as a hitter. The hitter you would least want to face with the bases loaded and two outs is Tony Gwynn.

Q: *What kind of pressure do you face as a Christian to live the right way?*
John: People are always going to judge you as a Christian, and they're going to wait for you to do something wrong. That's why it's a constant struggle to make sure you're doing the right thing. It's got to come from within. It's got to be something you're willing to accept and make a sacrifice for.

Q: *How has your wife been a help to you in your career?*
John: Dyan and I have both grown over the years. She has been through so much with me as a major league baseball player. It's not been easy. In 1991, 1992, and 1993, baseball consumed me more than I would have liked, and I'm sure more than she would have liked. She's been patient and such an encouragement. When we finally won the World Series, she had this look like, "It's over. We don't have to talk about that anymore." She has been there when times have been tough. God gave me her as an anchor.

THE ROAD TO THE MAJORS

- Signed by the Detroit Tigers as a free agent on September 22, 1985
- Traded by the Tigers to the Atlanta Braves for Doyle Alexander on August 12, 1987

Minor league stops: Lakeland, Glen Falls, Richmond
Minor league highlight: Named International League's top major league prospect in 1988

THE SMOLTZ FILE

Year	Team	W	L	PCT	G	SV	IP	H	R	ER	HR	TBB	SO	ERA
1988	Atl	2	7	.222	12	0	64.0	74	40	39	10	33	37	5.48
1989	Atl	12	11	.522	29	0	208.0	160	79	68	15	72	168	2.94
1990	Atl	14	11	.560	34	0	231.1	206	109	99	20	90	170	3.85
1991	Atl	14	13	.519	36	0	229.2	206	101	97	16	77	148	3.80
1992	Atl	15	12	.556	35	0	246.2	206	90	78	17	80	215	2.85
1993	Atl	15	11	.577	35	0	243.2	208	104	98	23	100	208	3.62
1994	Atl	6	10	.375	21	0	134.2	120	69	62	15	48	113	4.14
1995	Atl	12	7	.632	29	0	192.2	166	76	68	15	72	193	3.18
1996	Atl	24	8	.750	35	0	253.2	199	93	83	19	55	276	2.94
9 Years		**114**	**90**	**.559**	**266**	**0**	**1804.0**	**1545**	**761**	**692**	**150**	**627**	**1528**	**3.45**

Kurt Stillwell
Born to Play Ball

VITAL STATISTICS

Born: June 4, 1965, in Glendale, California
5 feet 11, 185 pounds
Position: Infielder
Throws right, bats both
Family: Married to Angela
1997 Team: Texas Rangers

CAREER HIGHLIGHTS

- Selected to National League All-Star team in 1988
- Drove in five runs against Minnesota, including a grand slam home run, on May 25, 1991
- Tied Royals record with three doubles in one game on April 26, 1990
- Selected to *Baseball Digest's* All-Rookie team in 1986

WARMING UP

Kurt Stillwell made the CNN Play of the Day once for a fielding opportunity. "I was chasing a foul ball down the third-base line at full speed and watching only the ball when I ran smack into the umpire. It felt like I ran into a brick wall. The umpire was Vic Voltaggio, who is about 6 feet 5 inches tall, and my chin hit his shoulder. I dropped like a rag doll to the turf. No, I didn't catch the ball."

FAVORITE BIBLE PASSAGE

Philippians 4:13. "When I was leaving home to play minor league baseball, my mom wrote it down for me, and I had it for a long time in the minors. It reminded me of her and of the fact that I can do all things through the Lord. It's basic, and it's a real powerful one for me."

Kurt Stillwell

As major league baseball father-son combos go, the Ron Stillwell-Kurt Stillwell duo may not rank up there with Ken Griffey-Ken Griffey Jr. or Hal McRae-Brian McRae, but it is an important part of baseball history.

In 1961 and 1962, the Washington Senators were toiling almost anonymously in Griffith Stadium and RFK Stadium in the nation's capital, making another futile attempt to interest District of Columbia residents in baseball. One of their infielders was Ron Stillwell, who played in fourteen games for the Senators in those first two years.

Three years after Ron's stint with the Senators, he and his wife were living in Thousand Oaks, California, when they had a little boy, whom they named Kurt. It seemed this was a kid who was destined to become a ballplayer.

"I tell people that baseball was in my blood," Kurt says. "One of the earliest pictures my parents took of me was with a bat and a ball in my crib. I've had a ball and bat in my hand literally since I was born."

Even though Ron Stillwell was no longer a major leaguer by the time Kurt was born, his influence was clear. "Unfortunately, my dad's career was cut short by an injury, so I never got a chance to see him play," Kurt says. "He tried to make a comeback, but he had a collision with an outfielder in Triple A.

He broke his cheekbone, had some depth perception problems, and was not able to return."

As a former major leaguer, Ron Stillwell was in demand as a coach, so he set out to show others how to play the game. He coached in both high school and college, but perhaps his greatest project was Kurt.

Not that the younger Stillwell needed much help.

By the time he reached high school, he was on his way to stardom. In four years at Thousand Oaks High School, Stillwell hit .440 with 50 steals in 52 attempts. In his senior year, he batted .552 and was named Southern California Player of the Year. Although his favorite player was Dave Kingman, the Giants' slugger of monster home runs, Stillwell's game was not one of power but of hitting for the average and fielding well.

Yet as good as Stillwell was, it appeared that a college career was his next step after his 1983 graduation from high school. "I was studious. I think I got that from my father. He was an All-American in baseball at the University of Southern California, and he was an academic All-American, too. I wasn't the smartest person in the world, but I was a hard worker and a studier. So I was bound to be a college student. That's what I wanted to be.

"I wanted to follow my dad's footsteps and go to USC and be a Trojan. As it turned out, I changed my plans and decided to go to Stanford. I was impressed with Stanford's whole scene. My cousin was an All-American athlete at Stanford, and I was really impressed with what I saw there."

So Stillwell, turning away from a chance to be a second-generation Trojan on the baseball team, signed a letter of intent to go to Stanford.

But he never went.

The 1983 amateur baseball draft got in the way. Being picked number one by the Cincinnati Reds changed everything.

"Although I had signed to go to Stanford, when the Reds called the night before the draft, I told them that my main goal was to be a major league player. They had to know [my intentions] at least the day before the draft because they didn't want to waste a pick. I had decided a couple of days before that my main goal was to be a major leaguer—not a lawyer or a doctor—even though I was a good student. I believe I made the right decision."

His mother wasn't so sure. "My mom was crushed," Stillwell recalls. "I had worked hard to be accepted at Stanford. I had taken the SATs three times to get in. My mother wanted me to go to Stanford."

Family reactions and decisions were important in the Stillwell household. They were a tight-knit bunch who loved each other and loved Jesus Christ. It was not easy, then, to make a decision that did not have everyone's total approval.

When it came to matters of faith, however, the family was in complete agreement. "I give my family all the credit in the world," Kurt says of his commitment to follow Christ. "I mentioned having baseball in my blood; likewise, the love of the Lord has always been in my family. I'm proud of my heritage and my family. We've had a long line of Christians. My grandfather was a pioneer in bringing the Salvation Army out to the West Coast. Both sets of grandparents were involved in the Salvation Army."

Stillwell's personal journey with Jesus began when he was a Little Leaguer. "I was ten years old when I accepted the Lord. My parents instilled Christian values, but Mr. Zaranandia, my Sunday school teacher, finally made the gospel hit home with me. My parents laid the groundwork, and Mr. Z did the harvesting."

When Stillwell signed with the Reds eight years later, he felt compelled to rededicate himself to God. "I remember telling the Lord that I would play baseball if it was His will, and that's what I've been doing for the past fourteen years. Rededications are important when you get out on your own. I had been raised in a good Christian home, but once I got out on my own, I had to take it upon myself to grow in my faith."

So with his life newly rededicated to God, a handsome contract signed, and visions of college life far behind him, Kurt left home. Instead of going to Palo Alto, he headed for Billings, Montana. The son of a major leaguer was headed out to make his own mark on the game.

It would be an auspicious beginning. In his first game as a paid baseball player, Stillwell went 4-for-5 with a home run and three RBIs. He went on to be voted the Pioneer League's best defensive shortstop, hit .324, and help Billings win the league championship. The Reds knew they had a winner.

As is typical with first-round draft picks, Stillwell was moved quickly through the Reds' minor league system. After a full year at Midwest League Cedar Rapids in 1984 and a year at Triple A Denver in 1985, Stillwell arrived at Riverfront Stadium to start the 1986 season. He was in the majors before his twenty-first birthday. When he stepped onto the field in his Reds uniform, the Stillwell father-son major league combination was complete. It would be several years, though, before the Ron-Kurt pairing would make a small mark on baseball history.

A faltering start in Cincinnati for Stillwell led to a two-week exile back to Denver, but he redeemed himself on his return trip to Ohio. Finally settling in, he hit .303 over the last eight weeks of the season and had 8 game-winning RBIs for the year, tying him with Will Clark for the most among rookies in the National League.

But there was an obstacle to stardom in Cincinnati for Stillwell. The Reds had another outstanding prospect at shortstop. He was a hometown hero named Barry Larkin, and his arrival spelled doom for Kurt Stillwell in the Ohio River city. In 1987, Stillwell became a very young utility player for the Reds, performing at second, third, and short, and hitting .258 in 131 games.

His moment in the sun during this final season with the Reds came early. On April 17, in a game with Houston, he clobbered his first major league home run. It came off Aurelio Lopez—Señor Smoke, as he was known. "The whole first year I was in the big leagues, I didn't hit one," says Stillwell of his first home run. "But the time I did hit one, my parents just happened to be there." Not only that, but that initial big fly was also a grand slam.

On November 6, Stillwell was traded to Kansas City in a deal that sent him and Ted Power to the Royals for Danny Jackson and Angel Salazar.

While with K.C., Stillwell experienced his greatest big-league thrill. He made the 1988 All-Star team. The best part, though, was that the game was held in Cincinnati. "It was a special time for me," he says. In the midseason classic, Stillwell played one inning at shortstop, but did not get a chance to bat.

His first year in Kansas City was also highlighted by his best-ever home run total of ten, which was perhaps not Kong Kingman-like, yet satisfying for Stillwell. And he played so well between May 16 and 22 of his first year with the Royals that the Senator's son was named the American League Player of the Week.

For the next four years, Stillwell was a fixture in K.C., averaging 130 games a year and pounding out 464 hits. Included in his time with the Royals was a 13-game hitting streak in 1988 that he wasn't even aware of when asked about it in 1996.

Despite a number of solid years, some observers might say Kurt's career has represented something of an unfulfilled expectation. First-round draft picks are not supposed to have .250 career batting averages. They're not supposed to be playing Triple A ball at age thirty as Stillwell did as recently as 1995 for Indianapolis.

Yet the former whiz kid from Sparky Anderson's hometown is not about to mope about what might have been. He's at peace with himself and the effort he has put forth.

"I feel blessed," Stillwell says. "I've spent nine years in the major leagues. I think I peaked early in the big leagues when I was twenty. Obviously, I don't have any big statistics or great numbers, but I feel thankful for what I've gotten. There is no way I'd regret it. I feel very fortunate."

Accompanying Stillwell on his travels through baseball since 1991 has been his wife, Angela. She became the best thing he took away with him from his time in Cincinnati.

During Stillwell's rookie year in the Queen City, he ventured south across the Ohio River one day in search of some clothes at the Florence Mall in northern Kentucky. While there, he met Angela Meeks, who was working at the shopping center. For the next five years, he and Angela dated—often by long distance after Stillwell moved on to Kansas City. Because Angela grew up in a church tradition that was much different from Stillwell's Baptist upbringing, he knew they had some spiritual questions to sort out before they could get married.

"We've come a long way in that department," Stillwell says. "We dated for five years until I was sure we were on the same page with our theology. It was the number one thing for us to settle before getting hitched." They were "hitched" shortly before spring training in 1991. Although Stillwell had been around baseball a long time by then, he was only twenty-five years old.

A high priority for the Stillwells through the years of their marriage has been getting involved in good churches. "We have locked into a good church at home in California, and we had a good church in Kansas City. That's where we got most of our growth as a newly married couple. We also try to get involved in Bible studies or small groups. And we try to go through a devotional book together."

Since Kurt and Angela have been together, his baseball odyssey has taken him to the San Diego Padres, the California Angels, and to the Texas Rangers. In the middle of all that, though, was the strong possibility that he would return to the Cincinnati Reds. Yet it would not be without some real soul-searching. In 1994, Stillwell signed to play with Indianapolis, the Reds' top farm team. He had a good season with the Indians, hitting .270. That may have led to great things on the horizon in Cincinnati if the strike hadn't changed so many things.

The work stoppage left Stillwell in a quandary when the 1995 season rolled around. He reported to spring training with the Reds and was soon given an ultimatum: either play with the replacement players or go home.

For Stillwell, who had been a union member for eight years as a major leaguer and had benefited from the advantages of the union, it was a no-win situation. If he played, he would risk ever getting back on the field in a regular major league game. If he didn't play, the Reds might never take him back.

Fortunately, the situation resolved itself before the replacement season began, and Stillwell's career was left intact. Again he went to Indianapolis, where he put together a year similar to his 1994 campaign.

Yet it would not be with the Reds that Stillwell would get his chance to reappear in a major league uniform. Instead it would be with the only team that would enable the Ron Stillwell-Kurt Stillwell connection to come full circle. On January 2, 1996, Kurt signed a contract with the Texas Rangers. When he put on a Rangers uniform in April of 1996, Stillwell became part of Ranger trivia: Who are the only two father-son units who played for the Washington Senators-Texas Rangers organization? The first were Dick (1965–67) and Robb (1993) Nen. (What's more, they represent a trivia question of their own: Who is the only father-son team in major league history whose last name is a palindrome?)

The second unit, of course, is Ron and Kurt Stillwell. The Washington Senators, an expansion team in 1961, moved to Texas and became the Rangers in 1972.

As a member of the 1996 Rangers, Stillwell was fortunate to hook up with manager Johnny Oates, a man with his own Washington Senators' background. In his first major league at bat on September 17, 1970, Oates singled off Dick Bosman of the Senators in a game at RFK Stadium in Washington. Dick Bosman was the Rangers' pitching coach in 1996.

"It is tremendous to have a manager of his character," says Kurt. "The quiet leadership that he has is great. I know he's a Christian, because I know where his heart is. I've been in the other boat too, where I was looked down on as a Christian. It's nice to know that someone in charge doesn't look at me that way."

Stillwell played in just 46 games with the division champion Rangers in 1996, but he contributed greatly to the team's success. He hit .273, his best mark ever in the majors. In September alone, Stillwell hit .357 for the Rangers.

It hasn't been quite the kind of career anyone envisioned in the early '80s when Stillwell was pounding the ball around high school baseball diamonds back in Southern California. Yet it has been deeply satisfying for Stillwell in ways that don't show up in the box score.

For one thing, he feels that he has successfully negotiated the pitfalls of life in baseball and been able to maintain his Christian testimony. And that alone is enough to get him excited.

"What lights my fire is trying to live by the Spirit," he says. "I'm not real vocal about it, and I've been in the game long enough to know that walking the walk seems to make the biggest impact on fellow teammates. The big talk turns them off.

"I love to see guys on fire for the Lord, guys who walk by the Spirit and let other guys see it. That's my passion. I want to reveal the fruit of the Spirit as much as I can and let people know that I'm a Christian by the way I live my life."

For a veteran journeyman, there is nothing certain about his baseball career. From year to year, there are no guarantees about where he might be—whether in the game or out. For Stillwell, the thoughts of what to do after baseball are never far away. In fact, he figured he would have faced those decisions long ago.

"I've been thinking about my future for years, thinking baseball was all over. But the Lord has kept opening doors for me. It's awesome to get a chance to return to the big leagues. I honestly don't know what I'm going to do with the rest of my life, but I know I'm going to try to continue to live by faith."

That's what Ron Stillwell did when his career was cut short by injury. And you can be sure that's what Kurt Stillwell will do when he has to close his major league locker for the last time.

He may have been born to play baseball, but he was born again to do more. And he's eager to find out what God has in store for him next.

Q & A WITH KURT STILLWELL

Q: *What do you think baseball has to do to bring the fans back?*
Kurt: Well, they're trying. It's been extra fun being on a winner in 1996. Texas is alive. It's been a thrill to get back to the majors and see the difference between 1994 and 1996. The big league teams are trying to get the guys to come out and spend ten minutes signing autographs. They certainly weren't doing that a few years ago.

Q: *What is the toughest thing for you as a Christian in regard to being a major leaguer?*

Kurt: Nothing, really. It's a great opportunity to shine for the Lord. You are under the public's microscope, as well as your teammates', and if you slip up, it could hurt your credibility and testimony. But this is probably true in all professions and walks of life. I honestly don't find this very tough, but it could be if you don't stay close to the Lord.

Q: *Who is the toughest pitcher you've ever faced?*
Kurt: That's easy—all of them! But one pitcher especially has had my number over the years—Gregg Olson. I've faced him something like twenty times and have struck out sixteen times with no hits. I did squeak a single off him in a spring training game once. He has a wicked curveball.

Q: *What do you like to do for relaxation when you're away from the game?*
Kurt: I'm a fishing fool. My passion is fishing for bass and trout. It is very relaxing for me. I also enjoy golfing, but I'm a real hacker. That is more like frustration than relaxation.

THE ROAD TO THE MAJORS

- Selected by the Cincinnati Reds in the first round of the June 1983 draft
- Traded to the Kansas City Royals with Ted Power for Danny Jackson and Angel Salazar on November 6, 1987
- Signed as a free agent by the San Diego Padres on February 28, 1992
- Signed as a free agent by the California Angels on August 1, 1993
- Signed as a free agent by Cincinnati on November 24, 1993
- Signed as a free agent by the Texas Rangers on January 2, 1996

Minor league stops: Billings, Cedar Rapids, Denver, Indianapolis

Minor league highlights: 1984 Midwest League's starting short-stop in the All-Star game

THE STILLWELL FILE

Year	Team	G	AB	R	H	2B	3B	HR	RBI	BB	SO	SB	BA	SLG
1986	Cin	104	279	31	64	6	1	0	26	30	47	6	.229	.258
1987	Cin	131	395	54	102	20	7	4	33	32	50	4	.258	.375
1988	KC	128	459	63	115	28	5	10	53	47	76	6	.251	.399
1989	KC	130	463	52	121	20	7	7	54	42	64	9	.261	.380
1990	KC	144	506	60	126	35	4	3	51	39	60	0	.249	.352
1991	KC	122	385	44	102	17	1	6	51	33	56	3	.265	.361
1992	SD	114	379	35	86	15	3	2	24	26	58	4	.227	.298
1993	SD	57	121	9	26	4	0	1	11	11	22	4	.215	.273
	Cal	22	61	2	16	2	2	0	3	4	11	2	.262	.361
1996	Tex	46	77	12	21	4	0	1	4	10	11	0	.273	.364
9 Years		**998**	**3125**	**362**	**779**	**151**	**30**	**34**	**310**	**274**	**455**	**38**	**.249**	**.349**

Dave Valle
Man of Hope

VITAL STATISTICS

Born October 30, 1960, in Bayside, New York
6 feet 2, 220 pounds
Position: Catcher
Throws right, bats right
Family: Wife, Vicki, and three children, Philip, Natalia, and
   Alina
1997 Team: Oakland A's

CAREER HIGHLIGHTS

- Led Texas to 14–8 mark when he was starting catcher in 1995
- Finished second among AL catchers with .995 fielding mark in 1993
- Led AL in putouts (881) in 1993
- Led AL in throwing out runners (43.9 percent) in 1989

WARMING UP

Dave Valle gets his message of hope straight from Scripture. "I've gone to prisons, I've gone to youth centers and talked to hardened kids who are tough to talk to. They don't see hope beyond their death. They say, 'Chances are, I'm not going to make it till I'm twenty, so why should I worry about my future?' But God's Word says, 'I know the plans I have for you, not for evil but for good so that you have a future and a hope.'"

FAVORITE BIBLE PASSAGE

"Trust in the Lord with all your heart and lean not on your own understanding; in all your ways acknowledge him, and he will make your paths straight" (Proverbs 3:5–6). "I like to sign Proverbs 3:5–6 on autographs," Dave says.

Dave Valle

The year was 1991. Dave Valle was the Seattle Mariners' top catcher. He was behind the plate in 129 games for the boys from the Emerald City that year—the second most games caught in one year in Mariners history.

Behind the plate, Valle was having his usual stellar season—throwing out 34 percent of the runners who dared to steal against him. Until May 10, he had played in 120 straight games without making an error, a streak that had begun in April of 1990. Valle was 39 games shy of the major league record when he finally made a miscue. For the season, Valle fashioned a .992 fielding average with just six errors.

Fielding was not a problem for Dave Valle that year. But when he doffed the catcher's tools, picked up a bat, and stepped up to the offensive side of home plate, his difficulties started.

Throughout his career, Valle has had an up-and-down record as a hitter. One year in the minors he hit .213, but the next year he hit .293. While playing in Calgary in 1985, he hit .344. The following season with the same minor league club, Valle pounded out 21 home runs and hit .312.

He proved during each step of his long minor league journey that despite the occasional down years, he could hit and hit for power.

But in 1991, nothing was going right for him at the plate. In May, he was 7 for 57 (.070), and in June he managed only three hits in 41 trips to the plate (.073). No matter what he tried, Valle couldn't shake the slump. At the All-Star break, Valle was hitting .135.

Things got a little better after that, but even a .261 average the rest of the season couldn't pull Valle's average above the Mendoza line. He hit just .194 for the season.

Careers have been killed by years like that. And for Valle, it was indeed a frustrating season. However, Dave Valle's outlook on life and on baseball had become so refreshingly unusual that he is able to look back on this most maddening of years as a career highlight.

It certainly wasn't a highlight year because the Seattle fans rallied to support him. "I got booed every time my name was announced in the Kingdome," says a man who is far too good a person to receive such abuse. "It was tough to go out there every day."

And it wasn't a highlight year because he was secure in his position as a major league player. "In the middle of that year, I wanted to retire," he says.

No, this worst of all times for Valle became valuable to him because of the help he received from the Lord. "God met me at every turn, helping me to realize that I was not alone."

Each day when he went to the stadium or began thinking about how he was going to step out on the field one more time while being weighed down by his hitting problems, Valle felt that God was saying to him, "Hey, can you handle today?"

In his heart, Valle would respond, "Yeah, Lord, I can handle today."

"Okay, that's all I want you to do," he would sense God saying back. "Handle today. We'll handle tomorrow tomorrow."

On one particular day in the middle of a hot July when Dave Valle was anything but hot, even God's promise of help seemed not to be enough. He was on the verge of becoming a baseball dropout. "I was hitting about .150, and I was ready to quit. I told myself, *That's it. I'm not coming back tomorrow.*"

After the game, Valle again felt God impressing an idea on

him—a biblical concept that he knew to be true. "Dave, this is for My glory," he sensed God telling him.

"Yeah, right, Lord," Valle said grudgingly as he dressed and left the Kingdome, still unsure of his future in baseball.

The next day, Valle returned to the stadium.

"As the game was about to start, I walked into the dugout and Alvin Davis was there," Valle says, referring to his fellow Christian on the Mariners. "He says, 'Val, check it out, man! That's powerful!' He pointed up into the third deck. There was a huge sign—must have been letters two or three feet high. It said, 'For His Glory!—Valle.' I almost started crying. My eyes filled with tears. It was like the Lord saying, 'Dave, you didn't hear Me last night. So I had to move somebody to write a sign to remind you.' The weight of the world was lifted off my shoulders that night."

Valle made it through that traumatic year at the plate, still able to look back with admiration at how God salvaged that year of hopelessness by giving him reason to continue. "It's very easy in this game to get filled with yourself because of the adulation pro athletes receive. But this game can also humble you. It can do that to anybody. God cares about His children, and He doesn't want us to have big egos."

Besides learning about egos and playing for God's glory, Valle learned from that 1991 season a valuable lesson in love. It's a lesson he shares with others when he does speaking engagements. He calls the way the fans treated him when he was struggling at the plate "a perfect example of *conditional love.*"

He tells his listeners, "If I do well, the fans love me. They cheer me. They'll give me a standing ovation. But if I do bad, they don't love me anymore. They boo me, they hate me, they cast insults at me, and they call my mother names. But God loves me unconditionally. He doesn't care what I hit. During 1991, I never wondered if God loved me. I went to Him for strength and refuge to get me through."

The 1991 version of Dave Valle's baseball career seemed to represent a low ebb on the field while his spiritual journey reached a peak. Both aspects of his life have been important to him for a number of years, but the love of baseball was instilled far earlier than a love for God.

Baseball began for Valle back in the late '60s, when he played stickball every day at a local school yard in New York City. "That was how we filled our days back then," he recalls. "You had to get there early to get a place to play."

And when he wasn't playing, young Dave was following his beloved Yankees, who, Valle recalls, were going through "the worst stretch in their history. My cousin and I would take the train over to Yankee Stadium." Or, if the long trip to the Bronx seemed too ambitious, they would visit Shea Stadium, which was much closer than the House That Ruth Built.

For the first eight years of his life, Valle's major influence in baseball was his dad, John. Yet when Dave was eight, his dad died of a heart attack. Just forty-one years old, John Valle died of a heart problem left over from a childhood case of rheumatic fever. His death left Marilyn Valle with the unenviable task of raising eight children by herself. "My dad was very involved in Little League," Valle says. "After he died, the Little League fields were named after him."

Another major influence on the youngest boy in the Valle family were his brothers. "All of my brothers played baseball, and whatever my older brothers did, I jumped in and did too. If they played basketball, I played basketball."

Valle played both sports while attending Holy Cross High School in Flushing, New York. "I loved basketball. It was a strong passion for me. We won two city league championships in my four years. In my senior year, we lost in the finals in overtime to a team that future NBA star Vern Fleming played on."

During the spring of his senior year, Valle faced a similar situation in the baseball version of the city league. And this time, he had a chance to change the outcome. He got a base hit in the bottom of the seventh and final inning to win the game for Holy Cross and capture the title. In addition to that strategic hit, Valle was named to the All-New York City team and the third-team All-American squad. During his senior year, Valle hit .550 with 10 home runs and was selected in the second round of the 1978 draft.

It would not be the team of Thurman Munson and Roy White who would draft Valle, however. "I dreamed of wearing pinstripes, because that was my favorite team," Valle says.

The Yankees were not interested, it seems, and Valle had to settle for the then-new Seattle club. "It was a good opportunity for me to get on an expansion team and try to move up." And it looked at first like Valle would make the jump from high school to the majors in short order. By the time he was twenty-one, he had already earned a spot on Seattle's Triple A Salt Lake City team.

Yet it would be five more years before he could leap that last hurdle and land in Seattle. "I had a lot of injuries in the minors," Valle says. "I had knee injuries. I lacerated my throwing hand one time, severing tendons. That certainly curtailed my advancement."

But what really threatened to put an end to Valle's career early on was the volatile combination of a hot temper and a party spirit. When Valle first entered pro baseball, he played in Bellingham, a Class A outfit in the Northwest League. There he met Dave Edler, a kindred spirit with whom he would party for the next few months. Oblivious to what they might be doing to their potential careers, the two of them did the drug and alcohol scene all summer. Not surprisingly, Valle hit a miserable .204 at Bellingham.

After a visit to the Instructional League, where Valle and Edler continued their escapades, they parted company for one season. Valle went to Alexandria and Edler played for San Jose. For both of them, it would turn out to be a split of monumental importance.

While Valle returned to his dangerous lifestyle, mixing heavy partying with drugs and alcohol, Edler was investigating a different way of living. He was given a copy of Hal Lindsey's book *Late Great Planet Earth*, and it changed his entire outlook on life. While on a road trip to Fresno, Edler sat in the back of the team bus in a McDonald's parking lot and accepted Jesus Christ as his Savior.

When it came time for the Arizona Instructional League, the two former teammates were reunited. Valle came sauntering into the hotel room that they would share and found something he never would have expected. Edler was reading his Bible. That initial scene threw Valle off a bit, but Edler's new life was so real and so different that Valle soon wanted to know more about it.

"I noticed that Dave was different," Valle recalls. "He didn't want to hang out and do the things he used to do. He presented the gospel in a way that was very real. He didn't browbeat me with it. He just kind of lived it, and he showed that God had made a difference in his life."

For Valle, it was time to wade through the things he had learned about religion earlier in his life and decide how he wanted to live. While his church background had filled him with knowledge, Valle soon discovered that his heart had never been changed.

Before long, he followed Dave Edler's lead and accepted Jesus Christ after a chapel service at Diablo Stadium in Tempe. "A real peace settled over me," he says.

No one has any way of measuring what effect such a decision can make on professional endeavors, but Valle realizes that his turning to Christ saved his career—and quite possibly his life. Gone were the wandering days of partying at night and taking pills to be able to play the next game. "It could have been the end of my career at age nineteen after two disastrous years in the minors," Valle says.

Instead, his career began to take off. The season after Valle put his faith in Christ and got his life straightened out, he batted .293 for San Jose. This didn't mean, however, that the Mariners were ready to call him up. In fact, Valle would spend four more seasons in the minors.

In 1982, another source of strength and help entered his life when he married Vicki Comella on February 6. Like Dave, Vicki was a native New Yorker, and he had met her through a good friend who had gone to high school with her.

Coming out of spring training in 1985, Valle had won a spot on the Mariners' roster. His September call-up the previous summer had been successful, and a good effort in the Cactus League earned him his ticket to the big show. But three weeks into the season, Valle was injured in a collision at home plate with Bob Boone. The deep thigh bruise would cost Valle three and one-half months of what should have been his first full season in the majors. It would be 1987—Valle's tenth year as a pro—before he could enjoy an entire season in Seattle.

Once he finally arrived, though, he stuck around a long time. From 1986 until 1993, when he left Seattle to sign with Boston, Valle gradually became the mainstay behind the plate for the Mariners. Finally fulfilling the expectations from his youthful days, he became one of the best defensive catchers in baseball.

While in Seattle, Valle discovered the value of good spiritual training as he was mentored by Chuck Snyder, who has a ministry for ballplayers. "When we got to Seattle, Vicki and I were still a very young couple. Chuck and Barb's ministry is to couples, and we attended Bible studies in their home. As I look back over my life as a believer, I see how God has brought people in almost every step of the way to continue to teach me and to instruct me."

Valle's spiritual growth was also helped by Jim Singleton, a pastor who lived in Lynn, Massachusetts, where Valle was playing ball shortly after he became a Christian. "He taught me principles I still use today," Dave says.

Another mentor was Ernie Tavilla, who was chaplain for the Red Sox in 1994 when Valle played in Boston. The two had met before, back in Lynn, where Tavilla was the minor league chaplain. Tavilla, who helped get Valle started spiritually, died in 1996.

The combined instruction of those teachers would be put to good use. While Valle was still with the Mariners, he discovered a way to relay to a large number of people the hope he had found in Jesus Christ.

In 1985, Valle went to the Dominican Republic to play winter baseball. While there, he was touched by what he saw outside the baseball stadium. As he and Vicki were leaving the stadium one night, they ran across crowds of children and young people who seemed to be in need of everything from shoes to shirts to their next meal.

"We saw kids who don't have shoes or food and their bellies were sticking out and they were begging for money so they could survive," Dave says. "Having grown up in New York City, I don't think our poor areas even compare to what you see in Santo Domingo."

What Dave and Vicki saw that night changed their lives. They decided that if they ever had the means, they would return to the Dominican Republic and help. In 1994, Valle felt he was ready to take the plunge. With the help of former Seattle teammate Brian Holman, Valle began Esperanza International. The word *esperanza* means *hope* in Spanish, and that is exactly what the organization tries to provide.

When Valle was in the investigation stage of the ministry, he sent a research team to the Dominican Republic to find out how he could best help the people. What they discovered was something that had been started in Bangladesh twenty years earlier. A bank had been opened, and small loans were made to poor women, who could then begin businesses to support their children.

"They found that if you want to help the children, you have to help the mothers," Valle says. "The bank had started giving money to the men, but they were using it to gamble or drink or go to prostitutes. Mothers, if they have discretionary income, will spend it on their children."

Now, through Esperanza, Dominican women are loaned $110 apiece. Then volunteers help them invest in ventures that will earn a good return. Some sell chickens. Some do laundry. Some make clothes.

"A bank is a group of twenty-five women," Dave explains. "We call it Bancos de Esperanza. The women are accountable to each other. If one of them fails to pay a loan, that bank has to pay that woman's loan. Unless all the loans are paid, no one in the group gets a second loan. It's peer pressure, but it also becomes a sense of community for these women. They want to help each other because they have a vested interest in it."

In addition to providing the start-up money and the means for the women to earn more, Esperanza also provides the women with spiritual help. "Every two weeks, they meet and make their loan payments. They hear a message of hope—a gospel message. Eventually, we want to work more with the local churches, trying to get them involved."

Beyond what is happening in the Dominican Republic, Valle and his wife have their eyes on another Caribbean island—Cuba. Vicki Valle is Cuban-American and would love to see this kind of ministry replicated in her homeland. "We made a trip there in 1985," Valle says. "It was Vicki's first trip back, and it was a powerful trip. We saw the oppression, yet the church is thriving, even if it is underground."

The years 1995 and 1996 might seem to have gone underground for Dave Valle's baseball career, yet he is not complaining.

After splitting the 1994 season among Boston, Milwaukee, and the strike, Valle signed a two-year pact with Texas on December 5, 1994. Although this deal would give him financial security and ensure the ongoing work of Esperanza, it didn't do any favors for his playing career. Valle was coming into Dallas-Fort Worth to back up one of the best young catchers in the game, Ivan Rodriquez, who was seven years old when Dave signed his first pro contract.

A backup role was all that would be available for Valle in Texas, but he refused to complain. "It's been incredibly wonderful for me in Texas," Valle says. "I've not played much, but I feel like I've had an impact on the team. I've found other ways to help—whether it be encouragement or exhortation. That's what it's all about. It's not about me.

"I want the players to know that I'm here for them." he said while with Texas. "I'll get them a drink of water. It's a simple gesture. But after a guy makes a great catch or hits a triple and he comes in, he's too tired to think of water. It's not a big deal, but it's thinking beyond your own interests."

Dave Valle has been thinking beyond his own interests for a long time now—ever since Dave Edler showed him how a Christian lives. He's the kind of man baseball needs more of—interested in his family, interested in helping his teammates, interested in helping those in need.

Q & A WITH DAVE VALLE

Q: *While with the Rangers, you played for fellow Christian Johnny Oates. What has it done for you to play for a man like him?*
Dave: Johnny Oates has been wonderful. He allowed my eleven-year-old son to go out on the field with me. That to me is worth every penny in the world. My son could ride to the park with me. He had his own locker and his own uniform. We would shag balls. I would throw him batting practice. I want to build memories with my son that he won't ever forget.

Q: *Is baseball doing all it can to bring the fans back?*
Dave: No. I believe in going the extra mile. The agreement was the first step. Now the owners and players need to bring back the love for the game. I'm afraid we've lost a generation of athletes, and we need to reintroduce young kids to baseball.

The part of Ken Burns's feature on baseball that really struck me was the one on the Brooklyn Dodgers. There was a love for that team. One of the reasons was that the players lived in the neighborhood. It was like Joe down the street happens to be a ballplayer. It was a neighborhood thing. The game is not that way anymore. There is a gap between players and fans.

Q: *Could you relate an incident from your visits to the Dominican Republic?*
Dave: I was there in December 1995. We met with three different banks [groups of twenty-five women who have been loaned money]. It was absolutely amazing to see these women. You've got to remember that I was in a shack—aluminum and cardboard stuck together. No running water, a dirt floor. And these women were standing up with such a sense of self-esteem and self-worth. They could say, "This is what I accomplished!" Nobody gave it to them. They are paying it back. It's all their own!

Q: *How do you approach a player who says, "Dave, I don't need Jesus. I've got everything"?*
Dave: I would tell him, "There's a problem, and it's sin. What

are you going to do with it?" These guys have heard every scam, every investment scheme. They are very leery of big plans. But the issue comes right down to sin. I can walk them through the Ten Commandments, and they'll see the sin in their own lives. All of a sudden, they start to realize that the standard by which they measure their live doesn't hold up. They need a Savior.

THE ROAD TO THE MAJORS

- Selected by the Seattle Mariners in the second round of the 1978 draft
- Signed as a free agent by the Boston Red Sox on December 30, 1993
- Traded to the Milwaukee Brewers on June 16, 1994, for Tom Brunansky
- Signed as a free agent by the Texas Rangers on December 5, 1994
- Signed as a free agent by the Oakland A's on January 6, 1997

Minor league stops: Bellingham, Alexandria, San Jose, Lynn, Salt Lake City, Chattanooga, Calgary

Minor league highlight: While playing in Calgary in 1986, Dave Valle hit 21 home runs and knocked in 72 runs while batting .312.

Year	Team	G	AB	R	H	2B	3B	HR	RBI	BB	SO	SB	BA	SLG
1984	Sea	13	27	4	8	1	0	1	4	1	5	0	.296	.444
1985	Sea	31	70	2	11	1	0	0	4	1	17	0	.157	.171
1986	Sea	22	53	10	18	3	0	5	15	7	7	0	.340	.679
1987	Sea	95	324	40	83	16	3	12	53	15	46	2	.256	.435
1988	Sea	93	290	29	67	15	2	10	50	18	38	0	.231	.400
1989	Sea	94	316	32	75	10	3	7	34	29	32	0	.237	.354
1990	Sea	107	308	37	66	15	0	7	33	45	48	1	.214	.331
1991	Sea	132	324	38	63	8	1	8	32	34	49	0	.194	.299
1992	Sea	124	367	39	88	16	1	9	30	27	58	0	.240	.362
1993	Sea	135	423	48	109	19	0	13	63	48	56	1	.258	.395
1994	Bos	30	76	6	12	2	1	1	5	9	18	0	.158	.250
	Mil	16	36	8	14	6	0	1	5	9	4	0	.389	.639
1995	Tex	36	75	7	18	3	0	0	5	6	18	1	.240	.280
1996	Tex	42	86	14	26	6	1	3	17	9	17	0	.302	.500
13 Years		**970**	**2775**	**314**	**658**	**121**	**12**	**77**	**350**	**258**	**413**	**5**	**.237**	**.373**

Walt Weiss
Blue-Collar Competitor

VITAL STATISTICS

Born November 28, 1963, in Tuxedo, New York
6 feet, 175 pounds
Attended the University of North Carolina
Position: Infielder
Throws right, bats both
Family: Wife, Terri, and two children, Blake and Brody
1997 Team: Colorado Rockies

- Had a career-high batting average, .282, in 1996
- Recorded fourth-best on-base percentage in NL (.403) in 1995
- Ranked second in fielding for NL shortstops with .977 percentage in 1993
- Named American League Rookie of the Year in 1988

WARMING UP

"He's not cute, but we all love Walt Weiss," Colorado Rockies pitcher and teammate Darren Holmes said in 1996, speaking on behalf of other Rockies pitchers. Moundsmen love Walt Weiss because he makes so few errors. According to another Rockies teammate, Bruce Ruffin, the pitchers talk about having a "ground-ball-to-Walt-Weiss" pitch because they know that anything hit near him will be turned into an out.

FAVORITE BIBLE PASSAGE

"Behold, I am coming soon! My reward is with me, and I will give to everyone according to what he has done. I am the Alpha and the Omega, the First and the Last, the Beginning and the End" (Revelation 22:12–13).

Walt Weiss

I f a young kid loved baseball and he needed one great piece of advice to help him prepare to be an outstanding player, the best tip he could receive would be "Watch Walt Weiss."

Walt Weiss may not show the power and flair of an Alex Rodriguez. He may not do flips on the infield and perform amazing acrobatics like Ozzie Smith. And he may not have the big-city pizzazz that Jerek Deter brings to Yankee Stadium. But that hasn't stopped Weiss from being one of the most successful shortstops in baseball since he showed up in Oakland in 1988 and won the Rookie of the Year Award.

With the determination and perseverance you would expect from a kid from a blue-collar family, Weiss has carved out a niche for himself in the baseball world.

Growing up in Suffern, New York, just a short drive from New York City, Walt knew his chances of fulfilling his major league dream were as slim as he was. "My number one dream was to play professional baseball," says Weiss. "I never really knew if I could do it, but no one was going to tell me I couldn't. I was going to do whatever it took to get me there. I grew up in a pretty small town, and I never knew anyone who played in the major leagues from my area."

One of the things Walt did as youngster to pursue his dream was attend summer baseball camp in Florida. The camp—run by Brian, Blake, and Denny Doyle, who are former pro players—gave Weiss the foundation he needed. "That's where I learned to play the game," he says. "Coming from New York and going down to Florida to play baseball was a big deal. To be around pro players was quite a thing."

What young Walt didn't count on was learning from the Doyle brothers about faith. "They were the first Christian people I had ever been around," he says. Like his baseball career that received a shot in the arm with the Doyle camp but matured later, so his introduction to Christianity took place during his weeks at camp but would bear fruit years afterward.

Another huge influence on Weiss as a kid was his father, Bill. Walt's dad, who ran a newsstand in Grand Central Station, was an avid baseball fan who had played some ball in his day. Therefore, when Walt expressed a desire to play at a young age, his dad was there to help. "He taught me a lot when I was young."

As a youngster, Weiss was also influenced by his sports heroes, including Yankee stars Willie Randolph, Thurman Munson, and Craig Nettles.

Yet with all these influences and with all his drive to become a major league player, there was one drawback as Weiss matured. He was never a standout player, never a big star.

For one thing, his slight build worked against him. For instance, when it came time to graduate from Little League to the higher levels of competition, Weiss had a huge hurdle. "The transition from Little League to the big diamond was tough," he recalls. "I was a pitcher at that time, and then we had to go to the big mound. That was a rude awakening. In Little League, I could just throw it as hard as I could and throw it by everyone. But when I got to junior high, I took a few lumps."

Then he moved to his more natural position—shortstop.

Even then, as he moved his way up to high school ball and developed as a solid infielder, there was no sense that his advancement to the professional ranks would be automatic.

"I was a guy who, probably even to this day, never stood out. If you saw me play over the course of a season, you would notice that I do a number of things fairly well, but nothing outstanding. I was never a guy who could hit the ball out of sight. I fielded my position pretty well in high school, and I could run and throw. But other than that, I never was a guy who tore it up."

Weiss had some help in getting the attention he needed, though. "In my junior year, we had a couple of guys on my team who were seniors, and some local college coaches came around to watch them. Those coaches noticed me at the time and began talking to me. That was the first time I got feedback from people at a higher level. That planted a seed that perhaps I had the ability to go to college and possibly get drafted."

Even the idea of going to college presented some new challenges for Walt's family, since no Weiss had ever gone to college. "I never thought about going to college. I never applied to any colleges."

But soon he was thinking about the possibility when coaches from Seton Hall and St. John's stopped by to watch him play.

But the real surprise for Walt came when Mike Roberts, the coach of the North Carolina Tar Heels baseball team, showed up unannounced. He was in the area on a recruiting trip the day Weiss's Suffern High School team had a game. He obviously liked what he saw in young Walt, for he dropped by the Weiss's household that night and inked the infielder to a letter of intent to attend the University of North Carolina.

"I knew that North Carolina was a good school," Walt says. "I used to watch their basketball team on TV."

Because he had not considered college as a possibility, he had not made the extra effort to accumulate a high grade point average. "If it wasn't for baseball, I never would have gotten in," he claims. "I always did just enough to get by." Now, though, he would have to apply himself in the classroom with the same vigor he had demonstrated on the diamond.

But not so fast. There was one more opportunity to forgo that college career and continue playing baseball. The Baltimore Orioles, who have considerably more baseball clout than the North Carolina Tar Heels, drafted Walt in the tenth round of the free agent draft that spring.

Weiss had a decision to make. Pro baseball or college baseball? Which would it be? "Even to this day, it has been one of the bigger decisions I've had to make," Weiss says. "I was scared to go play minor league ball because I didn't think I was ready. Physically, I was behind everyone else. I was small and thin."

The Orioles were offering $8,000 for a shot at a boyhood dream. North Carolina was offering an education and a spot on their baseball team.

Weiss turned to the man who had helped him so much in the past—Brian Doyle. Doyle, himself an infielder, advised Walt to go to college. "That's all I wanted to hear," Weiss recalls. "I didn't think I was ready to go play pro ball at the time."

So it was off to Chapel Hill for Walt.

"I grew up quite a bit at North Carolina," he says. "That was exactly what I needed for my baseball career. I would have just been a number in minor league ball. I just wasn't ready at that time."

After what Weiss describes as "a great three years," Weiss was again drafted by a major league baseball team—this time by the Oakland A's in 1985. He would be lost in the shuffle no more; Weiss was the A's first pick in the draft and the eleventh selection by any team. With draft numbers like that, he would be given every chance to work his way through the system.

This time, he signed on the dotted line and soon began climbing the minor league ladder. Playing just a half-year at each level along the way, Weiss moved quickly toward Oakland. By the middle of 1987, he had moved through the Rookie League, the Midwest League, the Southern League, and the Pacific Coast League all the way to the American League. On July 12, 1987, Weiss was in the big show replacing injured Tony Phillips.

The dream had come true. All those hours of instruction with his dad had paid off. Those trips to Florida to learn from the Doyle brothers had reaped benefits. That effort to go to North Carolina and defer those hopes and wishes while maturing had led to success. The son of a newsstand owner and an Avon cosmetics factory worker was a major league baseball player now.

The 1988 season brought the Oakland A's back to a familiar spot as one of the top teams in baseball. Loaded as they were with power and pitching, all they needed was solid defense. One of the key components of that dependable defense was Walt Weiss. His job was to replace Alfredo Griffin and solidify the middle of the infield. He did that and more.

By the middle of July, Weiss and platooning second basemen Glenn Hubbard and Mike Gallego had teamed up to help the A's record more double plays than they had during all of 1987. And Weiss, who had so won the confidence of player development director Karl Kuehl in 1987 that he had traded regular shortstop Griffin away, recorded a sparkling .979 fielding average in 147 games. After July 8, Weiss made just one error the rest of the season.

The A's won the American League West and played the Boston Red Sox in the American League Championship Series. In the play-offs, Weiss hit a hefty .333 and knocked in the game-winning run in Game 2 with a single off Lee Smith. The A's beat Boston in four games and won the right to face the Los Angeles Dodgers in the World Series.

The World Series that year belonged to the Dodgers and their heroes Kirk Gibson and Orel Hershiser, but a disappointing ending to his first full major league season could not tarnish Weiss's excitement about that year. Especially when the post-season awards came out and Weiss was named the American League Rookie of the Year.

"That was a shock," Weiss says in his typical humble fashion. "That was something I never even anticipated. I think it had a lot to do with my being on a very good team. A lot was made about my being a rookie shortstop on a World Series team. That's why I got a lot of mention for Rookie of the Year."

Of course a great fielding average, a flair for turning the double play, and a solid year at the plate (.250 batting average, 35 walks, 113 hits) didn't hurt. It became a common occurrence to see photos of the airborne Walt Weiss, after nailing a runner at second and leaping and firing a strike to first.

There's another good reason 1988 was a good year for Weiss. It was the year he met the woman who in 1990 would become Terri Weiss. "She was originally from Louisville," he says, "but she had been living in the Bay Area since she was eleven. Actually she lived about forty miles north of San Francisco in a town called Fairfield. We met through some mutual friends near the end of the season."

In 1989, they would experience one of the most bizarre scenes in baseball history. As with 1988, the 1989 American League season belonged to the Oakland A's. This time, they were slated to play the San Francisco Giants in the first-ever Bay Area World Series. There would be minimal travel as the two northern California teams battled for baseball supremacy in their own backyard. What could be more appealing than a crosstown-rival Series?

The appeal of it all ended at 5:04 Pacific time on October 17, 1989. As the teams were preparing for the game and as the fans settled into their seats for the third game of the Series, TV announcer Al Michaels was halfway through his pregame show. Suddenly, Candlestick Park began to shake to its foundations. Michaels cut into his monologue and said, "We're having an earth—" and the power to the stadium was interrupted.

The Bay Area, we now know, was under the throes of one of America's worst earthquakes—hitting 7.1 on the Richter scale. Everywhere there was panic as fans and players alike scrambled to find their loved ones.

Walt Weiss was on the field when the quake rumbled through the ballpark. He was warming up, running near the left-field foul line. "The feeling I had was that I had stepped in a hole, because I almost fell down. Now I know that the ground was moving. The last thing on my mind was an earthquake. I really didn't give it much thought. I didn't even know it was an earthquake until I started seeing news reports on TV monitors."

When he did discover what had happened, he did as the other players were allowed to do—get their families out of the stands and down onto the field. Family members from New York had come out for the game, and he gathered them up for the bus ride back to the hotel.

But he couldn't find Terri.

In fact, it would be several hours before he knew where his

girlfriend was. She had been on her way to the ballpark with her dad when the quake hit, and she'd never made it to Candlestick. It would be five long hours before Walt could get to her house to find out she was OK. "She ended up getting home about an hour before I arrived. It was a crazy day, an eerie day."

That World Series had started out so well for Weiss. Earlier in the 1989 season, on May 17, he had injured his knee turning a double play. When he came back, Gallego had run off with his position at short. Weiss had played in just 84 games during the season.

But when the first game of the World Series rolled around, manager Tony LaRussa went with Weiss on a hunch. In the fourth, the hunch paid big dividends as Weiss pounded a Scott Garrelts fastball for a home run, extending the A's lead to 5–0 over the Giants. It was just the seventh home run in Weiss' scareer, and it was his most delicious. "This goes a long way toward salvaging my season," he said after Game 1.

The A's also won Game 2, which is how the World Series stood for ten days as San Franciscans tried to put their lives back in order before baseball would resume. Games 3 and 4 also went to the A's, and Oakland had the World Series title.

That would be the last World Series appearance for Weiss, even though the A's went again in 1990. This time, an injured left knee kept him out of the entire Series.

During the '90s, Weiss had made several transitions. In 1993, after eight years with the Oakland organization, Weiss was dealt to the expansion Florida Marlins. Looking for experience in their infield, the Marlins dealt two prospects, catcher Eric Helfand and pitcher Scott Baker, to the A's in exchange for the sure-handed shortstop.

The one-year stay in Miami was the best of times and the worst of times for Weiss. Although he set career-best marks for games played (158) and hits (133) while finishing second in the National League in fielding percentage, it was a long season. Accustomed as he was to winning with the A's, he found that dealing with the travails of typical first-year mediocrity took its toll.

After just one year with the Marlins, Weiss headed back

west, this time signing on with the Colorado Rockies. They too were an expansion team, but they seemed to be headed toward success at a faster rate than Florida. Indeed, in their third year in existence, the Rockies won a berth in postseason play. In 1995, for the fifth time in his career, Weiss was playing in October.

Although Colorado did not make it to the next round of the play-offs, Weiss savors the success of that team. "My highlight as a Rockie was the 1995 season," he says. "Clinching a play-off spot on the last day of the season made it quite a year."

There would be another highlight in the life of Walt Weiss in 1995. It happened in November at a Professional Athletes Outreach (PAO) conference. PAO holds Christian conferences during the off-season for football, basketball, and baseball players and their spouses. Top speakers are brought in to help the players with various aspects of their lives, including financial concerns, marital problems, and other lifestyle difficulties—all based on biblical principles.

In 1994, Terri Weiss had attended a PAO conference for players' wives, and when she heard about the 1995 meeting for both players and their spouses, she wanted them both to go. Her husband was not so eager.

"I really didn't want to go," Walt confesses. "It was one of those conferences where I thought I'd really be out of place. I thought I would be an outcast there. I was really intimidated by the whole thing."

Yet it meant so much to Terri that she sent in the form on her own. Then she told Walt, "I sent it in. We're going."

"So we ended up going," Walt says, "and it ended up changing my life."

What changed his life was the gospel of Jesus Christ.

It wasn't something he hadn't known about. In fact, he had a respect for teammates who were Christians. "I had been around people before who were saved, and I always admired the way they lived and the peace they seemed to have."

For example, two of his teammates on the Rockies, Mike Kingery and Joe Girardi had impressed Walt with their lives. "Kingery is a special guy, and Joe is a really close friend of mine. So I wasn't oblivious to the whole thing."

In fact, going into the conference, Weiss says, he had a lot of questions about who Jesus was and what He did. At the conference, he got a lot of the answers he was looking for. "It was plain to me that Jesus walked here on earth, and He did what it says in the Bible. If that is the case, there is no reason for me not to open my life to Him. To me, it is either all true or it isn't, and it's all true. Let's go full bore with this, I decided."

So, while attending a conference he really didn't want to go to, Weiss prayed to accept Jesus. And things haven't been the same since.

Now Terri and Walt Weiss make it a point to fill their minds with good Christian literature as they grow spiritually. "We hit the Christian bookstores quite a bit," he says. Among his favorite books has been Josh McDowell's *Evidence That Demands a Verdict*, which makes the case for logical thinking and Christian faith.

In addition to reading books, Terri and Walt also benefit from Bible studies with other couples, including Bobby and Gari Meacham and Rockies' chapel leader Bill Rader.

With the same intensity that Walt Weiss pursued his dream of playing major league baseball, he is now pursuing his desire to be strong in his faith. It's a blue-collar, I-have-to-make-the-effort attitude that will bring great benefits as he walks through the Christian life.

Walt Weiss started out a little late in baseball, spending some extra time in college, maturing and getting ready for the tests of pro baseball. And he's started a bit late in life down the road of faith. But just as he excelled in baseball because of his drive and desire, look for great things spiritually from him as well. He may not stand out like some high-profile Christians in the game, but he'll get the job done. He always has.

Q & A WITH WALT WEISS

Q: *What has made you such a good fielder?*

Walt: I've always been blessed with good hands and feet as an infielder. I've always worked hard—extremely hard. I'm always willing to take more ground balls. Fielding is what got me to the major leagues.

Q: *You've been a leadoff hitter and you've batted eighth. Which do you prefer?*
Walt: I don't really consider myself a leadoff hitter. I'm probably more comfortable hitting second or eighth. I'm not a guy who has ever stolen a lot of bases, so I don't feel like I give the team what it needs in the leadoff spot. I just don't feel like I'm doing the team justice in that spot.

Q: *What do you think baseball needs to do to bring the fans back?*
Walt: I think it's just a matter of time. The key is having a good collective bargaining agreement. We need stability and not having that cloud hanging over the game. It's also a matter of players going out and doing their job the right way. Fans in America love this game, and as long as we don't mess it up too bad, they'll keep coming back. The players have to make sure there is some type of attachment to the fans. This gives the fans a sense of being a part of it.

Q: *What type of charity do you like to be involved with?*
Walt: When I was eleven, I lost a brother to Sudden Infant Death Syndrome. He was two months old. I still can't forget waking up to the sounds of screaming that day. As a matter of fact, my brother had just gone to the doctor the day before for a two-month checkup and had a clean bill of health. So, when I was asked to be involved with a charity, I picked SIDS as one group I wanted to help.

THE ROAD TO THE MAJORS

- Selected by the Oakland A's as their first selection in the 1985 draft
- Traded to the Florida Marlins on November 17, 1992, for Eric Helfand and Scott Baker
- Signed by the Colorado Rockies on January 7, 1994

Minor league stops: Pocatello, Modesto, Madison, Huntsville, Tacoma

Minor league highlight: Stole 23 bases for Huntsville in 1987

Year	Team	G	AB	R	H	2B	3B	HR	RBI	BB	SO	SB	BA	SLG
1987	Oak	16	26	3	12	4	0	0	1	2	2	1	.462	.615
1988	Oak	147	452	44	113	17	3	3	39	35	56	4	.250	.321
1989	Oak	84	236	30	55	11	0	3	21	21	39	6	.233	.318
1990	Oak	138	445	50	118	17	1	2	35	46	53	9	.265	.321
1991	Oak	40	133	15	30	6	1	0	13	12	14	6	.226	.286
1992	Oak	103	316	36	67	5	2	0	21	43	39	6	.212	.241
1993	Fla	158	500	50	133	14	2	1	39	79	73	7	.266	.308
1994	Col	110	423	58	106	11	4	1	32	56	58	12	.251	.303
1995	Col	137	427	65	111	17	3	1	25	98	57	15	.260	.321
1996	Col	155	517	89	146	20	2	8	48	80	78	10	.282	.375
10 Years		**1088**	**3475**	**440**	**891**	**122**	**18**	**19**	**274**	**472**	**469**	**76**	**.256**	**.318**